Era!

I hope you have
an amazing journey
and meet many people,
try new things and
have so much fun!
Maybe this book will
help you along your
way or inspire you to
make the most of it.
Will miss you, Alice X

ROYAL CHALLENGE ACCEPTED

". . . how to get there?"

ROYAL CHALLENGE ACCEPTED

ALISTAIR BOYD

"What I would like every University student
or graduate to be able to do is first of all
to work his way around the world on £5 . . ."

H.R.H. The Duke of Edinburgh

First published January 1962
Second impression April 1962

Published by
Ocean Media
19 The Porticos
384 Kings Rd
Chelsea
SW 3 5UW

Dedicated to

H.R.H. The Duke of Edinburgh, K.G.

AUTHOR'S NOTE

My journey round the world could never have been achieved without the friendship and hospitality of those I met on the way. A list of acknowledgements would fill many pages with names from twenty-two countries, and in order not to confuse the reader I have mentioned only a few of these in the text. To all who helped in this way, as well as those whose co-operation enabled me to leave England in the first place, I express my deep gratitude for their interest and generosity.

For obvious reasons, I have changed the names of certain persons, places and vessels mentioned in the book, but this in no way affects the authenticity of the events described.

That this book is written is due to the encouragement of my mother and to the patience and editorial assistance of my wife, who spent much time going over the manuscript.

CONTENTS

LIST OF ILLUSTRATIONS

ROYAL CHALLENGE ACCEPTED

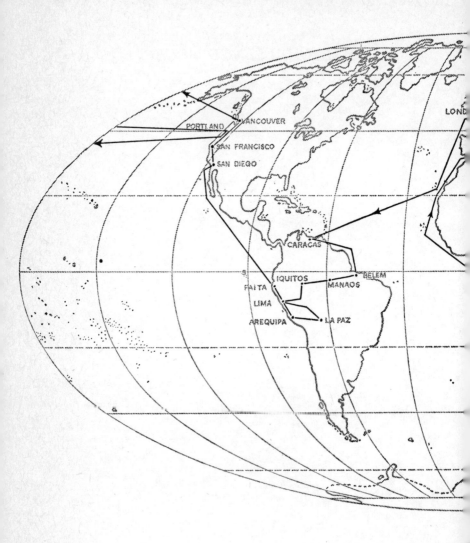

PORTLAND
VANCOUVER
SAN FRANCISCO
SAN DIEGO
LOND
CARACAS
IQUITOS
BELEM
FAITA
LIMA
MANAOS
AREQUIPA
LA PAZ

M

I

"*SEE YOU LATER. . . .*"

"The world is your oyster," pronounced the captain, some envy in his voice, "all yours for the taking."

Maybe, but oysters have to be prised open before they can be sampled; I had five pounds sterling with which to open this one. Could it be done?

We were out on the spray-swept boat deck, the captain of s.s. *Salop* gazing steadily seawards as he had done for the past fifty years, myself hanging over the leeward rail and not doing steadily anything. For him it was his last voyage; for me, my first, the beginning of my world adventure, only it felt like the end. The sea was riding rough, had been for three days. Typical Bay of Biscay weather they told me.

Abruptly I left the skipper on deck and groped my way back to the cabin. Never mind my world-oyster, or any oyster for the moment. I had no appetite for adventure.

The ship plunged into cavernous wave-troughs and rolled over crests. A crazy horizon looked into the cabin port-hole, sloped one way then another, fell out of sight and arrived again with a speed that was alarming. So much contrary motion everywhere was a torment to put up with. A Spanish steward entered bearing a cup of tea. He swayed towards the bunk as the vessel listed and encouraged me to swallow it.

"Señor's belly no like sea. Why come to sea?" asked the steward.

"Why come to sea?" I moaned. "Go and ask Prince Philip."

I wished I hadn't said that, for now the Spaniard stood in the doorway wanting to know what I meant. I told him.

It all began about five months back in the gloom of Oxford's examination halls. One of the questions I had to answer was connected with the Amazon in South America. For forty-five minutes I wrote down all I could remember of what many famous authors had said about the great river, adding bits of my own. Now I read through my answer. "The Amazon is four thousand miles long. It drains a basin of two million square miles. . . ." How meaningless! I couldn't envisage a river as long as the distance from London to New York. Fancy travelling all that way, week after week, into the wild, tropical heart of a continent. The idea took hold of my imagination: in fantasy I made that journey.

I was parachuting down upon South America from a great height. Below I could see the dense jungle roof and the tortuous winding silver veins that cut through this endless green, dividing and sub-dividing from the central artery like the branches of a tree from its trunk. In a flash I was in the midst of it, down amongst the hotly breathing Green Hell that was the heart of Amazonia. The silver artery was the River Amazon, thirty miles wide, the veins its thousand-mile-long tributaries. Crowding, pushing and swelling in an impenetrable mass was the eternal tropical growth. A crocodile gave me a nasty grin from his mud berth. A shoal of blood-thirsty *piranha* fish darted about in the water waiting to mop up the remains of me if I chanced a swim. An anaconda was lurking in the reeds ready to pounce. Night dropped in a hurry and the insects started their evening parade. Jaguars began to pad softly round me in circles. Sticky heat broke out all over me as I thought of my fate if I should fall into the hands of a head-hunting tribe . . .

Someone tugged my arm and the invigilator's voice said, "Time's up, you know. Sorry, but you'll have to hand in your paper now." Slowly, but with relief, I found myself in the Schools and realized I had finished my last paper. Thank God for that! But my brief, nightmare glimpse of the Amazon remained with me, and haunted me for the last few days of term.

Life was a rush. We had our College Commem Ball in the beautiful Wadham Gardens with Humphrey Littleton's trumpet troubling the Trinity dons. Term ended, goodbyes were said and a hundred new Wadham graduates were ready to pounce upon the world. I bumped into an old school-friend I hadn't seen for a long time.

"Hallo, Alistair, going down this term?"

"Yes, tomorrow, for good."

"Then what? National Service, I suppose, like everyone else?"

"Not likely. Had rheumatic fever in 1949. They won't look at me after that. I've got an itch to travel. Might have a shot at visiting the Amazon."

My heart thudded at the thought.

"The Amazon!" he exclaimed. "What's bitten you about that of all places?"

"Nothing really. Just that I'm looking for something different; exciting; off the beat."

My friend stared. "Take it easy, old chap. An Amazon safari's a noble ambition, but it's plumb crazy. Where's the cash coming from anyway?"

"I'll hitch-hike. Take a job on a freighter, steward on an aeroplane, anything that comes alone." I was getting into my stride as a budding, intrepid explorer: I would go to the Amazon. Nothing would stop me.

My friend began to believe me. "Well, if you're bent on this crazy project, you ought to take up the Duke of Edinburgh's suggestion, and travel right round the world."

Why not? I remembered now that Prince Philip had said to a group of students at Cardiff: "What I would like every University student or graduate to be able to do first of all is to work his way around the world on £5. . . ."

Prince Philip had flung out a challenge. I would take it up. I was eager to see new places and meet new people, but not as a tourist. Geography had taught me much about foreign countries, but it required a visual impact to bring them to life. Starting off with only a fiver I couldn't be a tourist. I should have to try my hand at any job that came along. Working for a living in foreign countries I might appreciate more fully their customs and way of life.

Globetrotting sounds a fine idea. I soon found out it wasn't going to be so easy. South America was my first stop. That had been decided in the examination hall. But how to get there?

I began with the airlines. Their managers were polite, but un-co-operative. They told me firmly that there was nothing doing in the way of a free air lift. When I suggested working an air passage they ushered me out. That left the sea. I wrote to Lloyds, to shipping companies and their managers, to superintendents and agents of foreign lines, stating my willingness to tackle any job whatsoever on a South America-bound freighter. Back came the replies, all ending on the same note. "We shall be delighted to let you sign the ship's articles, providing you work the round voyage." That meant a return passage—the very last thing a globetrotter wants. The sea looked to be a dead end too. I felt despondent.

Then at last I found one company superintendent with a more helpful attitude. He thought I should stand a much better chance with the tramp steamers. "They are less tied to regular runs than the larger freight lines." I followed up his suggestion and discovered that the tramping companies drew their crews from the Labour Pool. Down to Dock Street I trudged to join the Pool.

A burly docker opened the door. "No papers; no Union card! What's the bloody use of coming here? Go away and don't come back."

Defeat in Dock Street. But I wouldn't give up yet. I applied for a Union membership card. A week later the reply came. My application had been turned down. Every regulation seemed specially designed to thwart penniless globetrotters. August and September slipped by. South America remained as far away as ever.

There were difficulties even about getting visas for my passport. The Foreign Office endorsed it for most of the world. But when it came to visas for Latin America the consular authorities proved obstinate. They demanded good-conduct guarantees, financial bonds of a hundred pounds and evidence of a booked passage out of the country, none of which I had any hope of producing. As my route after Brazil was unplanned, I gave up the visa struggle and returned to the basic problem of how to get out of the country. No longer can you approach the master of a vessel and persuade him to take you on as a workaway. His hands are tied by laws, regulations and Union protocols. Wherever I went in the London docks it was the same story—shipping company rules, labour pools and the Unions—a vicious circle that seemed unassailable.

More weeks slipped by. The telephone rang constantly and my pen worked overtime. I got nowhere. I was about to give up the whole idea when a letter from a South American shipping company arrived.

"Dear Sir:

We have been informed of your intention to tour the world, and of your particular wish to travel to Brazil. We should be delighted to offer you our assistance over the first part of your journey. One of our freighters, the s.s. *Salop*, is due to sail from London on November 1st for Venezuela and thence to Brazil. We are pleased to offer you a passage on the *Salop* as a supernumerary workaway. . . ."

My wages were to be one shilling a month. I shouldn't accumulate much capital on that. But to get to Brazil was all that mattered. I read the letter over and over again just to make sure I wasn't imagining the whole thing. The days of anxiety, suspense and frustration seemed over for a while.

The weeks that followed were hectic. At last there was a reason for buying one hundred razor blades, a tube of iodine, nylon shirts and socks and a tropical linen suit. Then followed a bout of inoculations. The Institute of Tropical Diseases at Euston plugged my arm with shots for yellow fever, smallpox, cholera, typhoid and typhus. A doctor wrote out a certificate of fitness just in case anyone should query my general health, and the dentist was let loose on my teeth.

My mother and grandmother did their utmost to persuade me to pack enough and to spare for journeys through temperatures of a hundred plus and of sub-zero. But the essential thing, I maintained, was to carry as little as possible, preferably in one hand. The compromise was a suitcase and a hand grip. I packed a year's clothing and accessories. The suitcase was to keep my tropical suit in shape so that I shouldn't look a vagabond when demanding visas from stubborn consuls. The credit for that idea must go to the ladies.

A week before the sailing date the shipping company in Leadenhall Street telephoned to enquire if all my travelling documents were in order. They were not.

"The Brazilian and Peruvian consulates want some kind of good conduct guarantee," I explained. "Also a letter stating that I'm a *bona fide* traveller."

They said they would draw up some papers for me at once. I raced down to the office, acquired the necessary letters, and returned to the West End only to find that the consulates closed after midday. More complications arose at the consulates next morning. The Peruvian and the Brazilian officials each asked to see the other's visa in my passport before applying his own stamp. Peru gave way first, and the Brazilian visa soon followed.

A college friend presented me with an old German Floca camera. I was glad it had lost its shine and had a shabby case. In this state it wasn't likely to give me any trouble with customs officials or pilferers. I made a few last-minute additions to my luggage. That would be all I decided, except for—in my wallet, all alone, was the all-important fiver. It looked altogether too vulnerable in its isolation, something a stock-broker might tip his schoolboy son with or a housewife put down as deposit on her latest hire-purchase fancy. Better get it into small change right away. A couple of hours later I checked over a miscellany of foreign currency bought with my fiver. Columbian *pesos*, Brazilian *cruzeiros*, Peruvian *soles*—yes, five pounds' worth exactly. My preparations were complete; I was ready to go. The *Salop* was sailing in two days.

These were more than filled by the goodbyes of friends and relations, who seemed to be expecting me back in about two months by their manner. Some gave me the addresses of friends, or friends of friends of theirs, living abroad. "In San Francisco, dear, either twenty-second or thirty-second street, or possibly fifty-second. Or was it New York? But I'm sure they'll be delighted to help you." On the other hand they might not, I thought privately, but I wrote them all down and long afterwards was glad I had, for one or two turned up trumps when needed.

On October 31st, 1955, I swung off on the first lap of my adventure. s.s. *Salop* lay moored alongside the King George V dock. I approached her with awe. The gang-plank wobbled (or was it my knees?) as I climbed up onto her lower deck. It was a strange sensation joining my first ship, severing myself from the large, familiar, landsman's world to go into this little one close-bounded by the sea. I wondered what the crew would be like, what their nationalities and dispositions, how they would react to having an outsider planted in their midst and whether I should be able to get on with them. Naturally I had expected to share their sleeping quarters so prepared myself to join some uncomfortable shambles below. It was a tremendous surprise to find I was allotted the *Salop*'s stateroom! No other passengers claiming it, I supposed.

At a few minutes to midnight the *Salop*'s great propellers started to churn up the water. Two grimy tugs manoeuvred her out of the dock into mid-river; a deep-throated siren told them to lay off, and we glided down the River Thames under our own steam, bound for South America. Now that I had actually embarked, the immensity of the mileage I meant to cover temporarily overwhelmed my imagination. It would take me a year, more—perhaps two. Yet I still felt quite certain that I should make it, somehow, sometime.

This was the story I unloaded on the steward as he stood in the doorway, holding the tea-cup and maintaining a sort of bewildered attention. Probably he hadn't understood a word of it. But I must have felt better for the telling of it because after he'd gone, leaving me reflecting that I should be up against this problem of communication at every turn, I got out my Hugo Conversational Course for the third time. Now I was determined to progress beyond page one.

After Biscay the sea became calmer and I spent less time hanging over the rail. I helped the purser to duplicate the stores list on a gelatine tray. The gelatine was floppy and refused to set, so that every time the *Salop* heeled, a little more slopped out of the tray. The purser was a South African, so disgruntled with the way things were shaping in South Africa that he had given up his job in Capetown. Women didn't agree with him either and he had come to sea to avoid landing up with a fourth wife.

Once past the Azores, the swell eased off and I felt better. Captain Parry thought I now looked capable of working. The captain was a round jovial little man, past sixty, but a terror to anyone who shirked work.

"Been on any other ship before?" he bellowed across the mess the first morning I made the breakfast table. The mates were ready for me to say "the cross-channel steamers", and have a good laugh.

"Only a small sailing craft in Chichester harbour, sir." My remark was an anti-climax for the officers, but the captain could use it.

"Well, that's good enough," he conceded. "You should know port from starboard and the points of the compass. Start tomorrow on the four to eight watch. Take the wheel for a couple of hours. That all right by you, Mr. Taylor?" Mr. Taylor, the chief mate, said he would be glad of my company on the early morning watch. Later, he confided, "Can't talk to the seamen on the wheel, they're all Portuguese; be a change to have you."

"How about waking up in time?" I enquired.

"Don't worry about that. Someone will come down from the bridge at three-thirty. Expect you up there at five-to-four."

For the next three weeks I staggered up to the dimly-lit chart room at 3.55 a.m. There, I brewed a cup of tea for the retiring second mate and another for the chief mate who appeared on the dot of four looking quite blotto. We nodded each other good morning. I peered out of the wheelhouse ports to make sure that we weren't heading for an immediate collision and tried out an elementary Hugo phrase on the helmsman. Mr. Taylor snoozed for five minutes, but after that he got down to the business of preparing the long cargo manifests for the Venezuelan customs officials. "Every item from a piece of whipping twine to the last tiny shackle must be recorded," he told me. "There's plenty of trouble if it isn't." Then there were the sights to take. The mate spent half an hour working out our exact position on the chart, using four sextant readings he had obtained from the stars.

At six o'clock I took over the wheel from the Portuguese quartermaster. To steer a straight course required greater concentration than I had imagined, and once or twice during the two hours the *Salop* crept two or three degrees off her course. If the mate was on the bridge I edged her bows round on to the right course very gradually so that the movement on the helm was barely perceptible. I found an air of nonchalance the best attitude to adopt on these occasions. One morning, however, he noticed that I was a long way off course. When I asked him how he knew he pointed to the telltale twist in our wake several hundred yards astern. I was learning gradually to be a seaman.

Hot tea and toast from the galley were a welcome relief at seven o'clock. At half past, the captain would appear and ask how young "Vasco Da Gama" was faring. By eight o'clock I felt pretty hungry and joined the officers in the saloon. The bacon and eggs had barely slipped down before I was put to work again. This time on a variety of jobs. There was always plenty to do—whipping rope ends to prevent them fraying, oiling the oars and spars of the lifeboats and checking over their stores. Castaways, it seems, exist on barley sugar sticks.

"You can sew up the canvas potato covers," said the second officer one day. I looked at him blankly.

"The potato covers. To protect the spuds from the sun. But no fancy sewing mind you. We use homeward-bound stitches." I still looked mystified. "What the wife calls running stitches," he explained.

One day I was promoted to chief whistle-polisher. I climbed up the funnel, to within a yard of belching black smoke, and rubbed down the tarnished 4-foot-high whistle with Bathbrick and Brasso.

The *Salop* slept in the afternoon, and peace reigned until the steward came in with nauseating cups of tea. I usually managed to slip out before he arrived. For the next half hour I would walk round the boat deck—a most unexciting occupation, but an encouragement to the fruit salts. At eight bells I climbed the companionway for the evening watch. Four hours later I was always ready for bed. Each day for three weeks I went through the same routine.

Then at last *the* day arrived. After a voyage of four thousand miles, across the Atlantic, the *Salop* glided into the artificial harbour of La Guaira, Venezuela.

At a distance La Guaira looked enchanting with its gaily coloured bungalows nestling against a mountain slope. Drawing closer, neat bungalows became tattered shacks stuck precariously onto a cliff of cacti and scrub vegetations. Landslides are frequent and there was nothing to prevent the shacks falling a thousand feet into the Atlantic. The mountain rises straight from the sea and only a very narrow coastal strip provides room for the more permanent settlement.

The *Salop* was brought alongside the quay and moored astern of the Venezuelan President's yacht. Before the gang-plank had been down a couple of minutes the officers and crew were ashore and speeding along the highway to Caracas. Our cargo of sports cars for the nouveau riche of Venezuela would have to remain in the hold for a while.

All this enthusiasm was too much for me. Soon I was bowling along the highway to Caracas in the wake of the crew, a magnificent, six-lane super-highway tunnelling through the mountains and evidence of Venezuela's power and wealth as the world's second-largest oil-producing country. Twenty minutes out from La Guaira I was driven down ten-mile boulevards and avenidos flanked by a flaming bougainvilias in to the heart of a booming South American metropolis. There, colonial-type houses with bright red roof tiles stand side by side with slender glass-and-concrete skyscrapers; multi-coloured marble apartment blocks for workers are attractively sited on knolls around the city, their imaginative design putting London's council flats to shame. Wealth from oil has brilliantly modernised what was once an insignificant banana republic.

High incomes, however, are generally accompanied by high prices. In my circumstances I should have looked out for that. But in my pleasure at having reached the first of the strange continents I had to traverse, I launched out buying a round of beers—twenty-eight shillings down! Back on the ship I put away my diminished capital: three pounds, twelve shillings. Even in three currencies, that sum of three-twelve-nought looked meagre for a man who still had more than four-fifths of the world to cross over.

The *Salop* called next at Port-of-Spain, Trinidad, to pick up nine hundred tons of bunkering oil. As we moved southwards down the east coast of the island, the lights of Trinidad twinkled some ten miles away to port giving me something to stare at while keeping the evening look-out. The captain joined me on the flying bridge after dinner. He asked me to fetch the fog locker key.

"The fog locker key, captain?" I repeated, wondering what on earth was kept in a fog locker.

"Yes, ask Mr. Taylor for it," he said. "I'll stay here and keep look-out. Don't be long."

Mr. Taylor was poring over logarithm tables in the chartroom. He looked up. "What is it?"

"Have you got the fog locker key, sir?"

He stared at me over the top of his spectacles.

"Captain said that you would know. . . ."

"Oh, that's different," he smiled. "Afraid that the old man is mistaken, though. Ask the second engineer."

I clambered below. The second was in the middle of a heated game of poker.

"Sorry to bother you, second," I chipped in at the end of a round, "but the Old Man wants the fog locker key."

"Can't you bloody well wait until I'm through with this?" he snapped.

"I can, but the Old Man won't."

"Oh, blast the Old Man."

The second threw his cards down on the table and stalked off to his cabin. He returned empty-handed.

"The chief must have it." He resumed his game.

I hunted the entire ship for the chief engineer without success. Then I bumped into the captain's boy in the galley who had seen the chief on the boat deck about an hour back. With luck he might still be there. He was—fast asleep in a deck chair. There was nothing for it but to wake the chief, though I could imagine the flow of language that would result. When the invective subsided I was no nearer getting that key. He sent me off to the ship's carpenter, Chippy.

Chippy turned out to be a Spaniard who spoke no English and didn't attempt to understand mine. Instead he just grinned amiably. In despair I returned to my cabin for the Spanish dictionary and hunted through for the three magic words that might get me out of all this—"fog", "locker", "key".

"*Niebla, cajon, llave,*" I repeated in a variety of accents. Chippy nodded and I followed him out of the workshop where he handed me a four-foot sledge-hammer. I protested at once. But Chippy nodded vigorously to assure me that it was what the old man wanted.

Five minutes later I presented the skipper with the fog locker key. "Here you are, sir. Sorry I've taken so long, but I had a bit of trouble finding it."

The Old Man laughed. "Good old Vasco, not surprised you had some difficulty. You seem to have done the complete rounds. Actually there's no such thing as a fog locker key. Now you can take that thing back."

I felt like dropping it on his toe.

Two days before we reached Belem the *Salop* crossed the Equator. We were some two hundred and fifty miles east of the Amazon's mouth. Even as far off shore as this the silt brought down by the river changes the colour of the water from deep green to murky beige. Belem, gateway port to the Amazon, grew up on the neighbouring Para estuary joined to the Amazon by a number of very deep channels known as the narrows. All Amazon traffic must pass through Belem and the narrows.

The city was founded in 1613 as a fortress settlement and slave trading post. For two centuries it was only a small town, but its position close to the mouth of the largest river in the world guaranteed eventual prosperity. Belem bounced into wealth in the late nineteenth century with the discovery of Amazon rubber. Shipments from the interior flowed in an endless stream across her quays, and out of the rubber profits emerged a new Belem with luxurious mansions, magnificent public buildings and clubs for the tycoons. Then came the collapse when rubber cultivation began in the East, and Belem was reduced to a ghost city. The wealth vanished, leaving one inglorious token—a huge red-light district. Today there are signs of an economic revival, and bustling activity moves about her quays as new products of the Amazon find their way to the outside world.

The pilot took the *Salop* up the Para estuary on the rising tide. The first gang-plank went down at midday. We arrived in the midst of riots in the street and knife battles in the dimly-lit bars. These were repercussions of the October-November presidential *coup d'état* in Brazil. On our first night alongside the wharf an important notice appeared on the ship's board. It read—"Belem is officially under a State of Siege."

2

UNDESIRABLE ALIEN

"Undesirable alien," said the Belem immigration officer finally, closing up my passport book. I had only three and a half pounds, therefore the authorities considered me a future dependent upon the State.

"You can't be a European tourist with so little money. It isn't possible," another officer remonstrated. "You must produce a guarantee, otherwise you go home."

Well, that would seem to them a simple solution but I was determined not to turn back now whatever the consequences of my obstinacy. Unfortunately, my position was in no way improved by the attitude of a responsible British resident in Belem. Too loudly he voiced his objections to people travelling on a shoe-string.

"You want to go round the world, you say, and not content with that you think you'd like to travel to the end of the earth—up the Amazon to Iquitos. And with only three and a half pounds in your pocket! I don't suppose you have the slightest idea what it is like beyond Iquitos, or how you are going to cross the Andes, have you? The Amazon's still the most unfriendly river in the world. Suppose you forgot that in the rush of getting here? Why don't you think again, old chap?"

"You might say it is the spirit of adventure," I replied. My heart was set on an Amazon voyage and I was not to be dissuaded. All the same I *was* an "undesirable" here. These officials would be quite happy to hear I was sailing back to London on the *Salop*, their regulations obeyed. Deprived of argument I tried desperately to think of some loop-hole to put before them. Nothing occurred to me. I picked up my passport and left.

But this after all was Belem, not Whitehall. I hadn't taken three steps outside the office before I felt a tap on my shoulder. A voice whispered, "I might be able to help you; meet me at the Casablanca bar in about half-an-hour."

28

Someone glided away.

The Casablanca bar lay in a less respectable part of the town known as Tank Street. It was easy to find. Belemites know the place well and foreigners soon get to know of it. I made sure of the whereabouts first, then drifted in on time. The stranger, a European, picked me out and at once got to business.

"So you want to go up the Amazon to Peru—yes. Well, I'm skipper of a six-hundred-ton craft, taking her a couple of thousand miles up river as far as Iquitos. That any good to you? If it's what you want I could squeeze you in without the whole of Belem knowing."

"When do we leave, captain?"

"Tonight on the tide. We'll be right alongside the *Salop* at eleven to pick you up. You should find it an interesting voyage," he grinned, "most interesting."

Money was never mentioned; of course he knew I hadn't any. I started thanking him; as he would have nothing to gain by helping me, it was difficult to thank him enough.

"There's no need for you to worry about the police or immigration people," he added. "I'll fix them up all right!" We shook hands and left.

A city clock was striking eleven as the M.V. *Trebak* manœuvred along our starboard side. I wished the officers of the *Salop* cheerio, chucked my bags over the rail and jumped from the lower deck on to the *Trebak*'s flying bridge.

"Welcome. Well jumped," the captain greeted me outside the wheelhouse. "Engines full ahead, mate," he yelled through the doorway. "Must reach the narrows before daybreak."

"What's the hurry, sir?" I asked.

"Once we are there nobody stands a chance of finding you," he laughed. But I wasn't so sure that the authorities wouldn't catch up with me. The Amazon is a large river—the largest in the world. . . . A glass of gin put an end to my worries.

"Here, you must sign these," the captain handed me three different forms stating that I was a pilot trainee, a workaway, a tourist.

"What does all this mean?"

"The Amazon is riddled with red tape," he explained. "Brazil, Columbia and Peru all have back doors on the river. Their people don't understand your sort of travel the way we do in Europe. Once they see these papers, they should be quite happy. But I'll post them in Santarem. You should be out of the continent before they reach anyone important."

There seemed to be no limits to the captain's co-operation, but I hoped I could live up to my triple identity.

The *Trebak*'s crew sprawled over the wheelhouse, sitting on the chart table, leaning out of the forward ports, generally lounging about chain-smoking. It was past midnight and I was worn out after a day during which I had combated five people who objected to my Amazon adventure.

"Oh, for a bed," I yawned. "Where do I turn in?"

The captain grinned all over. The luxury of a bunk was the last thing to expect on the *Trebak*.

"You can sling your hammock between the funnel and the life-boat," he said. "You've plenty of company; look after it nicely. Bunch of parrots. Got a hammock and a mosquito net?"

I had neither. The captain unlocked the ship's safe and pointed to a hammock tucked away amongst the *Trebak*'s valuables.

"Belonged to a Brazilian botanist once, but he left it behind. It's all yours."

As I unrolled the hammock a bundle of *cruzeiros*, the local currency, fell to the floor. Everyone was just as surprised as I was.

"Your Eldorado," declared the mate, counting out three hundred of them. "That's about thirty shillings." It was a good beginning, if an unearned one. The botanist had been a thoughtful fellow; what a pity he had forgotten to leave behind his mosquito-net as well.

A silent electrical storm threw flickering flashes across the Amazon, giving me just enough light to sling my hammock between the lifeboat and the funnel. It was cool for the Amazon—about 65 degrees Fahrenheit—and already mosquitoes were investigating up my trouser legs; I climbed into my hammock and found it much more comfortable than I had expected. I was on the move again—travelling due west along the Equator—what could be better? I thought . . . Wonder what the voyage will be like? Hope the im-migration officers don't kick up too much fuss over it all. Funny to be on the Amazon at last! . . . I was sung to sleep by a mosquito.

An unusual noise woke me at dawn—like a piccolo player having trouble with the spit that collects in his instrument. The parrots were treating me to their early morning overture. I should suffer a repeat performance for the next three weeks. I lay back in the hammock with my toes protruding beyond the end. The bough of a tree passed close over our funnel. Trees? I swung round startled. Dark, impenetrable jungle loomed high on the river bank only a few feet from the ship. A mass of foliage collided with the bridge, sprinkling leaves and twigs on the foredeck, and missed the top of the funnel by a couple of inches. I dressed at once and rushed into the wheelhouse, anxious to know why we were so near the bank when the Amazon was supposed to be a hundred miles wide at its mouth.

"We're not in the Amazon yet," the captain smiled. "These are only the narrows. And for your sake I've chosen a course through a small one. The main river is another two hundred miles on." And pointing to the steaming foliage of the river bank, he continued, "That's the island of Marajo. The largest freshwater island in the world; about the size of England."

We stood on the flying bridge, ducking to avoid boughs that took extensive liberties over the water.

"The mate on my last ship got swept right over by a branch," remarked the captain. "Happens quite easily, so keep a good look out."

It was hot, humid, sticky. We sweated as the sun beat down through the gap where the trees from either side of the river did not quite meet in the middle. The jungle too perspired and dripped and was monotonous; trailing lianas, silk cotton trees and palms firmly staked their claims along the edge of the water.

Two days out from Belem the *Trebak* sailed into the Amazon proper. A faint smudge on the northern horizon marked the opposite bank of the main river, and quite often even that disappeared as the Amazon bulged to a width of a hundred miles. There were no other vessels in sight, but as there are so many islands in the river we didn't expect to see any. Ships the size of the *Trebak*, under one thousand tons, stick close to the banks when proceeding up the river. There they keep well out of the fierce current that rushes down the centre at speeds of three to six knots. On the outer edge of a river loop, where the rush of the water is always greater, our speed was reduced by half. On those occasions it took almost a day to round a complete river meander.

Rain showers fell every night between one and three in the morning. I tried to stick it out on deck, but soon exchanged my hammock for a floor-bed in the wheelhouse. Sometimes I offered to take a spin at the wheel still dressed in my pyjamas. The wheel-man enjoyed the break, and it gave me something to do while waiting for the rain to stop.

"Steer course 248". . . "Steady on 248, sir". . . "Port five degrees". . . "Port five degrees it is, sir". This way and that, altering course while the *Trebak* threaded her way between invisible mud-banks and deep purple islands. There was no time to doze on this wheel. The Brazilian pilots navigated with an unerring accuracy, never referring to the ship's charts. I could never understand how they managed this when shoals and mudbanks change their positions at the whim of every storm. At night they leant far out of the bridge windows to use their mysterious powers of navigation under a starless sky. During the day it was easier admittedly, but even then it was amazing how they could recognise every little landmark on a river pilotage 2,000 miles long. The helmsmen too were mystified, but they concluded that they navigated by 'guess and by God' —mainly by guess.

We had two pilots aboard and there was keen competition between them. Like all pilots they were intensely jealous of each other's skill and united only in the common aim to be regarded as super-natural beings. One night I discovered the secret. I saw the flicker of a pencil torch shine for a second on a small roll of paper. The pilot was very reluctant to be drawn into discussion, but some cigarettes I had brought off the *Salop* helped him to open out a little. He showed me the tightly bound paper. The secret was simple. He had drawn up the whole course of the river from Belem to Iquitos. In spite of this disclosure of their methods I still admired the skill of the Amazon pilots.

Close to the town of Santarem the 1000-mile-long river Tapajos discharges clear water into the murky Amazon. We stopped there to refill our fresh-water tanks. Above the confluence the water in the main river becomes muddy and unreliable, so most ships bound for Iquitos take enough water to last the whole of the Amazon voyage. Five hundred miles from the river mouth Santarem is the head of the tidal influence on the river, though the locals main-tain that sometimes the tide can be felt as far up as Manaus, another five hundred miles further on.

The day after we left Santarem the ship ran out of stores, a fact blatantly announced by the cook at breakfast time. To confirm his statement he led us on a conducted tour round the bare shelves and empty cupboards of the galley. There was nothing left but tinned peaches—mountains of them. The captain was furious.

"Could easily have taken on some fresh stuff yesterday," he snapped at the cook, "but now, now of all times, to say that we're short. You've no ruddy commonsense." But the cook merely looked more miserable than ever.

"What do you propose doing?" he blundered on.

"What do I propose doing? Suppose you make the suggestion for a change. We can't live on peaches and whisky."

"We could have a good try," commented the engineer.

Finally we decided to try to replenish our store-cupboard at the next settlement. Sighting some huts in a forest clearing, the captain swung the *Trebak*'s bows shoreward and rammed her into the bank. There is an architectural sameness about all Amazon villages—bamboo-walled huts anchored to the river bank by long wooden poles. These poles support the houses above the level of the water when the river rises to its maximum height in March at the end of the rainy season. The huts are roofed with palm leaves which appear to give adequate protection from the elements.

Our arrival stirred the settlement into activity. Frightened faces of Indian half-breeds and Amazon *cobocoles* peered at us from under the banana leaves.

The captain conveyed our request to them by opening his mouth and pointing down it. There was no answer.

"*Una cosa a comida*," tried the engineer in his best South American, as he called it.

"We want something to eat," concluded the pilot in fluent Portuguese. A delightful babble of tongues suggested that we had at last scored a hit, and a short, wiry-haired man stepped forward to present his menu.

"*Tartaruga*," he announced. We all looked towards the engineer for enlightenment from his 1901 dictionary.

"*Podocnemis expansa*. Turtle," he read out. "Perfect for entrail soup." He was enjoying his importance as an interpreter.

"Sounds delicious," remarked the skipper flatly.

"*Ariranha*" came next, an otter; "*pescada*"—any kind of fish; "*carne*"—meat of nondescript origin. Black beans, looking as though a rabbit had been busy, and bananas by the ton, completed the list. This was our diet for the next two weeks.

No visitor to the Amazon ever forgets the night life. As soon as dusk descends, the air is filled with masses of whirring insects which taunt and persecute throughout the night, giving a special farewell nip at dawn. The miniature is the worst of all mosquitoes. Time means nothing to him as he works his way diligently through an abundance of clothing. It is always the ankles and wrists that suffer. Most of the day is spent suppressing the desire to scratch, but during the night the subconscious takes over with unpleasant consequences. The insects came with pugnacious promptitude and regularity. Some nights the wire netting over the engine-room door and the portholes was so plastered with bugs that I couldn't tell whether there was a light on inside.

Malaria struck down the second mate one morning, and sleeping on deck without a mosquito-net I expected to be the next victim. Mosquito-repellent was useless, but by taking mepacrine tablets I hoped to stave off the day when I should lie in bed shivering and sweating in 80°F. These tablets had worked so far and there was a good chance they might see me through the rest of the voyage.

One thousand miles from the sea, guarding the approach to Manaus, is a lighthouse. Beneath it lies the famous meeting of the waters—the pale waters of the Amazon (River Solimoes) with the black ones of the River Negro. I had heard a great deal about this spectacular hydrological phenomenon in which black and yellow collide, but for some reason it wasn't working that morning. Just beyond the *Encontro* of the two rivers appeared a far more mysterious and impressive spectacle. The dome of an enormous building pierced the green roof of the jungle and glittered in the sunshine. The captain added to my astonishment by remarking, "That's the Opera House." One thousand miles up the Amazon, in the heart of Green Hell—an Opera House?

I laughed, suspecting a joke. "I've never heard of anything so ludicrous. It can't be. . . ."

But rounding the next bend I saw the rest of the building, with a sizeable town sprawling around it. This must be the most useless two and a half million dollar extravagance in the world.

The captain told me the story. European tycoons in Manaus in the 1890's built it with the surplus of their fantastic rubber profits. They wanted a building that would gain the admiration of the whole world. They brought marble from Italy, glass from Austria and sumptuous furnishings from France and Germany. The greatest operas of all time were destined to be performed there. From Paris, Vienna, Milan, they came at the call of the millionaires. The Amazon quayside bristled with trade; rubber boomed; a resplendent future seemed assured for Manaus. Yet all this prosperity was doomed when an Englishman, Sir Henry Wickham, took some rubber seeds to Kew Gardens, from where they were sent to the Far East. Competition from the cultivated rubber plantations set up in Ceylon and Malaya soon burst the Amazon rubber bubble. As it was no longer profitable to exploit isolated rubber trees, the attention of Europe turned from South America to the Orient. The great Manaus reverted into an insignificant jungle town, as the rubber trade was abandoned. The operatic heyday became a romantic memory.

But today Manaus is recovering. Natural resources are being exploited. Her new products—manganese, iron ore, oil, rosewood, etc., and her position at the confluence of the Negro and the Amazon offer her a future of renewed greatness and prosperity.

What of the Opera House, whose white marble walls have been silenced for nearly half a century? Grand finales and curtain calls are still things of the past, but in their place you may now hear a timid voice announcing the date of the next local town meeting. The few inhabitants who remember the sumptuous early 1900's have faith in their idol and they patiently await an operatic revival in Manaus. The dome still glitters. I left Manaus hoping too that some day her "white elephant" might lose that sobriquet.

Staccato puffs from the engine room warned the captain of trouble brewing. The engines needed some careful coaxing if we were to reach Iquitos without a breakdown.

"Give them a rest at Tobatinga," the captain decided. "We've a few sheets of corrugated iron to unload there anyway."

Our flashlight scanned the bank for a suitable mud berth at Tobatinga. The beam drew excited natives from their hammocks even at three o'clock in the morning. They swarmed aboard, headed by a wizened grandma. The captain, who always reacted well on these occasions, seated them all in the saloon. Dark eyes flashed with greedy delight at the tinned peaches, in spite of an abundance of fruit in their village. Voluptuous Amazon maidens with their wiry black hair and plump faces, dressed in cheap imitations of western clothes, grew ecstatic over their presents of trinkets, while the older ones, some of them carrying babies, were highly satisfied with cigarettes.

By mid-morning we were all ashore, led by the elderly señora who took us round her clearing in the forest. Our progress towards the sugar plantation was impeded by children who scrambled

35

up the palm trees and dropped coconuts at appropriate moments missing us by a few inches. A direct hit on the head means instant death I was told, but this was just the sort of game that little Amazon boys like to play.

Beneath a roof of palm leaves stood the two crushing-wheels for squeezing juice from the sugar cane. They were normally turned by an animal and two men, but the animal had died and work was suspended. Once the cane is crushed the juice runs through a collecting funnel and into a frying-pan about four feet in diameter. Next it is boiled over a charcoal fire. The hot juice is then poured into wooden moulds and left to crystallize.

I drew the captain's attention to a small, palisaded garden.

"That's the medicine chest," he told me. "Most Indians keep a good stock of quassia, castor oil, senna pods and a hair tonic called *jaborandi*." "It stops the mosquito," added the señora in Portuguese when she saw me looking at some rhubarb-sized leaves. I picked a dozen leaves at once.

The entire crew of the *Trebak* entered the family hut up a series of log steps. We stumbled about inside, tripping over a heap of Brazil nuts on the floor.

Behind a lacework of hammocks stood a stack of blowpipes. The captain's eyes fixed on them while he calculated their commercial value on the European market.

"What can I give you in exchange for these?" He waved at them casually. Turning to me he added, "You know, my wife enjoys such—er . . . how do you call it—novelties? Souvenirs from the Amazon."

Yes, I could guess their value all right. The Indians hadn't until now been besieged by the experienced souvenir hunter. The captain glanced towards the second mate, who went out at once. He returned with an armful of tinned peaches.

"Two tins of fruit in return for one blowpipe and a quiver of darts?" the captain suggested. Food means existence to the mestizoes and they were ready to barter even on these terms. I noticed on the shelf a bag of flour with "Liverpool" written on it and a tin of chocolate on the shelf and felt proud that Britain's exports should reach these outposts beyond civilization. The deal was clinched: we made off with a dozen valuable curios. The mate and I snapped off a round of photographs to commemorate the visit and we returned to the *Trebak* after everyone had had a go at saying "*Muchas gracias*". The *Trebak* was the first foreign ship to call in at this homestead and the inhabitants were very excited as they waved goodbye to us. They would talk about us for a long time.

Someone was swinging my hammock. It was six o'clock and I had overslept, but then I had good reason to as during the night rain had forced me to seek refuge in the wheelhouse at least five times. The captain's son stood over me. "Come and have a look at the *Trebak's* new dart game." I slipped on my shoes after making sure that no creature had sought a night's lodging in them, and peered over the bridge. The mate had wedged an enormous bull's-eye between the anchor winch and the forward breakwater. The aft end of the blowpipe range was the bridge, so that even the wheelman could join in the game. From then on it was a competition, the half-inch tip of poison adding a touch of danger to the fun.

Indians have perfected the skill of making blowpipes through centuries of practice. They select two palms of straight grain, gouge grooves down the centre with the tooth of a *piranha* fish and bind the palms together with *jacitara* weed. The bore is as smooth as that of a rifle, quite an achievement since a sand pull-through is the only tool they use. The mouthpiece, a cup-shaped bit of wood, concentrates a gentle puff into the minute bore, then kapok at the other end punches all this force behind the lethal bamboo dart, giving it an effective range of at least 50 yards.

"Blow!" yelled the mate. My dart hurtled towards the bull and missed.

Ninety degrees Fahrenheit, and nearly one hundred per cent humidity. It was eleven a.m., siesta hour. The heat was oppressive —I felt lethargic.

"Let's have a bit of relaxation," suggested the Old Man. "It's too ruddy hot to work." We found some wicker chairs in one of the cargo holds, labelled for a "Dr. Carter".

"Don't suppose the doctor will mind us using them," he said, bringing the chairs on deck. "Only second-hand by the time they reach him. Quite an advantage carrying such a varied cargo."

I had been sitting for a couple of minutes when prickly heat started to work on my behind. I got up, sweated more under this exertion, taunted the parrots and received a hearty nip. Blast those birds! This was the Amazon that I had dreamed about. But it was hellish hot; a temper-fraying climate that turns minor irritations into nearly insupportable sufferings, that saps your strength, leaving you more lethargic at every turn of the river. You know damn well you should work to snap out of this state, but somehow you can't do anything about it.

My trickles of perspiration became rivers of sweat. I was frantic with thirst and ignored the skipper's experienced warning. "The more you drink the more you sweat, then your thirst is worse. So it's better not to start drinking."

The fresh-water tap trickled out half a glassful of brown-looking liquid and then gave up. The tanks must be dry. That was odd; we had replenished our supply a week ago at Salinas. Perhaps there was a blockage in the pipe. I decided to investigate the trouble without bothering the Old Man. The tank lay on top of the bridge and I climbed up to have a look at it. My curiosity drove me to work ten bolts loose. I removed the cap and peered in. Was I imagining things or had I really found the wine cellar? Groping into the tank I touched a wooden surface, straw, and then glass. I pulled out a bottle of Queen Anne whisky! No wonder the captain had promised me an interesting voyage. We were smugglers. Well, there was no backing out now. Of course I had to mention my discovery to the captain, but it wouldn't be easy to broach the subject.

In the saloon the captain was quietly putting away a bottle of Queen Anne. Perhaps he had seen me looking into the tank and thought this would ease the tension.

"Er—captain," I stumbled, "I see we have our own little distillery aboard."

He showed no surprise at the remark, and merely waited for me to continue. I regretted having opened the subject. Another minute slipped by before the captain broke the silence.

"And did you know," he asked pleasantly, "that we also have our own tobacco plantation?"

I made no attempt to conceal my astonishment.

"Come on." He got up. "Now you understand how we make a living, you'd better see all our ripening harvest. It's due to mature sometime during the next three hundred miles or so; I shouldn't like you to miss the fun. Anyway, I was counting on your co-operation."

No wonder the skipper had been so anxious to assist me in Belem. The events of the last hour had jolted the monotony of the daily routine. The Amazon was waking up at last, though not quite in the way I had expected. I followed the captain to the spare fuel tank in the engine room.

"Take a good look inside," he said, removing the cap-nuts, "such sights are rare these days."

I stared at the *Trebak's* supercargo—cigarettes by the million!

"What's the oil drum doing in the middle?" I asked.

The skipper laughed. "It's full of oil. Stands under the fuel gauge pipe in case a suspicious officer wants to check the amount of oil in the tank. His stick goes into the full oil drum. But most of them don't bother about the oil check; they've got enough sense to accept their share of cigarettes and liquor."

The engineer replaced the cap and painted over the screws to conceal the fact that they had been recently tampered with.

Whisky enough to inebriate all the people of the Amazon lay beneath groaning cement bags in No. 2 hold. And next to it were rolls of nylon which the sailors had been handing out to the river Indians.

"We must move all that whisky to a safer place tonight," said the captain. "We've some tough customers to deal with to-morrow."

He left a skeleton crew to run the ship while the rest transferred the contraband from the hold to a craftily constructed locker in the funnel. It was exhausting work and I wondered whether I should come in for any share of the rewards.

The *Trebak's* private mission was succeeding so far but there was always the grave possibilty that not every customs official could be induced to overlook such mammoth contraband. Fleeting visions of imprisonment in the heart of the jungle floated into my mind; my future seemed rather precarious.

A hard day's work in the sweltering heat justified some refreshment. The captain stopped the *Trebak* at a small village, Castro do Rio Solimoes. The entire crew went ashore and into the local bar. Remembering that disastrous round at Caracas I stayed by the captain. By midnight the tables were crammed with empty bottles and two of the Guianese members of our crew had become over-excited. When their vocabulary gave out they came to blows. Beer flowed over the tables and on to the floor in frothy puddles. No one knew what the quarrel was about and it was difficult to interfere. But when knives were drawn the police thought it was time to step in and break it up. The police officer declared he hadn't seen anything like it since a tribe had carried off a relation of his to supply the blossoming tourist trade in shrunken heads.

"Stop these men!" he yelled. "They kill each other. I have blame."

"Don't interfere," the captain rapped out. Obeying his order we all watched from the door of the customs house, a bamboo shack opposite the bar. Suddenly there was a piercing scream from the barmaid. "*Sangue! Sangue!*"

Blood was seeping through one man's jacket. This was too much for the authorities. The officer drew his revolver and fired into the air. There was a silence, and it seemed that all the night life of the forest awaited the outcome with bated breath; not even another scream from the barmaid; she had fainted.

The combatants fled into the jungle.

"What will you do, captain?" the officer enquired anxiously. He was reviving the barmaid with oil-of-rose-wood smelling-salts.

"You can treat them as deserters. Do anything you like with them: I'm not having them back."

The officer protested, no doubt wishing to avoid the responsibility of looking after them. But the captain was adamant. Anyway, they were as good as imprisoned here, a thousand miles from the sea. No other vessel was coming this way for at least six weeks.

Our party returned to the *Trebak* minus its two lively members. A few minutes later all the lights were out and everyone fast asleep. None of us suspected that mischief-making had only just begun.

Determined to have their revenge on the captain, the Guianese informed the police about the *Trebak's* private mission. The information stirred the whole bluecoat force of the town into action. The *Trebak* was invaded at four in the morning. The captain acted swiftly. Most Amazon locals are on the continual lookout for anything to brighten their material life. Whisky and cigarettes would be most acceptable bribes. So the Old Man saved the day by a well-timed sharing of his stocks. Of course he was generous. He couldn't afford to be otherwise. The whisky flowed and the cigarettes found their way into the hands of the law. The police needed no further confirmation that all was well aboard the *Trebak*. After giving them a helping hand over the gangplank we pulled up hook to continue our journey up-river a little sooner than we planned, and with the bulk of the supercargo intact. All Iquitos-bound vessels have to take on a police officer at Castro do Rio Solimoes, so one officer remained with us. But the moment his pals were off the boat, his swimming eyes registered the magical phrase "I no see", as they gazed upon another crate of whisky. He would play ball so long as the game ended in personal profit.

"We're unloading the stuff tonight," the captain informed us at dinner. "Expect to be called anytime after ten o'clock." He turned towards me. "Don't mind lending a hand, do you? You've pretty little choice in the matter, but if it's carried through without a hitch I'm sure you'll find it quite rewarding."

I woke up to a jangle of bells on the telegraph. The time was 2 a.m. The captain must have signalled slow ahead to the engine room. I tumbled out of my hammock and rushed to the wheelhouse, tripping over the policeman lying prostrate on the deck. He was breathing heavily and obviously wouldn't give us any trouble.

A long way to starboard, a number of small outboard motor craft were making their way towards us. The captain's careful arrangements were working out fine. We slowed down for the launches to draw alongside. "Damn fools! Wish they'd turn out their navigation lights; whole country will know about our little mission before we're through. How far are we from the bank, pilot?"

"A mile, captain."

"Good. Any spectators shouldn't notice that we've slackened speed." He leant over the flying bridge.

"All the stuff on deck?" he yelled down. "They'll be here in a minute."

I joined the men sweating in the hold, shifting hundred-weight bags of cement into the gaping hole where the contraband had been. Then six of us scrambled on deck to load the crates from the funnel locker and fuel tanks on to four craft now alongside. They were more than fully loaded, but there was still a mountain on deck to be squeezed on somehow.

"Too much, captain. No more room here," the helmsman on one of the launches shouted up.

"You *must* take it," came the Old Man's appeal from the bridge. "Can't risk it being found on board. Look, I'll have one of your men; easily drop him at the next village, but get that stuff off, and hurry."

Five minutes later the last of the launches was away. "Operation Queen Lucky", as the captain referred to it afterwards, had gone off without a hitch.

The draft of the *Trebak* had decreased from thirteen to twelve feet.

"We must fill all the forward tanks with water to give her the same draft as before," the Old Man told the mate. "Otherwise the customs at the next port might be suspicious."

He pulled out his log book and wrote under the date, "0200 hours engine trouble, steam-valve blown, speed reduced to three knots. 0230 hours, full speed ahead." Every detail was planned.

"How did you manage to load the cigarettes without arousing any suspicion?" I wondered aloud.

"Oh, quite simple," replied the Old Man. "Bought them two months ago, no trouble thanks to the co-operation of the customs officer. When the cigarettes arrived on the quayside he remarked that we were taking on enough for a transatlantic Cunarder. A hundred quid convinced him that we were all chain-smokers."

"And now, Mr. Boyd," he poured out nine glasses of whisky, "to the success of *your* trip."

At the frontier station of Piguayal, a rapidly-moving gun-boat brought the *Trebak* to a halt.

The presence of such a warship eighteen hundred miles from the ocean seemed incongruous. For a moment I wondered if the law had caught with the *Trebak* after all. However, it was only that all craft must stop and produce their papers here. While the ship's documents were being examined, the mate decided to take the *Trebak's* lifeboat for an evening expedition up a tributary river to the village of Piguayal. One of the pilots came with us and navigated with a torch. After stumbling up a mud bank to the village we came across the local pub, a bamboo hut lit by a solitary candle. There was no one about. Three dirty beer bottles laced with cobwebs stood on the shelf. Someone found a clay cup; we helped ourselves and drank a toast to our absent hosts. In twenty minutes we had emptied all the bottles. As the mate wasn't sure which country we were in, he deposited a generous amount of both Brazilian *cruzeiros* and Columbian *pesos* on the table. Before returning to the *Trebak* we serenaded the whole village with a rousing song.

We left the frontier station next morning. The *Trebak* hadn't long been under way when we saw a crowd of natives waving to us from the right bank of the river. "Probably want a free ride to the next town up-river," said the captain. "We'd better pull in and see."

The Indians disappeared the moment we came within calling distance. The mate waved back at the jungle to show them our friendly intentions, but there was no movement from the bank. Suddenly a barrage of rifle shots flew out across the water.

"Down!" yelled the captain. We dropped on all fours in the wheelhouse. "Get out the blowpipes, quick. Let them taste their own bloody toys for a change. Pilot, turn her round; too ruddy slow against the current. We're a sitting target."

The *Trebak's* bows swung down the river to give her the maximum speed possible with a five-knot current behind her. The crew manned each of the starboard portholes with a blowpipe and poisoned darts. Our assailants rattled off their ammunition without taking aim, their bullets flying in every direction but that of the target. When at right angles to their line of fire the *Trebak* delivered her deadly broadside. "Blow!" roared the captain. "And again, blow!" Darts hurtled to the shore accompanied by the blood-curdling yells of the civilised crew. The savages on the bank were silenced.

Three weeks out of Belem, still celebrating her unorthodox victory with what was left of the contraband, the *Trebak* steamed into San Raphael, eighteen hundred miles up the Amazon. On the small floating quay a bevy of officials in grey uniform waited to receive us. One of them, the one heavily decked out in gold braid, strode aboard waving a document.

"Perhaps you will be good enough to explain, captain. A message informs us that this ship is carrying illicit cargo."

The captain's eyes scanned the telegram unflinchingly; it had come from the police at Castro do Rio Solimoes. He made no comment. The officer ordered him to surrender his keys and strode out of the saloon. We heard him locking the entire crew inside. I wondered how long he would take to discover that he locked the stable after the horse had gone.

"They don't want anyone around while they're tooth-combing the cargo," the captain grinned.

Seven noses flattened out against the saloon's portholes to witness the grand finale. It was enacted on the foredeck and portrayed frantic desperation. The police had been right through the ship and so far hadn't found a thing. Our cargo of cement bags was the last to suffer the relentless prod of the officers' knives. They piled all the bags on deck—this itself took them over an hour. Sweating revenge, they were certain that the stuff was hidden amongst the cement. They didn't stop to untie the bags but ripped them open. The light grey powder rose in clouds and worked its way over the deck and on to the quayside. Heedlessly they ripped open bag after bag. A strong wind sprang up with the abruptness of all Amazon storms. Cement powder swooshed into the air; then came the rain.

The captain drained the last bottle of Queen Anne as we watched a gang of twenty men begin to clear the cement off the deck before the sun hardened it. Someone quietly unlocked the saloon door.

3

THE END OF THE EARTH . . . AND BEYOND

"*Perla del Amazonas*" (Pearl of the Amazon), is one description of Iquitos. It is a pocket in the heart of the jungle, the same unchanging jungle stretching as far as one could see, though we were now in Peru. Here was the end of the voyage for the *Trebak*. I wished the captain good luck and thanked him for the lift.

"That's all right; glad of your company, as a matter of fact. Besides," he started a little grin, "you worked pretty hard as a deck-hand when you were needed. So here's a little 'hush' money to help you on your way."

He pressed a bundle of notes into my palm—three hundred *soles* when I counted them, about five pounds. Well, not bad. I had now over nine pounds in all, having almost doubled my original capital. So much for the Belem unbelievers and their fear that I'd become a charge on the State. Of course luck had been with me so far; it might not hold for the next few thousand miles, I reminded myself as the *Trebak* berthed. The warning thought could not prevent me from looking benignantly at the crowd of Iquitens come to welcome the boat in.

They were girls mostly, quite a bevy of local beauties. So Iquitos should have plenty of social opportunities to offer. A walk to the Plaza de Armas confirmed this impression. There an evening procession of beauty and grace strolled the square, utterly frustrated in its search for youthful beaux. The arrival of a newcomer, even of a penniless globetrotter, was an event. At least three pairs of dreamy eyes followed my movements, speculating and hoping. In Iquitos, work for young men was limited, and most of them had to leave town at an early age to seek employment elsewhere. Unless the girls were emancipated and also left home in search of employment, the position had little chance of levelling off. *Perla del Amazonas* is off the beat for most sailors, but those who do reach it think it well worth the stay.

Few visitors pass through Iquitos without spending an evening at the eighty-year-old local dance hall. "A rubber tycoon took a fancy to the building at the Paris exhibition of 1870," I was told, "bought the thing, had it shipped up the Amazon and re-assembled here as a gambling house. One evening he staked the whole building on the turn of a card—and lost."

By the time we reached the hall its dance floor was packed with a hundred couples gently swaying their hips to the rhythm of a samba. There were far more girls than men. Five señoritas rushed across the floor to greet me. The one I picked out for a partner introduced herself in a deep voice as Chirusa Arnais. She spent most of her time gazing at me through her large appealing eyes, which opened soulfully when I murmured "*bonita*" and "*simpática*". But my vocabulary of adjectives was very limited and I soon ran out of conversation. Chirusa lacked nothing. She was a good dancer but for the terrific speed at which she whirled me around the dance-floor. On our twelfth circuit the music stopped, much to my relief.

As the band struck up the introductory notes to the next number a colossus of a woman bore down on us and grabbed Chirusa. Wishing me "*Buenas noches*" she propelled her charge from the room. Perhaps it wasn't the "done thing" to spend so long with a chaperoned señorita. I pursued them across the floor and tried to remonstrate with the mother, but she turned a deaf ear. Iquitens around me fizzled with delight when they saw what had happened and I heard the mate of the *Trebak* shout across the floor, "Serve you blooming well right!" Disappointed? Well there were a hundred others to fill the gap.

Iquitens make their living out of the jungle and look to its undeveloped resources for their future prosperity. There was a business-like air about the town. Jeeps and omnibuses pounded along its potholed streets of crumbled mud and fine sand, always accompanied by a trail of dust that hung in a persistent cloud before settling down again.

Only one road penetrated the forest beyond the city, but it soon gave up its struggle with the vegetation and ended in a jungle entanglement. On three sides Iquitos was completely sealed in by jungle; the Amazon was her only life-line with the rest of the world. Two thousand miles from the sea, Iquitos held the unique distinction of having the farthest-inland harbour in the world for ocean-going vessels.

Along the waterfront straggled the native quarter, Belen. This

was a temporary home town for those who paddled down the river
to trade their fish and fruits in the native market. They remained
in Belen until they had sold everything before attempting the
difficult return journey up- or down-river to their *chacras* (home-
steads) several hundred miles away.

Belen's muddy streets were thronged with people. Native women
wobbled past with *ollas* (baskets) of bananas precariously balanced
on their heads. There were mules laden with water-bottles and
gourds, and scruffy children who struggled along, shoulders bent
beneath bamboo rods with buckets suspended at the ends. Young
children sat making beads from the *chacuna* shrub and colourful
fans out of fish-scales and feathers from the umbrella bird. They
spent siesta time diving off balsa rafts or kicking balls of chewing
gum, which awaited export to the United States, round the muddy
quay.

I left Belen before the smell overpowered me and called in at the
offices of a large transport firm run by one of the three Englishmen
in Iquitos. The director welcomed me with exaggerated cordiality.

"Come in, come in. My name's Harry Holdsworth. Delighted
to see you."

The enjoyment of meeting a fellow countryman so far away from
home was mutual and we talked quite a while before I tackled him
about my problem.

He listened patiently to my story. "I've got four hundred and
fifty *soles*," I concluded. "I must reach Lima somehow. What
are my chances?"

"Lima! On 450 *soles*?" exclaimed Mr. Holdsworth. "You must
be crazy. Asking for a miracle to happen. Lima's over a thousand
miles away. Take you at least a month to get there by launch and
truck. And with only that cash . . ." He looked at me with an assess-
ing gaze. "Well, give me a day. I'll see if there's a craft going up
the Ucayali River for you. Can't promise anything though. It's
the wrong season for up-river traffic, so don't depend too much on
my efforts." But all my hopes rested on his efforts; I *had* to depend
on them. Sure enough a few days later he had some good news.

"You're damn lucky. There's a small cargo-tug sailing for
Pucallpa tonight. The captain doesn't mind taking you, providing
you lend a hand."

"Of course, I'll do anything."

"And don't go expecting a bunk because you won't get one.
Food's another luxury on board so you'd better stoke up before-

47

hand. There's nothing else sailing up the Ucayali for some time, so it's this or nothing."

"Thanks a million for fixing it. I can manage with my hammock all right. Getting into the way of life on the Amazon. Another two weeks of it should be fun."

Mr. Holdsworth spun round and stared. "Fun! That's a strange way of putting it. Hitch-hiking round the world with empty pockets is one thing, travelling the old Pichis trail to Lima is quite another. Not the sort of fun I'd hanker after. Did you *have* to come up the Amazon? Just about the most uncivilized spot left on earth. A few years ago it was a sure way of committing suicide. Quite an interesting, original, exciting way no doubt. Iquitos used to be called 'the end of the earth'; few people dared venture beyond it. Hasn't changed such a lot since then, you know. Anything can happen on the upper reaches of this river. And just supposing you pull through the Ucayali trip there's still the Andes ahead of you, a much bigger proposition than you seem to imagine. And another thing, once the rains have set in over the mountains the track to Lima is blocked. If you don't hurry I'll be seeing you back in Iquitos."

His words were reminiscent of the cautionary tales I had heard at the mouth of the Amazon, but nothing could dampen my enthusiasm.

"Good-bye, anyway, and lots of luck." He moderated his tone a little. "You should be all right, but take care." He strode away from the quay in his spotless white trousers, and I wondered how long it would be before I should speak English again. From now till Lima I should probably have to rely on a Spanish dictionary and gesticulations.

There was no one around when I clambered aboard the tug *Jean*, so I sat on the saloon table and waited. *Jean* didn't look like a tug-boat. She was rectangular, thirty-nine feet long, eight feet in the beam, more like a cardboard box on floats. Two flat barges loaded with oil drums and cedar wood were fastened to her blunt bows. The saloon had a wooden roof but its sides were open to the weather. Snuggling below the saloon was the engine room. Beneath a pile of greasy spanners were two grimy plate rings—the galley. The captain and pilot occupied the only cabins aboard.

An unruly commotion on the quay heralded the return of the *Jean*'s inmates. They clambered aboard obviously past caring whether we sailed or not.

1. "One day I was promoted to chief whistle-polisher." On the *Salop* in the Atlantic.

2. An Amazon river settlement.

3. The tug *Jean* pushed a barge loaded with cedar wood—and Señorita Camilla's belongings. On the Amazon.

"Hallo," I greeted them cheerily. They looked at me in silence. The captain, whom I had managed to pick out by now, was temporarily lost for words, and I began to feel embarrassed. He probably hadn't taken Mr. Holdsworth's request too seriously. Just at that moment, however, it didn't seem to matter who I was or what I was doing on the *Jean* so long as I kept well out of the way whilst she got ready to move.

Half an hour later we were ready to go. The engines refused to start. The engineer flew into a rage and impatiently wielded a hammer, as though hoping to frighten them into action. Dreadful noises came from below, then a series of mysterious bangs. The *Jean*'s inside suddenly spluttered into life.

Fifteen canoes hooked on to our stern in two long lines as we manœuvred into mid-river.

"A tow for them saves many days of paddling against the river current," explained a young passenger standing next to me. It was a pleasant surprise to hear English spoken after all. "In return, wherever the *Jean* stops they must break away and catch fish for us."

At the moment fishing seemed to be far from their thoughts. In the faint glow of oil lamps they were drinking and gambling away their earnings. One after another lost all his money and dropped out. Some began to mend their nets while others made string hammocks to sell on the next visit to market.

Two hours later the lights of Iquitos were still visible. We hadn't progressed much against the strong current of the river. No wonder the shipping agents had warned me that the 700 mile journey to Pucallpa might take several weeks.

The deck saloon became a cabin for seven of us, including a señora who had forgotten her age but looked like an octogenarian. Amidst the chaos of undressing in this confined space she demanded a certain amount of privacy. Every night, four other passengers lifted up the table while she undressed beneath. She invariably got stuck putting her arms through the sleeves of her nightdress, but she staunchly refused any help.

The rest of us laced our hammocks in tiers and at last the *Jean*'s inmates settled down for their first night together. Someone put out the light and there was peace; but not for long. I turned over and my bottom grazed the top of the saloon table. Someone else's brushed to and fro over my hair. The captain's boy, a grubby nine-year-old, discovered that sleeping on a bench was not to his liking so scrambled on to the floor. The old lady announced that she had forgotten her pillow. We handed her my hammock bag stuffed with clothes. Within half an hour of settling down again most of us had to get out and tighten our hammock-ends. Every time someone switched on the lamp the saloon was invaded by insects. The mosquitoes had a delightful feast and the rest of the night was punctuated by exclamations, slappings and curses.

The *Jean's* community stirred early. When one person decided to get up, the arrangement of the hammocks compelled the rest to follow suit. The old lady started the ball rolling on our first morning because she couldn't tolerate the boy's smelly toes dangling a few centimetres away.

Washing presented no problems if you didn't mind using slimy yellow water. You merely threw a bucket overboard and poured the contents over your head. The same water was considered good enough for drinking. The señora saw me looking at the debris floating in my glass. "Don't worry," she indicated with vigorous signs, "it all goes down and out the same way." There was coffee and dry bread for breakfast. "The canoes have not fished yet," the young passenger called Romega reminded me. Lunch and supper followed the same pattern.

When the *Jean* stopped at dusk, the fishermen dropped their tow-ropes and paddled away. A sharp cracking noise echoed round the quiet reaches of the Ucayali as they beat the waters with long bamboo sticks to frighten the fish into their nets. It made us feel even more hungry. By nightfall they had landed ten of the two thousand varieties of Amazon fish. One was the *paiche*, the second largest fresh-water fish in the world. It had an enormous slit for a mouth which gave it a silly grin. From then on the *paiche* was served for breakfast, lunch and supper. Black beans boiled or fried bananas, rice and river soup completed the meal. There was little variety on the *Jean's* menu.

Indians would paddle over to us from the bank, hold up a squawking chicken, and if the captain liked the look of it he stopped the tug and bartered a gallon of petrol in exchange.

"A gallon for a chicken, captain?" I exclaimed after he had bought three birds.

"And what's more, petrol's only two *soles* [eleven pence] a gallon in Peru." I was installed as cashier and soon became quite skilled at measuring out a gallon of petrol by guesswork. By the third day I had collected ten chickens.

"How about a blow-out?" I asked. "We've enough chickens

for one each." I doubt if the captain understood but he nodded in agreement, so we treated ourselves to a succulent change in the menu.

At breakfast one morning the mate handed me a spoonful of yellow peppers. "It will help the fish down," he said gaily, and I swallowed them eagerly. I spent the rest of the day pouring gallons of water down my throat to relieve the acute burning. Everyone thought it a great joke. But I was wondering how my stomach would react to such a quantity of Ucayali river as up till then I had been drinking only a mouthful per meal.

The burning subsided in the afternoon. Romega was the only one to sympathize. "I'll show you something to make you forget all about your stomach," he said. "Have you ever seen a *piranha* fish at work?"

"No. I've heard a lot about them. Are they as deadly as people say?"

"You can see for yourself, if you want, but don't expect too much from them. They're only very small and most of their work is done underwater. I'll ask the captain to wait a few minutes at the next village. We must get some fresh meat to tempt them alongside."

The captain was glad to let the engines cool down a bit and stopped at Saquena. Romega dashed ashore and bought a pig's head from the market place. Back on the tug again we fixed the meat to some wire, then dangled it over the side. The *Jean* had been underway for some time; I was beginning to think that the *piranhas* were an old Amazon wives' tale when there was a sudden commotion in the water. The *piranhas* had caught up with us.

A flash of silver bodies, lured by the smell of blood, darted forwards and sank their fine sharp teeth into the carcase, greedily fighting over chunks of flesh. A few seconds later the orgy was over. Only bloodstained water remained a little while before the current carried it downstream.

"Dangerous bathing," Romega remarked, and for some reason everyone roared with laughter.

On Christmas Eve the *Jean* drew into the river town of Requena. Romega and I went ashore with the tug's engineer to look at the local celebrations. In every street children were skipping along in disorderly processions lit by candlelight. They yelled their Christmas carols in the tempo of a frenzied mamba. Several boys strove to get a note or two out of wooden instruments, whilst those less musically ambitious thudded tom-toms.

A few young people were acting the Christmas story in a wine cellar. The spectators enlivened their interpretation by letting off home-made fireworks. We stopped to eat avocados—the alligator pears—and drink the local wine from the wayside stalls. Later in the evening we went dancing. Everyone seemed to be holding a party. We progressed down the street from one house to another, joining in the merriment of our hosts who were fascinated by my unorthodox dancing steps. Many villagers turned out for midnight Mass in the Roman Catholic church, and although an Anglican I joined in the service.

Christmas day came and went like any other day on the river. The captain managed to open a tin of cheese in celebration, but fish soup, boiled *paiche* and bananas constituted the rest of the Christmas dinner, the six-inch rib bone of the *paiche* making a mammoth substitute for the wishbone. I found it difficult to think of the Christmas story and missed my home a good deal.

On Boxing Day tummy troubles started in full force. The peppers and river water weren't going to let me off lightly. An absence of modern sanitary convenience was a tribulation which now assumed immense proportions. The heat was insufferable. I left my hammock in the saloon and lay flat on cedar-planks on the barge. But before long the white-hot sun drove me back to the shade of the saloon. I learnt to stop moaning—it only brought teasing and ridicule from my fellow travellers.

The Ucayali had reached full flood, dislodging trees and long trailing weeds which floated down-river. The tree trunks offered a convenient roost for white egret birds, perched like a display of giant snowdrops. During the day the pilot could thread his way through, but at night the submerged trunks were a serious threat to navigation. We were often disturbed by loud bumps beneath the hull. This would be followed by a jangle of bells, then silence from the engine and more bumps. The captain peered from his cabin praying for the propellers. When the last of the bumps were over and the engines spluttered into action again, he would give a grunt of satisfaction and return to his bunk.

On a six-hour night watch the pilot's attention was apt to wander. One night, he must have been thinking of those señoritas in Iquitos. There were terrific bumps, then a twanging sound aft. Suddenly the *Jean* began to swing round in little circles. The propellers were out of action.

The captain stormed out of his cabin. "*Caraco!*" he bellowed. "What the hell are you doing?"

At first I thought that "Caraco" was the name of the pilot, as I had heard the captain mention it many times, but when I started calling the pilot that he didn't respond very well.

The *Jean* drifted helplessly down-stream, her whistle screaming for help. The captain stormed up and down the deck airing his usual vocabulary. We were drifting back, past bends in the river we had struggled round.

"Won't be long before we're back in Iquitos," the captain fumed. His expletives were interrupted by the arrival of a launch which had put out from one of the cedar plantations to assist us—for a fee. The captain well knew that this wasn't the moment to start bargaining; he agreed to the financial terms at once. The launch pushed us on to a mudbank and there the engineer dived into the water to look at the damage.

He came to the surface grinning mischievously. "Rudder is bent into a right angle—propeller shaft twisted," he shouted up to us. Both parts needed renewing and everyone had to help. Waist deep in mud and water we tried to sort out screws and nuts. The frightening stories of the Amazon's voracious inmates suddenly took on a fresh meaning. I couldn't forget the razor-toothed *piranhas* which I had already seen at work. In spite of constant assurances from Romega that *piranhas* never attack unless there was blood flowing in the water, they would be unwelcome swimming companions. Bloodthirsty leeches lurked in the river, as well as the electric eel, which throws out charges powerful enough to stun a man and make it impossible for him to swim. The very thought of this long, lethal monster wriggling through the water sent a tingling down my spine and made me screw up the nuts a little faster. The *Jean* was repaired by breakfast-time and we were all glad to leave the mud berth.

The sound of our engine drew excited Indian families from villages on the mudbanks. Naked infants, suffering from acute avoirdupois of the belly, stood high on the bank and waved frantically as they watched our little symbol of civilisation struggle past. How lonely and microscopic the villages looked against the jungle towering behind their defiant clearings. The river is the only means of communication with their neighbouring settlements.

A canoe-load of Indians passed close to us.

"Those are Chamas Indians," said the captain. "I'll ask them to come alongside for you. We can exchange some milk for bananas."

The Chamas were very shy at first and it took ten minutes for the captain to persuade them that our intentions were friendly before they would draw nearer.

Two women in the stern of the canoe covered their faces with long black skirts to hide a gold ornament which each had threaded through her nose. A lethal-looking spear longer than the canoe itself protruded from the bows.

"They've speared a *piraraca*." One of the crew grabbed my arm, hoping that I would share his enthusiasm. But the *piraraca* was hidden under a pile of bananas.

"It weighs anything up to two hundred pounds; its scales are six inches long," Romega told me.

The man in the bows was the only one to exchange greetings. He had an ugly crescent-shaped scar across his cheek.

"It's a tribal marking denoting infidelity," said Romega. "Probably ran off with someone else's wife. Lucky to be alive, the usual penalty is death." But from the Chamas' arrogant expression I imagined he was rather proud of his branding. "The Chamas are the only tribe around here to let them off so lightly," Romega went on. "Not so long ago they would have stood him waist-deep in a hole filled with hungry ants, feeding him to keep him alive as long as possible. And who knows," he paused, staring at the jungle, "what happens in there?" I hadn't any desire to find out.

The green of the jungle became even more brilliant against a blackening sky as an equatorial cloud-burst swept across the forest towards us. The full fury of the storm collided with the *Jean* in mid-river. Lightning like giant flash-bulbs; rain like pellets, saturating our baggage and clothing, trickling into the engine room where we used every available utensil to bale it out. The captain's cabin became the storeroom for personal valuables; for me, that meant my camera.

A heavy sea piled up and two canoes sank. The treasures of at least two families floated down the Ucayali, with several empty petrol cans and planks of cedar wood.

Twang! One of the barge hawsers snapped. The mate just escaped having it wrapped round his neck. The *Jean* might have lost the barge altogether but for the captain's swift action. He turned the tug down-stream until the crew had fixed another hawser. The squall went as quickly as it had come, leaving the steam rising off the jungle roof. But this was the *Jean*'s unlucky day. Rounding another elbow bend in the Ucayali, where the river current ran at nine knots, faster than any navigable water-way in Britain, she began to loose ground.

"She'll drift back until she reaches the quieter waters nearer the bank," explained the skipper. But the *Jean* never reached them. Suddenly she was caught in a mid-stream eddy.

"Full throttle!" barked the captain. But it was no good: we were in the clutch of a whirlpool stronger than the engine. The *Jean* and her unwieldly barge spun round in the vortex in ever decreasing circles like a toy plastic boat about to disappear down the plughole of a bath. The force of the water dragged some of the canoes under.

One of the fishermen moaned as he saw his livelihood break away and bob out of sight. He was only just restrained from diving after it.

The captain rammed the engines into reverse. This did the trick: at last we were out of the pool. But it was a nasty moment and produced a volley of "*Caracos!*"

Soon after we were under way I saw some crocodiles taking to the water. They might have had a tasty meal.

"Contamana! Contamana!" yelled the galley boy. We had come to his home town which straggled for some miles along the right bank of the river. The *Jean* was fastened to the bank by a loop of her hawser round the post, and we all went ashore.

"Hello there!" A voice hailed me from out of the crowd of villagers who had collected to welcome us.

I had grown so used to my environment that it was a great surprise to hear English spoken. I was welcomed by a cheerful American couple.

"I'm Ralph and this is Jane. Sure glad to see you. Come and join us for a cup of tea; you must be raving for one after living on that box."

I laughed. "Isn't iced coffee or 'Coke' more in the American line?"

"We haven't reached the stage yet of refrigerators on the Amazon, though it won't be long before we do," Jane replied. Seated before a pile of delicious "cookies", I wanted to know what Ralph and Jane were doing in Contamana.

"We're missionaries," Ralph explained. "There are seven of us in Contamana; sounds a lot but there's a lot of work to be done. To start with most of the people are illiterate, worshipping idols, knowing nothing about our Lord."

"How much do they understand your teaching, Ralph?" I asked.

"Depends on the missionary, his method of approach. It's no good trying to force religion upon the Indians. We have to educate them first and then preach the gospel."

I questioned whether the Indian and *mestizo* (half-breeds) were capable of absorbing modern ideas. Most of the Amazon lives in the distant past, with little desire to move out of it. Perhaps it should be left to better itself at its own tempo. Civilisation is not the only doorway to a better and happier life.

Ralph didn't agree with my view. "You must remember that there have always been backward people living in undeveloped lands. We can't just watch them stumble along without doing something. Of course the process of assimilating a civilised life is a slow one, and it's no good trying to rush it. We're gradually bringing them round to modern ideas to save them from the disasters of a sudden impact later on when the Amazon is fully opened up. Besides we have our Lord's command to 'go into all the world and preach'."

Life for the missionaries is hard. They are always threatened by tropical diseases and sometimes even by native savagery. Only a month after my visit seven missionaries were beheaded by Indians eight hundred miles from Contamana. The missionaries have other personal problems, particularly with children.

"We should send them back to school in the States," Ralph admitted. "The climate is very unhealthy here, but it's so far away we'd never see them. Out here they help us in our work. Children make friends regardless of race, creed or upbringing and they learn the language much quicker than we do. Through their friendships we approach the native parents much more easily; and of course it helps if the natives see we are just a happy family like themselves."

Six missionaries came to see me off in the evening. Perhaps there would be no more tea brewed until another Englishman sailed the Ucayali. "Our last callers came in May," Ralph told me. That was half a year back.

A new passenger joined the *Jean*. Señorita Camilla was tired of Contamana, and proposed to spend the rest of her life at Pucallpa.

The crew stacked all her belongings on the barge above the cedar wood—a cupboard, bed, chest-of-drawers (without the drawers), a dozen broken china jugs and a bag of clucking hens.

The señorita had no wardrobe. She had sold all her clothes except those she wore, intending to fit herself out in style at Pucallpa. She waved a hundred-*sole* note in the air. If that was all she had, I couldn't see her being clothed above the waistline. Perhaps that was as far as they went in Pucallpa like the Dyaks in Borneo.

At the village of Tiruntin we loaded more cedar wood for the mill up-stream. The deckhand secured the tug to a very tall and unusual type of tree. Eight feet from its base three flat pieces of wood splayed out into a triangle like giant buttresses.

"Those are its roots," Romega explained. "They spread out under the ground, and then turn up into the main trunk again." Competition for root room is fierce in the tropics. This is how the mightiest tree in the forest gets round the difficulty.

Night fell and the eerie shadows of the Amazon forest crept across the water. The tough vines hung like ropes, limp and still.

When I tried to get to sleep I realised that the quiet was an illusion. I was suddenly aware of the castanet band of Amazon grass-hoppers, shrill and persistent. Worse still the shrill whirring of the stick and leaf insects, slightly irregular, exasperating. For bass accompaniment there was the pathetic croak from the sore-throated tree frogs. Most irritating of all, was the drip, drip, drip of the bush rain—from the leaves to branches, from branches to the saloon top of the *Jean*. I found myself counting the drips.

The night grew more lively. I could hear monkeys, peccaries, tigrillos; vampire bats went about their whispering ways in search of blood. Processions of ants marched over everything, in a night-marish profusion.

I dreamt I was ashore with two of the crew. We were sent to pick bananas, but the captain knew this was just an excuse for a jaunt. We had been walking through the jungle for about ten minutes when we came to a lake, one of the discarded loops of the Ucayali. Green slimy moss covered its stagnant waters. The heat was stifling. There wasn't a breath of wind. The rushes stood motionless. This was the loneliest place in the world. The reed tops began to sway as if a puff of wind had passed over them. We waited to feel the refreshing breeze on our faces, but it never came. Something was moving stealthily through the rushes towards us. Curiosity and horror held us mesmerized. It was coming nearer now and with terrific speed. Suddenly the reeds parted. A long black snake slithered out.

"It's an anaconda, run for your life!"

Would I never reach the ship again, why can't my legs move faster? We scrambled and stumbled as fast as we could but the monster pounded down the track, determined to catch us. Just as we reached the river-bank, I stumbled over a tree root. I felt myself falling. This is the end, I thought. I imagined the huge shiny coils wrapping themselves around me. They could crunch my bones with an effortless squeeze. The snake would cover me with saliva first and then bury his enormous curved teeth into me. Oh, why hadn't I listened to all those warnings?

The anaconda leapt towards me, lashing the ground with its tail, its gigantic jaws wide open . . . CRASH! The end of my hammock broke and I fell on the old lady sleeping below. The whole company roused and immediately dissolved into laughter. Still sweating from my nightmare I didn't feel like joining in; neither did the old lady. The joke ended abruptly when the captain stormed out of his cabin, "*Caraco!* What the hell are you doing?"

We all settled down in our hammocks again but I couldn't drop off to sleep; were anacondas really like that?

It was mid-morning, and according to the pilot's reckoning we should be in Pucallpa in about five hours' time. While the *Jean's* engine was having its last midday rest, Romega and I went ashore to pick some mangoes. Ten yards from the river-bank dense jungle closed in on us, and we might have been miles away from the river. High above, branches intertwined like the vaulting of a cathedral roof. The atmosphere was still humid and sticky. The jungle glowed with a ghostly green. Friendly spider monkeys, looking stupid with their long thin bodies and hairy arms, extended great hands down as though offering hand-shakes. After fifteen stifling minutes I was glad to see a brilliant patch of light in a clearing ahead. We came to the edge of a crescent lake. There was something oddly familiar about the golden brown weeds that waded far out into the stagnant waters. Romega suddenly tugged my arm and pointed to some rushes moving on the other side of the lake.

"Must be animal, wonder what it is!"

I *knew*. Desperately I tried to make the others come away but they were much too engrossed in what was happening in the rushes. Just then we heard the *Jean's* whistle give two long blasts and I was saved from the humiliation of running back to the tug alone.

"There go the warning notes, we'd better hurry," I said, thankful to see the others turning back at last.

As we climbed aboard the captain gave orders to cast off and we were away.

"Pity we didn't have time to stay and see what was in the reeds," Romega remarked gaily as we drifted from the bank. Unable to explain my dream in Spanish, I must have looked as foolish as I felt. Romega said I was "*loco*". Thumbing through my dictionary later I found that "*loco*" meant "crazy".

Another storm broke over the *Jean* in the afternoon. The young children aboard arranged an elaborate design of shelters on the barge, using the señorita's furniture, the cedar planks and canvas sides of the saloon, for props. After the first downpour was over the canvas shelter rose in the air as the boys stood up. In the scrimmage that followed they accidentally pushed one of the señorita's chairs into the river. Señorita Camilla descended on their stronghold like a whirlwind, but under threat of having all her chickens let out of the bag was powerless to punish them.

Rows of sawmills suddenly interrupted the monotonous line of vegetation on the left bank of the river and I knew that after ten days, sailing a distance of 850 miles, we had reached Pucallpa; like all Amazon settlements it clings to one side of the river only.

My river journey was over. At times it had seemed that the voyage would never end. Yet now I was at the head of navigation on the Ucayali and some three thousand miles from Belem at the mouth of the Amazon. Even this far up, the "Amazing Amazon" is more than three times as wide as the Thames at London Bridge.

My days of smuggling were over. Ahead lay the Andes.

4

WONDER HIGHWAY OF THE WORLD

"You'll never do it," the barber repeated, emphasising his words with unnecessary bouts of hacking. "Hitch-hiking over the Andes at this time of year? Quite impossible."

This was a bad beginning and I wondered why he was so pessimistic over my chance of reaching Lima. Was it the bad road, the weather or just the impossibility of getting lifts over the mountains? Another customer explained.

"The rains, señor. Have you never heard of the rains? Ah, but I forget. You are a *gringo*, a stranger in these parts. Let me explain. Now it is the season of the Igapo, when the Sierras drink hundreds of inches of rain for five months in the year without stopping. You have never seen such rains. The track to Lima becomes a mudbath, and Pucallpa is isolated for nearly half a year."

I didn't like the implications of his words at all. Perhaps he was mistaken over the timing of the rains.

"They haven't begun yet, at least not in real earnest," I maintained.

"No, but they are six weeks overdue and will not hold off much longer. All the downpours of the past few days, that means they come in a week's time."

The barber brandished his scissors in agreement. He made a final chop.

"But I do not understand this delay. They must know you are coming; it never happened this way before." My reflection in the back of a biscuit tin showed that I had acquired a fringe, the latest, I supposed, in Chamas Indian coiffure. The charge was fifty *centavos*—twopence.

The warnings had been well justified. Clouds over the mountains foretold that the rain wouldn't hold off much longer. In the afternoon Pucallpa was drenched.

I visited every warehouse in town and struggled with my meagre

Spanish to secure a seat on a **Lima**-bound truck. The truckers were too exasperated to listen to me, most of them having waited three days for a clear road. Each one I asked came forward with some feeble pretext for refusing, the general theme being that three in a cabin is one too many for comfort.

At last the driver of a truck called "Lulu" agreed to let me ride with him.

"You can help if we have accident," he admitted.

As nobody else offered me a lift I decided to throw my lot in with him without enquiring into the nature or frequency of his accidents.

The trucker, his mate and I waited three hours for the signal indicating a clear road. Then just as the police were telling us we could leave, it rained again. So for the fourth day nothing left Pucallpa. I clambered off the truck.

"We leave tomorrow," the driver asserted glumly, "but if it rains again . . ." There was an ear-splitting clap of thunder overhead.

My prospects of reaching Lima dwindled with every shower of rain. I just couldn't afford to be stuck here anyway. True, I had no hotel bills to meet, for having hung on to my hammock when I left the ship it was easy to persuade the manager of a transport company to let me sling it in one of their warehouses. But food I had to pay for. The longer I stayed in Pucallpa the more I'd have to dip into my remaining eight pounds. With each meal I bought it seemed to me that the Andes grew more inaccessible.

I went along to the police station to see if there was an alternative way to Lima.

"No other route unless you go back down the river to Iquitos," the officer told me.

Iquitos was nearly eight hundred miles back.

"I don't think much of your chances either way myself, with only four hundred *soles*."

It seemed absurd that ninety miles of sticky mud could come between success or failure at this early stage in my adventures.

I realized my carelessness in not considering the importance of the wet and dry seasons in the tropics when making my plans. It was an anxious time; I was nearly a thousand miles from civilisation and felt imprisoned in the jungle.

Next morning the sun set to work soaking up the rains like a gigantic sponge. Nothing was likely to be on the move for some hours yet, so I walked towards the Indian quarter just up the river. The river settlers here lived in floating balsa raft huts on the Ucayali itself, in preference to houses glued to the river bank on long poles. The drop outside the front door of the pole houses might be anything up to an awkward fifteen feet, whereas the raft houses kept level with the rise and fall of the river. When the village gossip was exhausted you weighed anchor and moved down-river, where there were ample sites and opportunities to start life afresh. Many of these floating huts could be used as cargo-boats. They were steered with round-bladed paddles fourteen feet long, and were often loaded high with all the family possessions, including a cow or dog. Traffic went down-stream only, as the fierce river current defied all who tried to paddle against it.

The village people are Chamas Indians. Their wardrobe is not extensive: the womenfolk wear black ankle-length drapes, which hide the dirt, whilst the men have given up the jungle loin-cloth for trousers. Narrow expressionless eyes stared at me from beneath jet-black hair. The gold nose ornament glinted as it caught the sun; the chubby red-skinned faces portrayed a touch of arrogance, making them appear a proud, fearsome and almost inhuman people. The Chamas were curious because few Pucall-pans, and probably never a *gringo*, wandered beyond the river dividing the two encampments. I was curious too. When our stares met we laughed at each other.

Important news travels fast in Pucallpa. "The road is clear." Everybody knew it in no time. The lucky break in the rains had come at last. Pucallpa sprang into action. Mothers and children rushed in all directions and even the shopkeepers came out to watch, standing, arms folded, in front of their doors.

I tore back to the warehouse to collect my bags. The manager was waiting for me excitedly.

"Ah! you are very lucky, señor," he exclaimed, "there will be no more break in the rains, it is the last fine day. You must hurry, señor, no driver will wait for you when the track is clear."

I wished him a brief cheerio and made off towards the town centre. The truck "Lulu" was in the market place amidst a number of gaudily-coloured vehicles. She was ready to go. I slung my suitcase aloft and clambered into the cabin, greeting the truckers with a cheery "hallo!". They looked blankly at me. Why anyone should want to travel so far away from home completely boggled their imagination. As for going round the world, that was sheer stupidity. I was *loco*. They called me a *"vagabundo"* (vagabond traveller), but that was the nearest approach they ever made to me.

We were off, and judging by the roar of the engines, so was everyone else. All the trucks converged on the one road leading beyond the town, the Pucallpa-Lima track. The urge to hit the road with all speed was unbelievable. There were interlocked bumpers, broken headlights and clenched fists. The few police Pucallpa could muster were there too, but their meaningless gesticulations only received a string of abuse hurled down from accelerator-happy drivers. The mêlée included Guys, Morrises and Fords, but most of the vehicles had lost their distinguishing characteristics, their coachwork having been long since altered by unskilled hands.

Once beyond the town we settled down to a steady 10 m.p.h. through the rain forest. Lulu lined up thirteenth in the procession. After the first few miles our wheels became stuck in the muddy grooves of the preceding truck.

"Why do all the trucks have to leave at once?" I asked in halting Spanish. "They could easily stagger their departure so that each has a clear road." There was no answer. Ten minutes later the mechanic volunteered the remark that half of them wouldn't get through anyway.

We passed two trucks bogged down in the ditch, and he laughed loudly, determined to prove the point.

Attempts at further conversation seemed futile as neither trucker looked anxious to be matey. So from then onwards I sat in silence between the mechanic and the driver, my long legs entangled with the gear lever. There was nothing to say, nothing to do but stare into the blackness ahead. My travelling mates seemed quite contented just looking through the windscreen. They had done it for years and would do it for years to come. These were the first South American mountain people I had met and I didn't take an immediate liking to them. Their harsh features and shabby clothes reflected the rugged sierran upbringing. Elias, the driver, was short with the broad shoulders characteristic of sierran Indians. He wore an ingratiating grin that reminded me of a hungry crocodile but he was a little more human than his mate, on rare occasions almost polite. The mechanic was his closest buddy. Unusually tall for a mountain Indian, his long unkempt hair straggled round a crimson pimply face. I couldn't have chosen a more uncouth companion. His movements were elephantine, and when he spoke it was like a depth-charge exploding in the space of our cabin. I wondered what evil genie had presided over his cradle.

Nearly all truckers are single men, willing to risk their lives and property carrying cargo to and from distant outposts in the Andes. The few that are married often bring their families along with them since one trip may last three or four weeks. In the truck ahead of us four children lay huddled together in the little space that was available above the cargo, a cold, damp and dangerous home.

The truckers' outlook on life is that of complete abandonment; of recklessness rather than of courage. As long as they earn enough money to keep the beer flowing they are satisfied. Yet their role is vital, for they are opening up the undeveloped regions of the Amazon. Without them, the challenging forest lands of Peru beyond the Andean mountains could never be exploited.

"We stop here the night," said Elias, hauling into the bank beneath the jungle. I got out and squelched into a foot of mud.

"Where you go?" boomed the mechanic.

"To find somewhere to sleep," I answered hopefully. There wasn't a shack in sight.

He laughed loudly, menacingly shook his head to humiliate me further, and pointed to the seat I had just left, glad of a chance to pull the *gringo* down a peg. I clambered back into the cabin beside him. I tried to mould my back into the right-angled contour of the seat but I soon abandoned all hope of sleeping.

The engine suddenly·roared into action; the time, 3 a.m. I must have dropped off to sleep after all. The bumpiness of the road soon dispelled my drowsiness.

After a cooling swim in a mountain stream we had an appetizing meal of bananas and melons, all purchased for 20 cents (1d.). These were to serve us for breakfast, lunch and dinner.

Leaving the Amazon behind us we rose above its green roof and penetrated the great cordillera of the Andes. I was excited at the sight of the mountains after all those weeks of imprisoning forests. The narrow track accompanied a muddy river into the canyon of the Boqueron Abad. The route was almost smothered by tropical jungle that staked its claim along the sides of the gorge. Soon the track became no more than a narrow flint path edging the rock face. Traffic could move in one direction only. What happened when someone came along in the opposite direction?

Great waterfalls hastened the journey of the rains to the Amazon

4. The beginning of the Andes.

5. Changing a wheel 9,000 feet up in the Andes. The houses have a 2,000-foot drop at their back doors.

6. The world's highest standard-gauge railway, Lima to La Oroya. Over 15,000 feet.

7. With Bobby Plenge in Lima, Peru.

and once or twice the track completely disappeared beneath a newly formed cascade. Lulu and her load were drenched.

At three thousand feet, Elias became impatient and tried to overtake another truck. We skidded into the mud ditch. Elias fought desperately with the gears but Lulu wouldn't budge an inch. The thick slimy mud oozed over her right wheel hubs. Lulu was completely blocking the trans-Andean highway. Far from showing any contrition or dismay Elias and his mate seemed to enjoy immense satisfaction. We sat contemplating, while a queue of lorries piled up behind. But instead of becoming impatient over the delay or offering to help, the newcomers just settled down to the enjoyment of a siesta.

"Take off the cargo," said Elias, coming to this decision without even descending to estimate the situation. "All the bottles, but leave the Schlumberger."

"Bottles?" I queried, as we hopped out and made for the rear of the truck.

Elias heard me. "Beer," he roared. "Thousands of bottles."

But the bottles were empty—that was his joke. The truck held hundreds of cardboard boxes packed with empty Pilsner bottles and stacked round a heavy piece of "Schlumberger" equipment. I wondered what that was doing on Lulu but for the moment my hands were full, lifting boxes. Or rather they too often weren't. That car-washing we got on the way had pulped much of the cardboard. Bottles slipped through the cartons as they were moved and crashed on the road. Unloading became an impossible task as we struggled to hold soggy cardboard round slippery bottles. In the end it took us over an hour to stack what remained of the bottles by the wayside. Our labours were accompanied by a chorus of insulting comments and laughter from the truckers behind, who pretended to think that we were handling the aftermath of some great Andean orgy.

Five o'clock the next morning, after a night as uncomfortable as the last, found us struggling to free Lulu's driving wheels with cedar planks borrowed from another truck. By noon Lulu was on the road again at last. Now that I had worked for my passage the truckers seemed more kindly disposed towards me. I was thankful for this change of attitude, and felt much safer in their hands than before.

After a twenty-four-hour fast your stomach begins to pinch. We pulled up at an Andean version of the "drive in" café—a bamboo shack—where we quickly demolished several bowls of soup, rice, meat, and *yucca* (a vegetable), washing it down with beer. Just as we were leaving, two more dishevelled truckers appeared in the doorway.

"*Amigos*," they hailed Elias. Such a chance meeting of friends called for a celebration.

Eight hours later the beer session was still going strong. I left it and clambered into Lulu, and promptly fell asleep on the cabin seat. It was a welcome relief to stretch out horizontally. The orgy continued well into the night. I woke up just in time to remove the ignition key before helping the beer-soddened truckers into the cabin. Luckily Elias wasn't in a driving mood anyway. I spent the rest of the night sandwiched between two inebriated monsters who occupied far more than their alloted share of the cabin space. After pushing and pulling the gear lever in every direction, I found it less troublesome in reverse. But I stayed awake listening to a concert in which Elias and his mate performed both solos and duets.

The windows had been tightly jammed the whole night so that by daybreak we were close to being asphyxiated. An attempt to lower one was thwarted by the mechanic who promptly wound it up again. I fetched out the map for the tenth time. In four days we had covered only a hundred and thirty miles and Lima seemed as far away as ever. Time we were on the move again, I thought. I replaced the ignition key, nudged Elias hard in the ribs, and directed his hand toward the starter. Just in time I remembered the gear lever. "*Vamos*," he yawned, letting in the clutch. Lulu shot forward.

The first town we drove through was Tingo Maria, a market between two economic zones, the tropical rain forest and the more temperate savanna uplands. Here farms, cattle raising, tea, rubber and oranges are all in the experimental stage. Like most small routeway settlements, the single-storied houses are set well back from the road and straggle along the wide main street for a mile or two. As we passed by, the villagers stopped what they were doing to have a good stare at us, most of them pointing at me, yelling "*Gringo*" and bursting into laughter; I waved back at them.

We met several saloon cars and shooting brakes attempting a passage over the rugged road. They all ran into trouble with the high centre hump pushed by the trucks. Their difficulties merely produced triumphant grins from the truckers.

Early one morning Lulu started the ascent to the 9,000-foot summit of Carpish Pass. We drove through villages of bamboo and adobe huts, which cling like parasites to the outside edge of the road. A two-thousand-foot drop at the back door must have solved sanitation problems. The narrow track was a series of blind corners. There had been no oncoming vehicles for the last three hours. This couldn't go on indefinitely. On one of the S bends an approaching truck loomed in front of us. Even at a 10 m.p.h. crawl, Lulu's brakes were powerless to pull her up in time.

"*Petrolero!*" Elias exclaimed, suddenly noticing the petrol cans. He grazed the rock face as close as he dare and remained quite calm.

"Empty bottles—empty petrol cans," I prayed, grabbing the nearest thing, the gear lever. Then came the crash. The oncomer rammed our offside wing, but the weight of the Schlumberger held Lulu to the road. The petrol truck slid outwards and disappeared over the precipice. We sat in silence.

We listened for the final crash of landing. Was it a hundred or a thousand feet down the slope? But it never came—something must have caught the truck and held it just beneath the road edge. In the seconds that followed we heard the clatter of oil drums rolling down to the valley bottom. The jangling of empty beer-bottles told us that they weren't far behind in the three-thousand-foot race downhill.

We expected to find the truckers badly hurt, if not dead. Crawling on our tummies to the cliff edge we peered over the precipice.

Two jolly truckers, grinning from ear to ear, were busy freeing themselves from an entanglement of metal.

One of them patted a tree trunk and shouted up at us.

"This has saved our lives." The truck had wrapped itself round three solid trees only fifty feet below the road edge. Had it missed them it would have fallen another 500 feet.

Some of the worst damage was suffered by an isolated hut wedged on the steep slope. Flying glass had pelted through its thatch and the impact of an oil drum had removed a vital support leaving it at a rakish angle. The occupants were either killed or not at home to welcome the strangers. Elias, filled with rare emotion, scribbled on a scrap of paper and pinned it to a post.

"*Me peso mucho.*" He was genuinely sorry.

Apart from a smashed wing and a broken headlight, Lulu was all right. But most of the bottles that hadn't joined the oil drums were now little pieces of green glass.

Studying the debris gave me gruesome thoughts of endless punctures to passing traffic, but in keeping with the cheerful attitude of

my companions, I broke into a song unfamiliar to sierran ears—
"And if one green bottle should accidentally fall, there'll be no
green bottles . . ." We laughed now that it was all over; what about
I didn't know. We dropped our new acquaintances at a road house
in Acomayo some ten miles further on.

"Will they retrieve anything from the wreckage?" I asked Elias.
His grin told me they wouldn't.

"If one green bottle," sang the mechanic in English.

"Should accidentally fall," I prompted.

"Should accidentally fall," he repeated.

Bawling out odd words in three different languages—Spanish,
Quechua and English—our voices echoed down the valley bottom
and rang through each sierran village. People scattered as Lulu
careered down the main streets, and gaped at us from the doors of
their bamboo houses that seemed to quiver as we tore past.

Still singing at the tops of our voices, we stopped at the bottle
store in Huanuco. Elias jammed on the brakes just as we repeated
the last line for the hundredth time, and a tinkle of glass from the
rear made a fitting conclusion to our song.

The manager was standing outside the warehouse. He found our
arrival less amusing than we did. As Elias backed into the building
to unload what was left of the bottles, little pieces of glass dropped
on to the concrete floor. The manager was livid, and the four walls
echoed to the blast of his language.

Elias's reaction was typical: a carefree grin and shrugged
shoulders. A look of innocent ignorance masked the mechanic's
delight at the scene. My presence was ignored, but I suppose I
looked on a par with my companions then. The grand count up
indicated that ten per cent of the bottles had survived the ordeal of
the last few days. The mechanic loosened a wheel-nut and tightened
it up again.

We escaped from the warehouse and ambled towards the centre
of the town. It was Twelfth Night and the townspeople were
making merry. The market place was a scene of gaiety and amusement, of spangles and baubles, dancing, singing, buying and selling.
We returned to the warehouse empty-handed. Elias fully expected
to find himself relieved of his post, but for reasons he couldn't
understand his services appeared to be still wanted.

Early next morning the mechanic withdrew a grimy head from
under the bonnet and solemnly announced that the strain of the
accident had been too much for Lulu; her driving days were over.

Feeling that we had lost a friend we transferred the ubiquitous Schlumberger to another truck which the mechanic christened "Lulu II". Since there were higher and more difficult passes ahead it was no good setting off in a vehicle with mechanical faults.

We left Huanuco with the manager waving us good-bye. He was affable now, for if his letter ever reached Lima these truckers wouldn't be coming this way for a very long time—that was his plan for getting even with them. However I was the bearer of the letter, and "there's many a slip . . ."

The valley gouged out by the river Hullaaga provided the only way of ascending the Peruvian altiplano. Once again the track narrows; for mile after mile the route winds up, up and up. Just below a village built entirely of mud and leaves, I saw an upturned truck lying in the river. There was a small crowd on the roadside discussing the catastrophe, which had just happened. We stopped for a breather and learnt that there had been no survivors. My companions said nothing. It was obviously a common sight.

Frequent surprises by oncoming vehicles required Elias's undivided concentration. The passing of another truck was nearly always accompanied by an outside dual wheel crumbling the road edge. A shrug from Elias was the only acknowledgement of their precarious situation; but that fatalistic lift of his shoulders meant that we might find ourselves at the bottom of a thousand-foot ravine through the unlucky spin of a wheel.

Lulu II struggled wheezily in second gear until we reached the large mining and commercial centre of Cerro de Pasco. At last we were on top of the altiplano, fourteen thousand feet up. The town was entirely different from any other I had seen in Peru. Instead of the bamboo shacks and grime of the valley settlements there were stone houses and rubbish-free streets. It looked like a little English mining town. The Quechua Indians were well wrapped up in layers of blankets and llama fur. No one sat in the streets; siesta hour was apparently unknown at such heights. Indians ran along the cobbled streets, too cold to stop and chat. Their alertness contrasted sharply with their compatriots in the forest region below. These mountain people work in the electrolytic copper refinery, zinc, and the lead and silver mines round the town.

It was bitterly cold, some sixty degrees Fahrenheit below the temperature we had just left behind. We had to stop and refill the petrol tanks and cans.

Bang!

A puncture. It would happen at this impossible altitude. The tools were like icicles, and my woollen socks proved a poor substitute for gloves. All three of us jumped up and down on the brace simultaneously, hoping to loosen the wheel-nuts, but the physical effort in this rarefied atmosphere set my lungs gaping for air.

After thirty minutes we had had enough. We made for the cabin and waited until our fingers had thawed a bit before resuming the task. We fought with the wheel-nuts for an hour before succeeding in levering off the wheel.

While the other two mended the tyre I climbed into the snows to take a photograph of the copper mines. Standing on a knoll five hundred feet above the town I could see the altiplano stretching to infinity beyond Cerro de Pasco; bare, bleak, cold, terribly lonely. Away to the west the peaks of the great cordillera were a white smudge on the horizon. They marked the outer rim of these high pampas lands. After the grotesque knots of mountains on our way up to the table land, the flatness on top seemed unreal. There were a few groups of houses clustered round the mining shafts, the only evidence of human life. The most striking feature of the altiplano is the complete absence of trees.

Elias hung grimly to the wheel that night. "Too cold to stop for long at this height after dark," he muttered. A brief stop for some soup at Junin town confirmed his view. It was well below freezing point. At the mining centre of La Oroya the road crossed the Rio Mantaro, the most westerly Amazon headwater tributary, four thousand miles from its mouth.

I thought we might stop at the local inn for what was left of the night, but hints of fatigue were drowned by the noise of the engine. Elias was in a driving mood. So for the last time Lulu II roared in low gear, to bring us to the summit of the Anticona pass, almost sixteen thousand feet above sea level. We were higher than Mont Blanc, but just then I didn't feel very enthusiastic about mountains. For all I cared we could have been twenty thousand feet up, I was so tired and cold.

Elias handed me some paper. "Stuff that under your jersey." Then he decided to let the exhausted engine cool off. Lulu II had been working overtime, and this wasn't the moment or place to flog her to death. A familiar hissing sound sang in our ears. No, it couldn't be, not again. It was—another puncture. We agreed unanimously to attend to it at daybreak, three or four hours away.

"Sleep, oh for some sleep," I yawned, but my hopes were shattered by Elias who revved the engine every ten minutes to keep the cabin's temperature above zero. The old, familiar smells returned in force, but this time there was an added tang from a ferocious mountain fox. This was the mechanic's latest acquisition, and he was determined to hang on to it, regardless of drawbacks. A *zorra* suited his temperament admirably. Every time it started to scratch, he tortured it, gloating over his superior strength.

I had almost fallen asleep when a shattering screech from the pedal lever jerked me into life again. The *zorra* had stuck his head behind the accelerator just as Elias's foot was bearing down on it.

Morning arrived suddenly. Elias had given up his struggle with the accelerator and was noisily asleep. His companion was chuckling to himself and the *zorra* was either dead or asleep. We were resting on the roof of the world, the watershed that separates east and west South America. Recalling the events of the past two months I seemed to have been away from home for a very long time. On the Amazon time had been meaningless. The scenery, weather and food had offered no variety for three thousand miles. Now with the Amazon and the Andes behind me I knew that the immense effort of getting to South America had been well worth while. But this wasn't the moment to be complacent—there were thousands of miles to go before I was even half-way round the world. Ahead stretched the Pacific, and that must mean more trouble and even greater problems to solve.

"Ticlio." Elias interrupted my thoughts, and waved his arms towards a railway tunnel. This was the highest standard-gauge railway in the world. Somewhere above us a train was struggling against the steep gradient with asthmatic wheezings. Ticlio station is 15,806 feet 9 inches above sea level and snowbound for much of the year. Yet it is kept pretty busy handling mineral ore and the passenger trains that ply between Lima, La Oroya and Cerro de Pasco. These trains have a hospital atmosphere for there are oxygen respirators for passengers overcome by the *soroche*— mountain sickness.

It took us two hours to change the wheel, then we set off on the final lap of the journey praying that there would be no more punctures. The road dropped steeply, tunnelling and bridging the massive canyon walls of the river Rimac. Next to it ran the railway, through its sixty-eight tunnels, over sixty-one bridges, falling sixteen thousand feet in the hundred miles between Ticlio and

Lima. Road and railway cross and recross each other like snakes and ladders—a welding of foreign engineering and local ingenuity.

We arrived at Matucana, home village of the two truckers, and I wondered if we should be in Lima by the evening.

"How long are we going to stop here?" I asked Elias, but in answer to my question I was ushered into the family house for a meal of fish, rice and *yucca*. There were no windows to the hut and three rooms were separated by flimsy bamboo partitions, stuck over with musty yellow newspapers. In the blackest corner of the main room, a saucepan boiled on the peat stove with an old lady bent over it stirring the family brew.

The family circle expanded as the village learned of Elias's unexpected arrival. When they found that he had brought along a *gringo*, the wide eyes and gaping mouths multiplied even more rapidly. In a rash moment I produced my camera. "*Fotografía!*" the cries went up—and soon the entire village was demanding photographs. I could little afford the ill feeling that would arise if I refused them, but with snaps costing sixpence a time, I couldn't afford to reel off a dozen films either.

Excitement rose into hysteria as I snapped some eighty photographs without raising the shutter lever. It was a dirty trick and I had to act quickly and convincingly. Showers of thanks and addresses came from a very highly-impressed gathering, but I turned away to attend to my luggage before they became too embarrassing.

The bags had been exposed to the weather in their place above the cargo, and most of my clothes were ruined or at the best stained. Soap removed the worst stains, but a stubborn and embarrassing yellow patch decorated the rear of my linen trousers for all future ambassadors and consuls to see. That night I had the truck to myself and relaxed horizontally for the first time since the night outside the Andean pub. Even that seemed a long time back now.

Next morning I rose early and fought with the icy waters of the river Rimac, using a rusty razor blade to remove a week's stubble. I drank a cup of black coffee with Elias's mother and then rejoined Lulu, which had now turned into a passenger vehicle. Elias took this opportunity of driving into Lima his entire family—almost the whole village it seemed—from a grubby three-year-old to the omnipotent grandmother. It would provide a day's outing at the Company's expense. Inside the cabin tempers started to fray as the new tarmac road shimmered with desert-like heat, so I was more than thankful when Lima's skyline came into view between the curly locks of a second cousin, sitting on my knee.

"Where to?" came Elias's voice above the family chorus.

"Anywhere," I shouted back. "Anywhere at all provided it's cheap," but my reply was lost amidst a vocal explosion close to my left ear. Grandma was beginning to exert her authority. The *zorra* would not be tolerated any longer, and as her protests came in deepening crescendos, so the *zorra* clung into her stocking with greater zeal, to the delight of the children and the mechanic who gave it plenty of encouragement.

We stopped somewhere in the suburbs of Lima, exactly where it didn't matter. I just longed for fresh air and fresh company. Wishing cheerio to the party took longer than I had expected, but then there were thirty hands to shake.

Worn out from the excitement and lack of sleep of the last week, I stumbled into a roadhouse.

"A bed for the night, please," I asked, waving my passport before the goggling eyes of the proprietor. He showed me the room, handed me some keys, and I sank down onto the bed, which was moderately clean—one couldn't expect perfection for two shillings.

Before dropping off to sleep I checked up on my finances. A mere two pounds ten shillings remained in the kitty. I must find some way to increase my funds, but I was too tired to plan anything just now. Rummaging through my bag I noticed that my pen and silk scarf were missing. I wonder which of the relatives is learning to write with a fountain pen.

I still had the letter from Huanuco. The transport manager would be surprised to see those two truckers back on the job, after all.

Recalling to mind the events of the past week I was glad to be in civilisation again, and in a bed for the first time since leaving Belem—ten weeks back. The Andean mule track had more than lived up to its reputation: six days of driving, sixteen thousand feet of climbing, twenty-four hours' sleep, four punctures, and two thousand broken bottles. This was indeed the wonder highway of the world.

5

THE LOST CITIES . . . AND ALL THAT

The police officer looked at me with a sardonic smile meant to imply that of course I was guilty, and to emphasize his infallibility.

"The hotel manager has just told me," he said in a precise little voice, "that you arrived in Lima yesterday, spent the night in his hotel, which has never been slept in by a tourist, and that you wish to leave Peru today. It is very strange." He paused, expecting some explanation but before I had time to compose a suitable reply in Spanish he started up again.

"Señor, if you will not talk, I will. There are a few points which need explanation. First I wish to know where you have just come from."

"Iquitos."

"By air?"

"No, land and water. By truck over the Andes from Pucallpa." He found that difficult to believe.

"How much money have you?"

"Enough."

"How much is enough?"

"Hundred and twenty-five *soles*," I said, waving two pounds in *soles* before his startled eyes. He became more suspicious.

"That is very little. You cannot be a tourist, so what are you?"

"A *trotamundos*," I tried. "*Trotamundos! Vagabundo turista*, someone who '*Vuelta del mundo*', only with no money."

The officer shrivelled up to half his size. Both he and the hotel manager looked at me like stuffed penguins, obviously wondering whether I was completely *loco*. Perhaps they couldn't understand my Spanish, or I had said something rude. The latter was always a possibility with my Spanish.

Any further explanations seemed pointless and I decided to clear out before the officer could trump up any likely charges for placing me under arrest.

"Well, hope I've been some use to you. Don't expect I'll see either of you again, but *hasta la vista*, all the same."

"Where you want to go, señor?"—came the voice of a taxi driver. I knew only one address in Lima but that was likely to be miles away and an expensive taxi ride. I gambled on the fact that most Spanish and Latin American cities have a central plaza.

"To the Plaza Central," I said boldly.

"Plaza San Martin, señor?"

"Yes, of course."

"Ah, señor! You want Hotel Bolivar. I take you there. It is the best hotel."

"The best? Then I certainly don't want the Hotel Bolivar," I hastily assured him, casting off my grand manner immediately. Five minutes later I asked how much the fare was going to be as I had very little money.

He had heard that one before. "It is quite cheap," he added in a matter-of-fact way. "Twenty *soles*." Twenty *soles* came to about seven shillings.

"Twenty *soles*? That's ridiculous."

"It is the price these days. Costs a bit extra for the European tourist, of course."

"But I'm not a tourist."

"What are you?"

He appeared to believe my story and just as I had finished it we arrived at a large square.

"The Plaza San Martin," the driver announced. "I hope you enjoy Lima, though you will not be able to make much money here. There is no harder work than looking for work."

I stepped out of the taxi and asked him what he wanted for the ride.

He gave me a sheepish grin, "Seeing you not ordinary tourist—four *soles*."

Thanking him for letting me off at the locals' rate, I carried my bags over to the centre of the Plaza and sat down on them wondering what to do next.

Earlier in the day I had telephoned an acquaintance in a large oil company. He sounded glad to hear from me and asked me to call at his office during the afternoon. There was the problem of finding more lodgings but that would have to be solved later. In the meantime I deposited my baggage in one of the luggage rooms of a large hotel.

Empty-handed and dressed in my tropical suit, I walked into the International Petroleum building. An attendant took me up to my friend's spacious apartment. That evening I was dining with his family at their home in a Lima suburb, San Isidro. This hospitality was quickly extended to include a bed for as long as I wanted to stay in Lima. The building was completely European in décor and I revelled in a civilised life. I was deeply grateful to the Plenge family for this very pleasant interlude in my wanderings.

The following day I hunted the city for work. As I had to accumulate some money before continuing my journey, I walked the *vias* and *avenidas* hoping something would turn up in the way of a job.

By tea-time I had spent about eight shillings on bus fares and I was still no nearer earning a penny. The last link in the chain of suggested "tries" led me to the University of San Marcos.

"So you wish to give some English lessons," said the university tutor. "Well, suppose you tell me something about yourself first. Where were you educated, for instance?" At the end of a brief viva he handed me a piece of paper, saying, "You're a lucky chap. As it happens I have several students wanting private tuition. That would probably suit you better than a class. You can arrange your own time-table. Here's a list of their names and addresses if you wish to contact them."

I wrung his hand a little harder than he had expected or thought necessary, and raced back to the Plenges with the good news.

Within a week I was teaching eight pupils, including a nine-year-old Czechoslovakian boy who already spoke four languages fluently.

Along with the more serious of the student enquirers came deeply-tanned señoritas who soon heard of my efforts to raise cash. They flocked to my door in embarrassing numbers, but to charge them seven shillings a lesson seemed a trifle unfair when I usually came away at the end of an hour with an increased knowledge of Peru. However, the hard-earned profits from the classes were soon frittered away on beach parties and dances organised by these glamorous pupils.

In moments of leisure I laid plans for the next stage of my journey. Regretfully I decided that to include North America would be an unwise deviation from my route westwards.

Anyway the States weren't so very far from England and I could probably get there later in my life. I set my heart on the Far East and introduced myself to nearly every shipping agent in town, hoping to find a vessel in which I could work a passage. Most of the agents suggested that I stood a better chance of picking up a ship from the port of Callao only ten miles away. I had already learned that a personal approach to the master of a vessel goes a long way to secure a job aboard, so I took the tram for Callao immediately. There were only two cargo vessels in port, a ship of some Japanese line and an India-bound freighter operating under the British flag. Both were sailing for the Far East the following week.

"Ver' sorry," apologised the Japanese captain, "but my company's regulations forbid any foreigner to work on a Japanese vessel," and nothing I could say would change the black-and-white of that statement.

The master of the other vessel gave a surly refusal.

"Why come to me with your troubles? Why should I personally and no one else be expected to help you? Got enough to worry about without damn globe-trotters demanding free rides. Anyway, we've got a Lascar crew. You couldn't possibly work with them."

"All right, all right. Of course neither you nor anybody else is under any obligation to help me out." The interview was at an end.

There were no more Asia-bound ships due in port for at least three weeks. My plans, so far as I had any, had come to a full stop. The Pacific was going to be just as difficult to work my way across as the Atlantic.

Meanwhile my lessons continued and so did the generous hospitality of my hosts.

The Plenge's youngest son, Bobby, was a handsome young Peruvian of nineteen. He was an enthusiastic party-goer and managed to rope me in for quite a few of them. At one I gained a useful introduction to an American who ran a west-coast fishing company. Perhaps it would lead nowhere, but anything was worth a try now, so I dropped in at the company's office in the Edificio Atlas.

"Sure I know all about you. Followed your exploits in this morning's newspaper," the director cut in before I had told him the reason for my visit. "I was wondering whether you planned to travel up to the States. My company runs a few Tuna clippers between Paita in northern Peru, and San Diego, California. Glad to assist you in any way. Matter of fact, one of our ships is leaving around February 20th. If you want a ride ask the skipper to sign you on as a workaway."

I hadn't been thinking along these lines, but then I wasn't in a position to brush aside such a generous offer.

"Sounds grand to me."

"How about your visa?"

"I should be able to get one from the American Embassy here easily enough."

"They don't dish them out to anybody, you know, but I guess if you apply for one now they ought to have it ready for you in three weeks. I'm going to Paita myself around the twentieth, so I'll see you there. Well, that's the best I can do for you. Now I expect you want to be along."

"Thanks a lot." I got up. "Last night I'd no idea how I was going to start the next stage of my travels. Now, thanks to you, it all seems settled."

The decision to go north after all had been made in a moment, yet this seemed to be my only way of getting out of South America. Yes, I was very glad I hadn't rejected the plan. Elated by this turn in my fortunes, I walked triumphantly into the United States Consulate.

"I wish to apply for a tourist visa for the United States," I told the vice-consul.

"Are you a resident of the United Kingdom or Peru?"

"The United Kingdom."

"Why didn't you apply for a visa before you left London?"

I explained that I couldn't pick up an Asia-bound vessel from South America and intended to try my luck in North America, probably Canada. He didn't show much enthusiasm.

"So, you intend hitch-hiking up the west coast of the States to Canada? How many dollars have you got?"

"By the time I leave about fifty."

"About fifty!" he exclaimed. "Do you really imagine that fifty bucks will last you more than a couple of days in the States? No, Mr. Boyd, if that's all you have I can't even send in your application for a visa, unless you provide me with a financial guarantee from someone inside the United States."

"All right," I said boldly. "I'll get a guarantee somehow, but to save time could you send in my application for a visa now?"

The consul agreed. "I'll cable your request to London soon and see what they can dig up about your past. I'm afraid you will have to pay for the cost of the cable."

I handed over three precious dollars. One day's earnings down the drain, I thought, but worth it if I obtained the visa in the end.

"By the way," he continued, "where were you at college?"

"Oxford University."

"Oh! Were you a member of any communist organisation?"

Thirty minutes later, after swearing some oath about "subversive activities", I was allowed to leave the building.

That evening Radio National del Peruana rang up and invited me to do something they must have regretted later. "Would you mind being interviewed on the radio?"

"Of course not," I said. "Be delighted. When? . . . Tonight? . . . Oh, fine, I'll be along."

I arrived at the studios a quarter of an hour before the programme was due to begin. My interviewer was at the door to meet me.

"Ah, Señor Boyd, I am so pleased that you could come. We are all looking forward to hearing about your wonderful adventure. Let us run through a few lines so that we get the—er . . . feeling of it, shall we?"

We entered the recording box. The red light flashed and my interviewer began reading from a typescript. "*Señor Boyd, Haganos el favor de contarnos como se origino el viaje que lo ha traido por estos lados?*"

I stared. There was a long pause while I tried to compose a suitable reply in Spanish.

He looked at me, horrified.

"What is the matter?" he cried, wringing his hands. "Don't you understand me?"

"I thought the programme was in English," I stuttered. The next ten minutes we blundered through with the broadcast. My services were never again required on the South American radio, nor, I imagine, were those of any other globe-trotter. But as the announcer said afterwards, my laughter covered up some of my worst grammatical howlers.

I was enjoying drinks at the cricket club with a crowd of the Lancashire-born who for some unknown reason collect in Lima. Most of them were playing dice, the national sport of Englishmen in Peru.

"I suppose you're a stranger to these parts?" One of the on-lookers asked me, "New resident or just on a business tour?"

"Neither. Just a visitor trying hard to pick up some cash."

"Oh, a visitor. Well, have you seen much of Peru yet? Inca-land for instance?"

"Not yet, but I want to spend a few days there before I leave the country. I've read quite a bit about their wonderful civilisation and how it broke up, but no one I've asked has been able to tell me how it all started. Suppose you haven't got any ideas on that?"

"Well, of course there's the old story," he said. "It's only a legend. You've probably heard it before. The Sun god looked down upon the world and he saw a land of barbaric and disorganised people. So he sent his children, Manco Capac and Mama Oello, husband and wife, to civilise mankind. They rose from Lake Titicaca carrying a golden staff and had to keep on marching until the staff sank into the ground and disappeared of its own accord. Wherever that happened they were to found the centre of a great civilisation. The miracle occurred at Cusco. There the Inca empire had its roots and from there it expanded far into Ecuador, Bolivia and Chile. Of course that's only one of the theories," he concluded. "Now you're in Peru you must get to Inca-land, Cusco, Machu Picchu, Titicaca, La Paz. . . ."

"What's the cheapest way of getting there?" my enthusiasm needed no more encouragement. Besides it was up to me to accept any challenge to go hitch-hiking if only to keep in practice.

"It's difficult at this time of year. The rains began in the mountains a week or two back, so road travel is impossible. You could go by bus as far as Arequipa and take the train from there, but that's a week's journey. Why don't you try the local airlines and see if they can produce any joy-rides. Ask for the manager. Probably be glad to help you."

The next morning I called at the offices of the Faucett Airline company. "I'm sorry, the managing director is away," said the clerk. "Can I help you?"

When asking for a free air passage, the clerk or even the traffic manager is the last person to approach, as it is his job to ward off such enquirers.

"I'm afraid not, thank you. Only the managing director can help me."

The clerk was apologetic and asked me to call again in the morning.

At my third attempt I was ushered into the managing director's office—a spacious room overlooking the Plaza San Martin. For five minutes he listened attentively to my story. "I've only got three more weeks in Peru," I concluded, "And I want to spend one of them in the land of the Incas. The trouble is that I haven't the time or money to take the overland route to Cusco and Titicaca, I wondered if your company could help me?"

The manager eyed me suspiciously, trying to decide whether I was a genuine penniless globetrotter or just cadging a free lift. At last he made up his mind. "All right, we'll fly you to Cusco on Sunday and back again a week later from Arequipa. That should give you plenty of time to see something of the Incas."

After thanking him profusely I made a bee-line for the Peruvian Corporation which operated most of the railways in Peru. They and the Ministerio de Fomento co-operated in the same way. I was now equipped with tickets for all the railroads in the Andes. Finally I called at the Touring and Automobile Club of Peru who obliged with an introductory letter to their agent in Cusco.

My thoughtful host packed seven tins of condensed milk and a box of biscuits into my bag, "Just in case you can't afford a meal anywhere," and drove me to the airport. At seven o'clock on Sunday morning I was airborne—on my way to Inca-land.

Three hours after take-off, Faucett's DC3 aircraft dropped into the Vilcanota valley and skidded to a stop at the end of Cusco's water-logged runway, eleven thousand feet above sea level. A large crowd awaited the arrival of the bi-weekly plane. A newspaper reporter darted from one passenger to another. I made a good opportunity for him to try out his English, with strange results in next morning's newspapers.

Ten little Indian boys all wanted to carry my bag, and could each show the señor a hotel far cheaper than the others. A dapper young man in a grey suit forced his way through the clammering horde and introduced himself as Pedro.

"I'm from the Touring Club. Our office in Lima telephoned me last week to say that you were coming. Don't take any notice of these kids, I'll find you a really cheap hotel for the night."

He took me to a sierra pension where two shillings secured a brick-hard bed and eiderdown. There was no other furniture in the room. We dumped my bag and went for a quick look at the city before dusk.

As we walked down its narrow streets Pedro told me the history of this old capital of the Incas.

The gold and the wealth of the fabulous palaces attracted the plundering Conquistadores. What Pizarro and his gang could not take away, they destroyed so that nothing of the Incas should remain. But they couldn't destroy the magnificent buildings. Pedro pointed at the stonework in the wall flanking the street of Loreto. "Perfectly cut and fitted stones, so smoothly finished that they didn't need any binding materials."

I could hardly believe it had been built long before Columbus discovered America. In many Spanish buildings the original Inca construction is incorporated into the lower half of the walls. It has weathered the centuries far better than the adobe and plaster of the later Spanish workmanship. More than once earthquakes have crumbled the upper half and left the lower part untouched.

We climbed to the Inca fortress of Sacsahuanan, towering high above Cusco and guarding the north-eastern flank of the city. Some of the stones used in its construction are twenty feet high and weigh as much as fifteen tons, irregular in shape, but all cut to fit with the highest degree of exactness. Crowning the fort is a waterclock some forty-five feet in diameter. Below it stretched the Inca armies' parade ground, and beyond that an intricate series of trenches.

Near the fort I noticed a curious smooth gully some fifty feet long. Pedro laughed and told me it was the Inca's *rodadero*—a shute, one of the many formed by an ice movement in the Andes millions of years ago. They must have borne many Inca behinds since then. Just to show that it was still in perfect order he produced a twenty cent coin and persuaded a little boy standing close by to slide down into the pool of water below.

Pedro invited me back to dinner to meet the rest of his family. After a meal we sat round the table drinking *pisco*, the sierran brandy. He asked me where I wanted to go tomorrow.

"The lost city of Machu Picchu," I replied with no hesitation.

"It's quite a long way from here. About an eight hours' journey. You cannot make it there and back in one day. But there is an inn by the ruins and you can spend the night there. I know the manager and I will give you a note for him."

I was the only foreigner aboard the Machu Picchu train next morning. All the other travellers were Quechua Indians. They smelt as though they rarely washed. I had been told some didn't bother to change their clothes either, but were content to wrap new ones around themselves when the old ones disintegrated.

The men wore long baggy trousers or the traditional breeches which stop just short of the knee. All had the *poncho* draped over their shoulders, a gaily coloured square blanket with a hole in the centre for the head. Indians don't usually wear shoes and even if one is lucky enough to own a pair he will probably carry them over rocky ground to prevent their soles from wearing out.

The Quechua sitting opposite me spent the entire journey taking lice from under his clothing, crunching them in his mouth and throwing the remains on to the carriage floor.

Another pulled a *coca* pellet from a pouch slung around his neck and began to chew it like a ruminating animal. *Coca* is collected from a plant growing in the Yungas, the eastward facing valleys of the Andes. For the Indians it has changed from being a luxury to a necessity of life. Without *coca* they would be unable to build up the necessary stamina for their rigorous life and the physical strain of living at such high altitudes. It has a deadening effect making the Indians slow-witted and easy-going.

The gradient of the railway became less steep after a while and the train gathered speed as it cut across the highest grazing land in the world, twelve thousand feet up. Herds of cattle browse on the tough Andean grass of this altiplano valley. Not long ago the toughness of the grass wore down the animals' teeth. Many died of starvation. Today the old tough grass is burnt off for them and that risk greatly reduced.

At every station along the track, an excited cluster of Indians awaited the train, squatting round food stalls. They dipped their grubby hands into even dirtier-looking pots of cassava and toasted barley flour. Some passengers descended for a feast, others ate leaning out of the carriage windows. Papayas, corn, succulent *cachon* (pork) and beef, deliciously tender, were added attractions. The meal was swilled down by *chicha*, a local drink made from maize. Quechuas regard a train journey as a holiday so everyone was very happy and talkative. Carefree travellers seemed as ready to bargain for dead daisies as for the huge orchids blazing colour along the steep slopes of the Urubamba River gorge.

The train left each station very slowly so that everyone could finish bargaining. Those who didn't pay found vendors jogging alongside the track for a mile or two, hands outstretched. Some of the travellers had no intention of paying and taunted the seller as he ran outside. Many coins never reached the right hands and usually went to the fastest runner or fell onto the track. A squabbling heap of Indians ran to pick up the coins from the sleepers. The less nimble stood astride the line shaking clenched fists at the rear of the train. The whole carriage broke into uproarious laughter.

The railway dropped steeply over the eastern rim of the altiplano, and six hours out from Cusco we drew into Machu Picchu. The station was a cluster of buildings clinging to the canyon walls, standing only a few feet above the rushing waters of the river Urubamba. I was the only one to jump off. Nearby a signpost pointed almost vertically upwards, "To the ruins." Above me towered four thousand feet of rock face.

"*Roto, roto automovil,*" cried the stationmaster when I pointed vaguely in the direction of the signpost and repeated "*Los ruinas*" several times. The truck was broken and he was very sorry but the señor would have to walk.

I set out along the winding track. It began to rain. As each step brought me nearer to Machu Picchu, I tried to imagine what a lost city should look like. Was it a bare heap of stones? Or an archaeological gem against a backcloth of tropical vegetation? An hour later I had the answer. Machu Picchu rose majestically out of the clouds—ghostly. From a peak above the cemetery I looked down on the city that was once the pride and glory of the Incas. House, halls, steps, bathing pools and fountains, all were wonderfully preserved. But nobody strolled across the great silent forum which five centuries back had held twenty thousand shouting men. The city was bereft of all human life save mine on that dull grey day, and the white granite buildings towered with dramatic splendour in the heavy stillness.

The buildings in Machu Picchu have withstood six hundred years of Andean climate with barely a blemish. They are one and a half stories high with tall gables at either end. But all the roofs have disappeared; I wondered what they had been made of. In the royal apartment of a princess, I came across a stone bed that stretched across the room from one wall to another. How uncomfortable it looked. Adjoining the palace was the banqueting hall. I looked back into far away centuries and saw a great feast, with Incas clad in fine vicuna fur, wearing diamond ear-rings, gold circlets and jewels in their long black hair. Gold too were the thrones, the dishes and goblets. Legend has it that they never used the same dish twice. No wonder the Conquistadores were lured to Inca-land.

As the light faded I climbed a sweeping flight of steps, which only a little weeding would have restored to its former glory, to reach the Intuatana resting on the highest point above the city. The Intuatana is a stone sundial, the national symbol of the Incas, "the stone to

which the sun is attached." The Sun god was their creator and
benefactor. I wonder what they thought about a wet, cloudy day.
It was probably a bad omen, particularly at festival time when the
fire for the sacrifice of the lamb should come from the sun's rays.
Below me lay the Temple of the Sun with its sacrificial stone
weighing two tons.

On all sides Machu Picchu's natural rock walls drop three quarters
of a mile down to the roaring waters of the Urubamba. Tiers of
agricultural terraces, only three yards wide, cling to Machu Picchu's
mountain face—Inca farming must have been extremely efficient to
feed the twenty thousand mouths off such a small allotment—and
beyond the Urubamba rise even greater mountains.

Machu Picchu was lost for four hundred years. As Hiram Bing-
ham told the world when he rediscovered it in 1911, it "lies in the
most inaccessible place in the most inaccessible part of the Andes."
No wonder it has remained deserted.

Next morning I began the journey to Cusco. The inn station
wagon was running again and drove me down to the station. The
rumblings of the approaching engine echoed along the walls of the
canyon long before it came into sight. The station master signalled
it to stop, but the engine driver had no intention of even slowing
down. The next train wasn't due for another twenty-four hours, so
I pelted down the track; catching up with the last carriage, I threw
my small bag on to the footplate and jumped on myself. A second
later the blackness of a tunnel surrounded me. The carriage was
crammed full and for an hour I couldn't get further than the footplate. Perhaps this was just as well. I didn't fancy sharing a seat
with a lice-ridden Quechua, a llama, or an Andean chicken.

One Indian was intrigued by my socks. He pointed them out to
his friends. So I gave him a worn-out pair. He tried them on his
hands and I suppose they will stay there until they disintegrate like
the rest of his clothes.

The train zig-zagged down to Cusco station and I was very glad
to see Pedro waiting on the platform.

"How did you enjoy it?" he enquired as I jumped down.

"Magnificent. Wouldn't have missed that for the world. Thanks
for the introduction to the inn keeper. He was very helpful. The
train ride was good fun but I couldn't see any difference between
the classes."

Pedro smiled. "You'll only notice the difference when the train
breaks down. Then the first-class passengers remain seated, the

second-class get out of the train and the third-class get out and push."

The next visit was to the Church of La Merced.

"Only a few visitors are allowed in," Pedro told me, "but the bishop gave me special permission to take you this afternoon."

A priest greeted us at the entrance, and then led us through massive wooden doors, into a dark-panelled chamber. He opened the safe and before us stood the fabulous and dazzling five-foot tall, solid-gold cross, glittering under six spotlights.

"It weighs fifty-six pounds. It has fifteen hundred large diamonds, six hundred and fifteen pearls and countless rubies, sapphires and other precious stones. In the centre is Peru's fairest pearl."

My exclamation of awe was quite involuntary. The sight of the cross was breath-taking. But after the first moments of admiration I began to wonder what was the use of such a precious treasure locked away in a safe?

In the early morning I left Cusco by express train for Puno, about two hundred and fifty miles away. After a long, tedious climb to the head of the Vilcanota valley, fourteen thousand feet above sea level, the train stopped at Aguas Calientes. Everyone hopped out and rushed to the hot steaming streams which bubble up alongside the rail track. For many it was probably the first hot-water wash of their lives.

At Crucero Alto, one hundred and fifty feet further up, a woman passenger fainted. She was unacclimatised to the rarified air, and was only revived with a dose of oxygen from a trolley wheeled by an attendant from one end of the train to the other. Towards evening we arrived at Puno, a small port on the western shores of Titicaca. I had always wanted to visit this beautiful and mysterious lake which is higher than any other navigable piece of water in the world. I knew that it was somewhere up in the Andes, but its existence seemed legendary. Out of Titicaca came the mythical children, Manco Capac and Mama Oello, founders of the Inca race. On its southern shore was the centre of the earlier Tiahvanaco civilisation, from whom the Incas inherited their knowledge of building and social organisation. Some historians claim that Titicaca was the apex of a vast empire of which the Andean civilisations of Chavins, Tihuanas and the Incas were merely offshoots. The religion of the Aymara Indians of the altiplano is bound up with the lake. When Titicaca floods it is a sign that their gods are displeased. In

Bolivia a hundred years ago it was believed that Noah's flood was in fact the waters of Titicaca rising and overspilling onto the lowlands.

Now standing on the shores, I felt that Titicaca was some mirage of its own mythical past, an illusion still. The effect was broken by noisy officialdom which had found its way up here and soon dispelled illusions. Aggressive immigration officers insisted that we were about to enter Bolivia. After filling up forms and wading through questionnaires, fifty angry and ruffled passengers at last boarded the motor ship *Inca*, determined never to set foot in Bolivia again. By ten o'clock she was under way and the beauty of Titicaca made us forget most of our grievances.

On deck there was a crisp wind blowing from across the lake. I sheltered on the leeward side of the funnel and leant against it to keep warm. One of the ship's officers on routine deck rounds had the same idea and we started chatting. I wondered where the *Inca* was built and how she was brought up to Titicaca.

"In England, about 1900," he told me. "Sailed out to Peru under her own steam and was dismantled at Mollendo. That's in South Peru. She was taken over the mountains by the Southern Railway. They had to rebuild her at Puno."

"Quite a feat!"

"Nothing compared to the *Yavari*, her predecessor. She sailed to the west coast a hundred years ago. In those days there was no railway between the coast and Titicaca. Indians had to lug her on their backs four hundred miles to the lake. And that meant climbing over fifteen-thousand-foot passes."

Everyone was up early in the morning to see the snow-capped peaks perfectly reflected in the transparent waters of the great lake. Well over thirty miles away they looked deceptively near in the clear atmosphere. As the *Inca* drew alongside the quay at Guaqui, a fleet of balsas set out on a trout-fishing expedition. These craft have hulls and sails made of the *totora* reeds around the lake shores; they are identical with those of the Incas, and probably of the Tiahuanaco civilization as well.

As I was disembarking, the chief steward came running after me. "Señor! you have not paid your bill."

"But that's all been settled. The corporation gave me a 'gratis' ticket for the journey from their head office in Lima. The purser has it," I assured him.

"I know, Señor, but the ticket does not include the price of your bunk."

He wouldn't let me go until I had handed him thirty *soles*—fifteen shillings—for my bunk.

I joined the La Paz express feeling a bit disgruntled. No sooner had I sat down than more trouble appeared. The customs official became intensely interested in my tins of sweetened milk. He eyed me suspiciously and gabbled off a series of unintelligible questions. When I made no attempt to reply, he stalked off to fetch his chief who was checking baggage further down the train. The chief handled the tins of milk in the same suspicious manner, and asked me what I was doing with them. All the people in the carriage crowded round as if they were somehow involved in the matter, their curiosity fanned by an unusual incident.

"I'm going to drink the milk, of course," I said in halting Spanish.

"You realise that you are breaking the law by bringing milk into this country?"

"Breaking the law? How absurd! I never knew you had such a stupid law."

This made the officer furious but he wasn't sure what to do. Could anyone be arrested for taking a few tins of milk into the country, I wondered?

Yes, it was just the exasperating sort of thing that could happen in South America. Our attempt at discussion reached a deadlock. They couldn't understand what a young visitor to Bolivia was doing with milk in his bag and I certainly demanded further explanation of this peculiar "law" before I budged from my seat. Meanwhile the train was speeding across the highland plain to La Paz.

Just then a young English employee of the railway came down the carriage.

"What's the matter?" he asked, seeing me surrounded by a large crowd. "Done something wrong?"

"I wasn't aware of it," I grinned; "perhaps you could help me out of the jam." He tried everything to humour the officers, interpreting my statement word for word to them, and after some rapid muttering and hostile glances they reluctantly put the milk back in my bag and moved on.

"Bad luck you chose to bring milk into the country," said my rescuer. "There's some kind of revolution going on. Apparently La Paz is being starved of milk and bread, and milk prices have soared to a fantastic figure. No one's allowed to relieve the shortage from outside. The other day a woman thought she would make a fortune by smuggling in some milk. The customs discovered it and fined her a sum that'll take a good many years to pay off."

Of all the things I could have brought with me it had to be the one commodity banned by the Bolivian government. To avoid any more trouble of this sort I promptly punched holes in the remaining tins and with the help of my benefactor, finished the contents.

The altiplano ends abruptly at El Alto. Here it looks as though someone has been along with a gigantic spoon and dug a two-thousand-foot hole in the plateau. Nestling in the foot of this amphitheatre lies La Paz, the capital, looking from above like a toy town. It was half an hour before the train pulled into the station at the bottom.

I got talking with an American who was standing outside the station. He introduced himself as Joe and said I looked a bit lost. "Come along with me to the hotel. Guess you're staying at least one night in La Paz." He hailed a taxi. "Hotel, and drive fast." The driver nodded and trod on the accelerator. We tore down the main street.

"Gee, so I'm in La Paz at last." Joe sat back. "You know, the one thing I wanted to do more than anything else in my life was to visit every capital city in the world. Spent the last twelve years making my wish come true, and now," rather sadly, "I've seen the lot. Last week, though, I made a little blunder. I stopped the night at Sucre. Always thought Sucre was the capital of Bolivia. Going home to my little steel mills in Chicago last Thursday I met a Bolivian on the plane. I told him how much I had enjoyed the city. Just as we touched down in Chicago he let me know I hadn't been to Bolivia's capital at all. It shook me a bit that did, so I hopped on to the next plane, telegraphed the folks back home to say I'd been delayed a few days, and, well, here I am."

Apparently spending one day in each captial was Joe's idea of seeing the world. He was thirty-three, too young to be a self-made steel magnate and I suspect that his father subsidised his extraordinary safaris.

The driver dropped us at the hotel. One glance told me that it would be far beyond my pocket. I hovered in the background whilst Joe strode up to the desk.

"I want a suite of rooms for the night," he said, pulling a bundle of dollar bills from his hip pocket.

"That will be two thousand five hundred *bolivianos*," said the clerk.

"Two thousand five. . . ." Joe spluttered. "A room cost only a few dollars in Sucre." Then he grinned at me. "Guess it's a little more expensive in the capital." He dumped five dollars on the counter. "Reckon that'll settle it."

The clerk shook his head. "Non, non, Señor. . . ."

Joe casually pulled out another five bucks and the clerk's eyes nearly shot through the ceiling. "*Uno! uno! uno!*" he exclaimed.

"*Uno?*" At last Joe understood. "Gee, one dollar. Incredible!" When he was handed his room key and a bundle of notes as change, he turned to the clerk and pointing at me said, "Book another suite for this gentleman."

I admit that I saw just as little of La Paz as Joe did, but I became very familiar with the inside of certain public buildings, notably the immigration offices.

Government offices appeared to be crammed with employees reaping a financial harvest from the present state of emergency in Bolivia. In one room A opened my passport, B found the right page, C scrawled his signature, D applied the official stamp, E the officer in charge of handing it back was in the middle of his coffee break. A call at the police station produced a shower of further decorations for my passport, so that within twenty-four hours three pages had been covered with scribbles and stamps. If they continued at this rate elsewhere in South America I should soon be needing a new passport.

With permission to leave Bolivia I trudged along to the Peruvian consulate. Before I had left Lima the authorities there had assured me that I could re-enter Peru on my existing visa. When I approached their consul in La Paz for a return permit it was a different story.

"I can't help what anybody told you," he said, "I know my instructions, so you need not try to tell me what they are. If you show me the ticket on which you are leaving Peru I will issue you another visa."

"I'm sorry but I haven't got a ticket. I don't require one. A fishing company is taking me to the United States. I'm going as a deckhand."

The consul laughed disbelievingly.

"If you cannot tell me how you are going to get out of the country without making up a story, I cannot be expected to let you in, can I?" This was the kind of remark that made me boil, but it wasn't quite the moment to blast him, blast his country or blast anybody else. I kept my temper somehow.

"When I arrived at Iquitos, Peru, two months ago," I explained patiently and deliberately, "the regulations did not require evidence of a through passage."

"No?"

"Then why should you suddenly demand it now? The regulations couldn't have changed since I arrived in Peru."

"No?" he pointed a menacing finger at a copy in front of him. New regulations came into effect as from the first of January.

I had come slap up against a wall of bureaucracy. Officially there was no way out of my dilemma. The only thing to do was to talk and go on talking in the hope that he would make me an exception. I appealed to the goodness of his nature, to all that was best in Peru, and for the adventurous spirit of youth the world over, if he would only waive aside the new restrictions, just this once. After all I simply *had* to return to his wonderful country again, I pleaded. At last I even suggested, when I saw my entreaties were getting nowhere, that a transit visa would be better than nothing.

The office closed at midday and when the consul saw I wasn't going to move until he had done something constructive, he suddenly gave way, grabbed a stamp and scribbled *Ocho dies valida* across a transit visa.

"*Gracias, señor, muchas gracias,*" I murmured as he strode out of the door. The visa was only valid for eight days and I had another two weeks to wait in Peru until the tuna clipper sailed, but at least it allowed me back into the country. I should have to deal with the problem of an extension later.

The train to Guaqui was scheduled to leave La Paz in two hours' time. I walked along the modern thoroughfares, thronged with people. Groups of Quechua and Aymara Indians, as well as a mixed breed called Cholos, squatted on the pavement at every street corner, somehow finding a living by the roadside. The women dress in gaily-coloured *polleras*, pleated skirts that flow out at the hem. Round their shoulders is slung the traditional *poncho*, a shawl of llama fur, or woven vicuna for the more wealthy ones. The shape of the women's hats differ from one part of the Andes to another. A visitor to La Paz can be recognised as a Cuscoan by her pancake style of hat, or as an inhabitant of Titicaca by a pudding-basin model. But in La Paz the women wear bowlers, in brown and white. This is a recent addition to the native dress.

I seldom saw an Indian or Cholo woman without a baby perched on her back with the chicken, fruit and vegetables. Baby was tightly swathed in yards of coloured wool, unhappily trying to breathe. Both mother and baby relieved themselves in public with no inhibitions. Some years ago, Harold Osborn remarked, "along the main streets of La Paz and on the steps of public buildings you may see a nightmarish phantasmagoria of warm brown breasts with their purple areoles exposed to the greedy lips of children, approaching you." I had the same nightmare.

Close to the railway station a crowd of Indians were displaying piles of fruit on the pavement. Trade didn't seem very brisk. They all preferred to barter their stuff rather than take money for it, but those who adhered to this rule looked as if they had been sitting there a whole week without doing much business.

Friday, 5th February, I was on the *Inca* once again as she made her return ten-hour voyage across the lake to Puno. This time I didn't have to stump the fare. Another passenger, the manager of the Southern Railways, applied his god-like signature to my bill and that was as good as saying it was paid. The *Inca* arrived at Puno in time to catch the train which runs twice a week to Arequipa.

At every stop along the line, Indian vendors with armloads of hand-knitted woollens, vicuna skins, alpaca furs and grotesque wooden images invaded the carriage, and made a bee-line for the tourists. At least two couples became the unwilling buyers of badly reproduced models of the balsa craft, and others couldn't resist a "bargain" in outsize vicuna slippers.

As the train climbed above the rolling lands of the altiplano we passed through the land of some of the most industrious women-folk in the world. For mile after mile there were women battling in the fields against the stubborn earth, and while the women toiled under the load of babies on their backs, the men, dressed in trousers made from sugar bags and peaked caps with long ear-flaps, sat around the station waiting for the arrival of the bi-weekly train. Aymarian men retire early in life.

The sun was falling fast by the time we arrived at Arequipa. Long after it had dropped over the horizon its glow reflected on the snow-capped peaks of the three volcanoes, El Misti, Chachani and Pichu-Pichu. These are the "gentlemen of the Andes", all about 18,000 feet, and I wondered how many civilisations they had seen pass this way.

Two American women stood on the platform at Arequipa amidst

an enormous pile of suitcases and hat-boxes. I helped carry their bags to a taxi, and was about to leave when one of them asked me where I was stopping the night.

"Oh, I expect I'll find an hotel somewhere in the town." "Why not come along with us for a drink first," she suggested. "You need fortifying before you go hotel-hunting."

"Delighted," I replied with an effort at gallantry.

The taxi drew up at Peru's most famous guest house, the Quinta Bates. Kindness and hospitality was a Bates family tradition well kept up by Mrs. Consuela Genth, grand-daughter of Mrs. Bates, who insisted that I stay the night free of charge. Amongst the signatures in the four-volumed visitors' book I found that of Noel Coward's, with a few verses beginning—"No wandering nomad hesitates to patronise the Quinta Bates."

In the morning I had an unforgettable breakfast on the flat roof of the guest house. Above me towered the purple mass of one "Andean gentleman", below stretched the adobe and plaster houses of this attractive town still visited by llama and alpaca trains. Later Consuela Genth drove me to the airport and once again I was flying high above the coastal desert lands of Peru. When I touched down in Lima late on Sunday morning, it seemed impossible that I had only been away a week, travelled two thousand, three hundred miles and spent only fifty-five shillings —thanks to the generosity of the Peruvians.

Now that I had returned to Lima, I appreciated its life even more than before. The friendly people bubbled with gaiety, and preparations for the carnival were in full swing. Within a week all was set for the three-day festival beginning on February 12th. South Americans celebrate Mardi Gras with gusto. Men and women used to squirt perfumed water at each other during the carnival, but today the fashion is a water balloon bomb loaded with coloured water, hurled by the younger folk in a battle between the sexes. Toy plastic water-pistols have been superseded by life-size machine guns that hold a pint of water. Victory is won by completely soaking your opponent. Bobby Plenge and I accordingly set to work on bigger and better water-balloon bombs. On the last day we were caught at a street corner by a truckload of señoritas waging a stirrup-pump warfare against any man in sight. We returned home drenched.

The glittering lights of Lima have lured thousands of Indians in the hope of easy employment and a quick fortune. But the

Indian is rooted to the infertile plateau lands and the moment he forsakes his plot in the sierras, all that is best in him is lost. He seems unable to adjust himself to urban life. The result is a slum area of ramshackled bamboo shacks on the desert fringe of the city or behind high plastered walls, rarely seen by the casual visitor.

In strange contrast to these hovels are the new buildings, artistically blending American with Spanish architecture. Windows at odd angles, glass walls and brightly coloured plaster work are imposed upon the traditional patio and archway with their iron scrollwork and barley-sugar columns. Unfortunately the high price of ground space is based on the width of the frontage, so that the owners build on top of each other with claustrophobic effects. Between the gay buildings the modern avenidas are lined with flowers and trees, even though there is practically no rain in Lima. They are all watered artificially by deep ditches branching off from the main aqueduct. The water travels at least fifty miles, down from the western cordillera.

The city streets were crowded with *colectivos*, communal taxis that pick up and set down passengers anywhere along the bus routes. They provide quick travel for those who cannot afford to run a car, at only double the bus fare. It is an efficient system which might well solve London's traffic problem by replacing most private cars. On the city trams you could buy anything from popcorn to the South American edition of *Reader's Digest*.

When the carnival was over it was time to think about leaving Lima. The tuna clipper was sailing in a week's time from Paita, a small port on the Peru-Ecuador border. The company wanted me there on Monday, February 20th. It might take as long as two days and nights to hitch-hike the five hundred miles to Paita. This would waste precious time, so I chose to pay two pounds fare and travel by Sud-Americano motor coach. I had managed to get a financial guarantee from an old school friend now in New York. It arrived by the late morning post on February 18th, and I rushed into the American consulate to pick up my visa with only half an hour to spare before the office closed for the weekend.

Five happy weeks in Lima came to an end on the afternoon of February 20th. I was getting into the swing of life in the city and regretted having to break away. But a globetrotter's life is a succession of farewells. Of one thing I was immensely glad—I was going to the United States after all.

6

HOLLYWOOD . . . OR BUST!

A shining aluminium jerry crowning a pile of baby clothes occupied my seat on the Sud-Americano coach. I had booked the window position, but clearly the real choice lay with the person who got in first. Someone had beaten me to the post. Rather than cause an uproar by moving the pot and other articles I resigned myself to the inside corridor seat.

At 5 p.m. the coach driver climbed on to his perch. "*Vamos!*" he yelled. Before he had time to let in the clutch a peremptory hammering on the coach door announced the arrival of a late-comer. Reluctantly he slipped off his seat and opened up. A bulbous, sierran lady squeezed in. She floundered through the sacks of clucking chickens in the gangway and advanced down the coach. In her arms lay an equally grotesque baby screaming under a volley of slaps, hands and feet waving frantically in little circles. I took an instant dislike to them both. Pity the person sitting next to that lot. Thank goodness it wasn't . . .The señora's smile froze too when she saw that she had a *gringo* for a travelling companion. She squeezed past me and deposited the baby on my lap together with a pile of llama-wool nappies. He doubled the volume of his complaints but Mother took no notice. She flopped into her seat and her flesh bulged outwards, forcing me against the armrest. The pressure was terrific. She snatched the yelling child from me without a word, then sighed very loudly in the hope of receiving sympathy in her tribulations.

I attempted to make conversation. I asked if she was going all the way to Paita, hoping that she was not, but the señora didn't understand my Spanish. She gesticulated madly and appealed to the crowd for support, and the other travellers were only too ready to make fun of the *gringo*. So we settled down for a long silent journey, interrupted regularly every hour by baby calling for his pot. More than once during the night I was left foolishly holding it to the amusement of the other passengers.

Revolutions are always popping up in Latin America. I had arrived in the middle of one in Brazil, and what looked like the beginning of one in Bolivia. Two months had passed without any trouble in Peru, but this situation couldn't last. The Peruvian revolution began on February 16th in the jungle town of Iquitos, where I had been eight weeks before.

The first intimation we had came when the coach was abruptly halted before a road barrier. The passengers heard that it was a revolution and they became very excited. "Will anything happen to us?" I asked a fellow traveller.

"Nothing at all," he assured me. "The police block the roads to prevent the trouble spreading. That's normal procedure when there's a riot. They might ask to see our travel documents, but nothing more."

"Our travel documents?" I realised with a sinking feeling that my passport came under this heading. The immigration authorities had refused to extend the eight day transit visa that I had wormed out of their consul in Bolivia. It was now out of date. I wondered what the penalty would be—prison, perhaps?

A police officer stepped aboard the coach. He looked around and I shrunk back in my seat and tried to merge into the señora's bulk. As a Britisher my papers would be scrutinized, but fortunately the booking clerk in Lima had recorded me as a Peruvian on the passenger list. The officer consulted the passenger list, counted the heads and left the coach. I sat up. It wasn't so difficult to scrape through a road barrier after all.

Another stop two hours later brought more inspectors on to the coach. These took nothing for granted and systematically examined everyone's papers. There was no escape for me. I should have to be brazen or apologetic, according to how they reacted. The inspector took my passport and showed surprise that it was British. He scanned the list in his hands, and then examined my eyes. They are blue. All Peruvians have brown eyes.

"Señor, you are not down here as British. Why is that?"

"The clerk in Lima must have made a mistake." My explanation wasn't convincing.

He looked at the passport again, and was obviously puzzled by the number of stamps and signatures.

"Señor, I cannot understand this passport. You must see my chief."

An attempt to argue in Spanish would get me nowhere, so I followed him out.

As he led me off the coach I glanced at the driver and asked him to wait for me. "Please," I pleaded, "I won't be long."

The driver promised to wait, though his expression belied his words. It seemed to imply that I should soon be behind iron bars.

I was led into a dimly-lit room and told to stand at the end of a long table. Seated at the other end was the perspiring police superintendent. Three junior officers stood respectfully behind him.

"Now, Señor Alistair," he began.

"Señor Boyd."

"Señor Boyd, then, if you will kindly give me your passport we can clear up this little trouble, yes?"

Handing it over I felt enmeshed in a web of red tape. For a minute or two the superintendent studied the passport upside down. Then he noticed the photograph and realised his mistake. Turning it up the right way, very deliberately he thumbed through the pages until he came to the tourist visa with which I had originally entered Peru. He passed it to the others to scrutinize. An almost imperceptible nod of the head told me that he thought this part quite satisfactory. Round one to me. He turned back a few pages and examined the Brazilian visa, then forward to the U.S.A. one. It was touch and go whether he would discover the out-of-date Peruvian transit visa. I had carefully stuck a number of medical certificates over it but they didn't hide the stamp very effectively. His clumsy fingers turned the pages first one way then the other and I began to sweat. These minutes seemed like hours. The suspense was getting unbearable. He was growing inquisitive; beginning to bend back those medical certificates. Only a miracle will save me now. I had to say something, I couldn't help it. Just then the bus driver tooted his horn.

"Er . . . officer. . . ."

He looked up, closing my passport abruptly. A huge lump slid down my throat, and I just managed to hold back a tell-tale sigh of relief.

"Yes?"

"Er . . . don't you think it's time for me to return to the coach?"

"Si, si, Señor, so sorry to trouble you. Of course, I was forgetting. You must go now," he murmured, handing back the passport. So he hadn't noticed that I had been to Bolivia since my arrival in Peru, and he thought the first Peruvian visa was still valid. I walked out of the room rather dazed. All the passengers except the señora shook me by the hand. I didn't quite know why; perhaps they thought I was a victim of injustice.

Five hundred miles down the road the coach stopped in the centre of Piura. By this time the señora had grown a little more friendly: we actually shook hands before I clambered off the coach. But that would be my last coach-ride in Peru I decided. I dumped my bags on the road outside the town and soon picked up a truck going all the way to Paita.

The gleaming white sands of the Atacama coastal desert separate Paita from the green of the Andean foothills. On her other side is the sea, a deep azure. The rainfall is almost nil, the heat unbearable; I felt like a dried apricot. It was off Paita that the Greek, Onassis, had his huge Pacific fishing fleet confiscated by the Peruvian Government for trawling within its territorial waters, but apart from that incident this little town lays no claim to fame.

The tuna clipper *Puerto de Sol* swung at anchor in the bay. Swarms of lighter barges brimming with frozen tuna fish were going out to her from the wooden quay. Hopping aboard one of these I was ferried out.

"Come in," the captain bellowed, in answer to my timid knock on his state-room door. He was stretched out on his bed clad only in his underpants.

"Well, what do you want?" he rubbed his eyes and hitched himself up on one elbow. He spoke with a foreign accent.

"Sorry if I disturbed you, captain. I'm Mr. Boyd. Er . . . I believe your office in Lima has already spoken to you about me, or . . ." He regarded me quite blankly. "I'm the one going round the world." But it was no good.

He sat up a little higher.

"What's that you say? Going round the world? No, never heard of you. Now that you are here, what do you want?"

I started on a brief explanation.

He interrupted me with a wave of his hand. "So you want to work your way to San Diego? Well, I have no objection and so long as the company agrees you can sign on as a workaway. Sleep aft and use a paint-brush during the voyage. We are not leaving for a day or two, possibly Saturday, so you can do what you like until then. And by the way," he added, "I'm afraid as a workaway you will have no pay. I am sorry."

I was sorry also but to expect pay as well as a passage would be a strain on their generosity. Anyway in ten days' time I should be in California two thousand miles away.

"You go ski-ing, Señor?" an old gentleman asked while I sought the cooling shade of the tuna factory's warehouse on the quay.

"Ski-ing here?" The veteran grinned and explained the Peruvian fishermen's version. They build a balsa raft, attach a harpoon spear to one end of it and paddle out after sharks. When the harpoonist scores a hit the shark kicks off at a high speed towing the raft with its rider standing astride the stern in proper ski fashion.

"It's skilled work to keep the raft upright," he said. "If it turns over you play with the shark." The old man disappeared round a corner muttering to himself. I didn't feel like trying Peruvian ski-ing.

One day in Paita was sufficient to discover that fishing was the only occupation. Dried fish hung outside every hut like part of the fabric, and the beach was littered with their remains. A persistent smell hovered over the town.

An hour before the *Puerto del Sol* left Paita, a luxury motor-yacht glided into the bay. She dropped anchor a hundred yards astern of the clipper. I was standing on the quay waiting to be ferried out, and was soon surrounded by the entire population who had assembled to gape at the newcomers. A white pinnace darted towards us bearing three gentlemen in tropical suits. Appointing myself spokesman for the motley crowd, I welcomed them on the quay.

"Hi. I'm MacMillan," one of them said, withdrawing his cigar. "Say, can you tell us the quickest way to a hospital? Our Captain's ill. Needs treatment at once. He fell sick while we were catching specimens of tropical fish from the Galapagos."

I directed them to the manager of the Paita-Piura railroad.

"Thanks for your help. What do you do for a living? Officer on the clipper out there?"

"Oh no, just passing through on my way to the States. Leaving on the *Puerto del Sol* this afternoon."

"He's going right round the world." We were joined by the manager of the tuna factory who started on a long account of my travels.

"That's great," said the visitor. "Coming to Canada at all?"

"Only Vancouver. Don't expect I'll have much time to see any more of the country."

"Well, that's fine. You don't need to worry about the rest. But just you make sure you stop off in Vancouver. When you get there, look us up in the University. The names are Mackenzie and

MacMillan. Can't miss us, and we shall be glad to see you. Cheerio, and have a good journey."

The *Puerto del Sol* sounded her whistle and I jumped aboard the last tender leaving the quay. As the tuna clipper got under way she blew a farewell whistle to the smaller fishing craft. The people on the quay shouted and waved and the toucans perched on the rafts lowered their oversize beaks as if they were sorry to see us leave. Very soon the skyline of South America was lost in the heat haze. We were out on the Pacific.

"Stow away the hawsers!" the mate yelled, a few inches from my eardrums, reminding me that I was aboard to work and not on a Pacific pleasure cruise. By six o'clock I was ready for my American-sized steak.

The strenuous afternoon on deck in 88 degrees had exhausted us and nobody stayed up long after dinner. I shared a cabin with an Italian steward, a Yugoslav bosun and a Peruvian greaser. They were stretched out on their bunks with towels round their waists, reading comic strips. All three lowered their literature to stare at me when I came in. They said nothing. The throb of the engines and the whir of the electric fan made their silence less noticeable. There would be language difficulties right from the start, I thought. The bosun swore at me in his Slavonic tongue when I staked a claim to a square inch of room on the table and to one hook in the communal cupboard. It was hard work trying to smooth out the difficulties that cropped up. Half the time I didn't know what they were all about.

Twelve different nationalities were represented amongst the crew of twenty-one; we were a little "United Nations" of our own. In the officers' mess, English and Swedish predominated, but in our mess Spanish held the floor, with little bits of Italian thrown in by the donkeymen who preferred to argue in their own lingo.

On the second morning out I trudged up forward with my paint-pot and began to plaster a coat of pale-grey on the deck and another of glaring white on the superstructure. At the end of the day the bos'n rigged up a shower with the fire hose suspended from a tripod. Showers were extremely popular and became even more so when he made out an hour's overtime on the paysheets at the end of the week for the time spent under them.

Whales were only occasional companions on the trip but black dolphins visited us daily, leaping and diving alongside our bows, following us for miles before they finally gave up and headed out to

sea again. Every day and all day the flying fish skidded away from
the bows, scattering particles of water that sparkled and formed
miniature rainbows in the sunlight. Every morning the bosun went
round the deck collecting the fish which had jumped aboard during
the night. He returned to the galley with a bucketful for breakfast.
Their bodies retained an ethereal blue shimmer. But such aesthetic
considerations did not interfere with our enjoyment of them for
breakfast.

The *Puerto del Sol* steamed close to the desert coastlands of the
Baja California state of Mexico. One afternoon a dense cloud
suddenly rolled across the water towards us. The mate hurried
forward. "A bloody sandstorm," he shouted. "Get inside," but
before he had finished speaking the clipper was enveloped in a
swirling mass of sand. Everything was blotted out, and above
where the brilliant blue sky had been a minute before there was
nothing but dense blackness. The storm was fierce, but short-lived.
After a few minutes we emerged into clear skies.

"*Caraco!*" yelled the astounded carpenter when he looked at the
superstructure. The paint which we had applied in the last two days
had been completely sanded off on the windward-facing surfaces.
Once again I trudged up forward with my paint-pot.

One morning early in March, the *Puerto del Sol* steamed slowly
past mist-enshrouded Point Loma to dock in the quiet waters of the
Marine Terminal at San Diego, California. I packed my bags.
Armed with forty-nine bucks I stepped on to North American soil
for the first time.

After Paita's sandy streets, grim bamboo shacks and fishy smell,
I was overawed by the "freeways", the skyscrapers and the clean-
liness of San Diego. The contrast was shattering, and for a while
I just stood and marvelled at my new environment. But I couldn't
do that all day. I must find somewhere to sleep, always the
first consideration when arriving in a new place. For years I had
read of American friendship and hospitality, but I expected to find
the reputation very exaggerated. I was wrong. Within three hours
of stepping ashore I sat in the luxurious home of Mrs. Ethel Jordan,
drinking tea.

"I shall be really delighted for you to stay as long as you wish,"
came Mrs. Jordan's voice from the kitchen and at these welcoming
words I sank further into the easy chair and dozed off. I had never
met Mrs. Jordan before, but this hospitality was the result of a

complicated exchange of letters between Lima, London and San Diego.

A sudden high-pitched scream jerked me into consciousness and a strange gurgling noise came from the kitchen. I rushed in to see what was happening.

Mrs. Jordan laughed when she saw my startled expression. "It's only my garbage-disposal machine," she explained. "It pulverises all the rubbish in the sink before sending it down the drain."

I wondered what happened to teaspoons. This was one of the dozens of modern gadgets in her house. There was a special fan over the cooking-stove to take away the smells. The garage and back doors opened by an electric beam so that Mrs. Jordan could go from her house to her Oldsmobile without having to open any doors by hand. Like that of most Americans her life could run smoothly without the help of domestic servants. Her house was built on an open plan, in which tall cupboards or tiers of shelves rather than walls separate the rooms.

"Guess we ought to let the television studios downtown know you're here." Mrs. Jordan dialled the number before I had time to say anything. I found life much less of a strain now that I was amongst English-speaking people again. I no longer felt like a dumb mute and I could almost understand what they were talking about.

"Well, that's just fine," Mrs. Jordan was saying over the 'phone. "He'll be along at the studio in a few minutes." Just what has she let me in for now, I wondered. She replaced the receiver and called out, "Say, Alistair, hurry up with that unpacking. You're on television in half an hour." Life in the States was going to be a strain after all.

Thirty minutes later I was making my debut on the screen, telling San Diego's viewers on channel 9 K.F.M.B. that it was simply wonderful to be in the States. After the show several well-wishers telephoned me to say how good it was to hear "old England on the telly", and one dear old soul said, "mind you have a drink on my Bert that's left me and runs a pub on the Old Bath road called the Red Lion."

Soon I was swept up in the whirlwind life of San Diego—luncheons, dinners, socials, dances. As an "Atlantic wetback", the English Speaking Union asked me to address a dinner meeting. For a ten minutes' talk I was presented with twenty dollars. Easy come.

And easy go. This I found out very swiftly. My hair had been neglected during travels in places where an Indian length of thatch passes unnoticed. I felt conspicuous here. So I walked into a downtown barber's saloon—and quickly walked out again on seeing that the price of a hair-cut was one dollar, thirty cents. Thinking that I must have stumbled into a de luxe establishment first time, I tried others. Everywhere I hit the same price-level— nine shillings minimum! I couldn't part with that, just for a hair-cut. Why ever since that catastrophic round of beers in Belem I had been teaching myself that miserliness was one of the conditions of my continuous motion. Firmly I retraced my steps to the Jordan home, hair still flopping over my ears.

"I can't possibly afford a hair-cut here," I told Mrs. Jordan.

"Can't afford a hair-cut?"

Her obvious astonishment made me feel embarrassed as I went on to mumble, "The last one I had cost only threepence. Downtown here they are asking nine shillings—er, one dollar, thirty."

She still looked puzzled; I think one dollar, thirty sounded the usual price to her. However she must have seen to it that news of my plight got round the San Diegans, for one morning a doctor's wife rang up to say she would be "mighty proud to shear the lad's hair." And she did, efficiently.

Also a couple of temporary jobs showed up for me. One, in San Diego, was so temporary it ended after one day but brought me in ten dollars; the other, on a ranch thirty miles out of town, gave me three full days' employment weeding the owner's private airstrip. "Weeding" was just the local name for the operation that followed, I decided. It seemed more like forestry to me as I struggled to eliminate "weeds" that had obviously taken to the American way of life in a big way and in less-democratic lands would have called themselves "saplings" or "bushes" at least.

When I'd got the strip smooth enough to take a tractor at thirty-five miles an hour I reckoned a plane should be able to land there in perfect safety, so my job was done. Returning from the airstrip in the tractor and driving on the wrong or "British" side of the road, I almost crashed into the rancher, Mr. Thompson, Jr. He leant out of his Oldsmobile to give me an urgent message, "Someone called you from Hollywood—they'll ring back in ten minutes— drive like hell and you'll make it."

I was outside the ranch door in a few minutes, then racing to the telephone. Hollywood! Perhaps they wanted to put me in a film.

Can't be! Could be! What else? Perhaps it's only an Englishman wanting to meet me. But someone must have gone to a lot of trouble to find out where I was staying. Hollywood! That's where they do things like that and work miracles over-night. Alistair Boyd, the new film star! How's that for size? The suspense of waiting was agonising; I strained my ears for the slightest tinkle on the phone, my fingers gripping the receiver.

At last. This was it!

"Yes, this is Mr. Boyd speaking. Yes, I was on television last week, that was me, yes. Tuesday week—no I'm not doing anything. I mean I'm free, yes. Yes."

In five minutes it was all arranged. Not a glamorous film role as from the Hollywood of yore but an appearance on the C.B.C. Television Network, a set-up typical of Hollywood today.

"You will be interviewed next Tuesday by the well-known Mr. Art Linkletter in his House Party programme," the voice said, and rang off.

Art Linkletter! Great guy by the sound of it, but I mustn't show my ignorance.

My total earnings in America now added up to the princely sum of twenty-eight pounds. Hollywood, here I come.

A freshly crew-cut monster called Sam welcomed me at the door of his fraternity house in Los Angeles. His shoulders slouched forward a little, both hands were plunged well down into the front pockets of his blue drain-pipe jeans and he chewed gum. Sam was a student of the University College of Los Angeles.

"Yeah, that's right. You're staying right here. Step in and make yourself at home. Ethel J. Jordan in San Diego wrote me. Said you were on your way up to L.A. Glad you managed to make it. Hitch-hike?"

Wading through a stack of empty beer cans in the hallway I followed him into the living room, where he introduced me to his fraternity brothers. A chorus of "Hi's" went up round the room and I luckily remembered to keep my hands firmly planted in my pockets.

"Right glad to know you," one of them drawled. "You've arrived in time for a mighty fine feast. Sam's won a raffle to-day."

"First prize is a dinner cooked by the six beauty queens of the University, with a seventh to wash up."

The feast started with giant rump steaks, and I very nearly failed to get through the first course on the menu.

In the morning Sam took me along to one of his lectures. "Guess you'd like to see how we do it in the States, huh?" The subject was anthropology. There was none of the hushed, reverent atmosphere of the Oxford lecture hall. Students badgered the professor into long, pointless arguments about the difficulties of racial classification. They were evidently specialists in red herrings. And all the time Sam's hands remained firmly embedded in his jeans.

Early Tuesday I presented myself at the Television Centre in Hollywood, slightly unnerved by its size. A guide met me at the entrance and led me through a maze of glass doors and marble halls where our footsteps were muffled by sound-proofed floors. Art Linkletter's House Party was warming up for its morning programme. As we entered Studio II there was a general buzz of excitement. Art, coolly perched on an uncomfortable-looking stool, directed floor operations through an entanglement of studio telephones. He was perfectly composed. All round him electricians were laying down last minute wires for the unwary to trip over and operators were moving massive cameras noiselessly across the stage. So much activity, not a sound. A huge packet of cake-mix surrounded by several chocolate cakes stood on a table with brightly-coloured advertisements behind. One hungry technician had already approved a sample of the product.

Four tiny tots were also led through the studio—they were to appear on the same programme before my turn. A schoolgirl pranced round the stage full of the smug assurance of a practised performer.

"Do you like going on telly?" she asked me.

"Well, I haven't done much television work yet, you know."

"Oh, I see. You're new. Of course I've done lots. It's all so easy but gets a bit boring."

"Bored? At your age?" I said in surprise. "What do you do then?"

"I have to cram a thick chunk of that chocolate cake into my mouth and look as if I am enjoying it. But I've been doing it for *years* now. I sure was glad when they changed to chocolate. Used to be raspberry, you know."

Art Linkletter's House Party was on the screen at 11.30, with the four shy tots sitting on the stage.

Art was compère. "Hallo, all," he said. "Now as you know, kids, I'm just gonna ask you a few mighty simple questions, so be darlings for once and answer them for me, will you? That's right."

He went over to the little girl at the end of the row who turned all coy and hugged an enormous doll.

"What's your name?" Of course there was no answer.

"What does Mama call you?"

"Sugar," she replied in a tiny voice.

"Well, Sugar, how old are you?"

"Four—" a little pause, "to-day."

"When you are a little older, Sugar, what do you think you would like more than anything else in the world?"

"Children," came the prompt answer.

"Well that is a nice thought and I hope that you have lots of little sugars. Then what do you want to do?"

"Get married." She smiled up at Art and a roar of laughter came from the studio audience.

Five minutes later Art said, "To-day we have an amphibious Englishman in the studio. He's travelled all the way up the River Amazon to be with us this morning." I was pushed onto the stage.

"Well, Mr. Alistair Boyd, twenty million housewives are looking in at you at this very moment. Suppose you tell them what Amazon housewives are really like."

"Well, er . . . they have, er . . . two of most things."

"Oh, you don't say," cut in Art, amidst howls of laughter from the audience. "I thought . . ."

"And they're the most beautiful women in the world," I added hastily before he had time to expand further on my opening statement.

Five minutes later the interview ended and Art motioned me off the stage.

At the end of the programme he showed me a wooden crate. "It's all yours."

I prised open the lid, half suspecting that this was some kind of a joke for suckers. Inside was the very latest wonder washing-machine. It left me speechless.

"Well, what do you think of it?" said Art. "Round the world with a washing-machine?"

"Yes, very handy. What the heck can I do with it?"

"Convert it into bucks."

We got rid of it for a hundred dollars that very afternoon.

I left Los Angeles two days after the show expecting to cover the four hundred and fifty miles to San Francisco before dark. Hitch-hiking a lift from the middle of Los Angeles is impossible. Six lines of traffic stream past at fifty miles an hour. Once clear of the town, however it was easier to pick up long distance lifts. By lunchtime I was in Fresno, California's raisin centre. Next I crossed the San Joaquin River whose flow, I was told, had been reversed by American engineers in order to irrigate the Great Valley of California. My last lift of the day took me to Menlow Park, and so to more American homes. As a result of my talk in San Diego, the hospitality committee of the English Speaking Union put me in touch with two doctors' families in San Francisco. Each welcomed me as a guest over Easter weekend.

One night a sorority girl, Jean, from the University at Berkley took me for a tour of the night clubs. It was a great success until we came to a low dive in the Latin Quarter. We had poked our noses in through the plush curtains and were persuaded to sit down and watch the floor show. The proprietress about to open the programme, planted her twenty-stone figure in front of the microphone. Clutching it with a dimpled hand she shrieked out a popular song, then another and another. After thirty minutes we couldn't stand any more. The moment we got up she abruptly left off and screamed, "Don't go! I'll strip." "No thanks. You needn't."

That was my undoing. Two tons descended on me like a meteorite and hauled me up onto the stage. "Say, you're a Limey, I guess," she drawled. "What d'ya think you're doing in Frisco?"

"Passing through."

"Passing through?" she repeated hoarsely. "Oh, so you're not stopping. Just passing through, you say. Suppose I couldn't persuade you to stay a bit longer. Guess you'd go down all right on my show, and honey," she whispered, drawing me a little closer with her ape-like arms, "we've gotta nice English piece backstage. She's undressing for the next act. Wanna introduction?"

After a bit of a tussle I wrenched myself free of the arms and we cleared out as fast as we could go. Jean didn't seem at all embarrassed by this interlude, but I resolved never to get in the limelight again in an American night club.

Last on the evening schedule was a rushed visit to the "Top O' the Mark"—the skyroom of the Mark Hopkins Hotel. Half-way up in the lift, the attendant shrieked,

"Say, you're the guy I saw on T.V. the other day."

We were in the limelight again and on reaching the skyroom so many drinks were showered on us that when I got round to looking at the famous view the lights of San Francisco swam beneath my eyes.

If there had been any chance of signing on an orient-bound cargo ship from San Francisco I might have grabbed at the opportunity of leaving North America. But after several telephone calls to port authorities I realized that the Unions were insuperable, so I had to get to Vancouver.

I set out on Highway 101, the great Redwood Highway. My first lift of the day took me across the Golden Gate suspension bridge with its 4,200 foot span. My driver commented that this bridge still had an irresistible fascination for suicides.

Hitch-hiking on the open highway was a lonely sport after all the hospitality and friendliness of the past few days. The drivers streamed past my waving arm, mostly the solitary businessmen who are always in a hurry and pretend not to notice you until the last minute when it's too late to stop.

At last one car stops and you run as fast as you can to catch it up so as not to cause the driver even more inconvenience. You gabble off a well-rehearsed sequence of "thank you very much, terribly good of you, I come from . . . " often ending up with whole life histories. Each listens to the other's yarn while the miles of grey tarmac are swallowed up in front of the windscreen. Some drivers often unburden their most closely-guarded family secrets to a hitch-hiker whom they never expect to see again, others treat you to a long intimate history of their ailments and operations, down to the last gruesome detail. But that is the hitch-hiker's fare and the price is low.

A sleek-looking Pontiac picked me up at Greysoris and it turned out that the woman driver was another who had seen me on television. Perhaps Art had been right about those twenty million housewives.

"What a coincidence meeting you here," she chuckled. "How far up the Redwood Highway are you going?"

"All the way. I'm aiming for Vancouver."

"Yeah, that's right, I remember. You said on the T.V. you were hitch-hiking up to Canada. Sure glad to have picked you up. Guess there's plenty of time to run you a couple of hundred miles on your way."

We drove through the Chandelier tree in Underwood park. "The older trees here were planted when the Pharaohs sat on Egypt's throne," she told me, and this one was as tall as Big Ben and it was possibly the oldest living thing on earth. I gazed up its three hundred feet. The road burrowed straight through the trunk.

I hadn't been waiting at the wayside very long before I was scooped up by two woodsmen going north for a week's holiday. They were huge, thickset, with ham fists, bronze skins and jaws set square. Their speech was as rugged as their appearance. I understoood about one word in five. The rest were lost in drawl, most sentences ending up with a string of "reck'n so's." I perched on a pile of dirty old clothes that filled the space where the back seat should have been and was thankful to be taken another hundred and fifty miles further up the highway.

About ten o'clock at night we stopped on the outskirts of a town, by a neon sign which said "The Hitching Post." It sounded the obvious place to try my luck for a night's lodging.

I pushed through the swing doors. The barmaid recognised me at once for a "Limey", probably by my tie, as west coasters rarely wear them. She served a round of drinks on the house as a welcome (there were only two others in the room). There was no accommodation at "The Hitching Post" but a shabby old gentleman sprawling across the bar said I could have a bed if I didn't mind roughing it. I offered him a dollar which he snatched out of my hand.

When he showed me the room I thought I'd been generous with the dollar.

"I'm a writer," he said over a cup of coffee. "Magazines and so on. Done quite a bit of it in my time." I noticed that his dirty clothes were splattered with paint so assumed he hadn't been very successful and had taken to the brush.

I didn't enquire further into the success or otherwise of his literary career. He was up and away before I woke at five-thirty next morning. Perhaps he was a decorator after all.

The morning was cold, bleak. Depressing grey clouds leaden with rain hung above me as I waited by the road to Grants Pass, speculating on my chances of reaching Seattle before nightfall. The band saws of the lumber yard behind me had whined endlessly and the garage opposite had played the same record sixteen times before I got my first lift of the day.

Three jolly Texans, well primed with spirits, released me from the pavement. Then followed a long exasperating "pub crawl" over Grants Pass as we found one liquor store after another, closed. When it was time to part company some sixty miles further on, I knew that everything in Texas was pretty stupendous and that the United States was mighty fortunate in having such an important locality, and that their little ol' Texas was three times the size of England, Wales, Scotland and Ireland all put together.

Breakfast and a mid-day snack went by the board that day. I was determined not to lose the chance of a lift. A low, sleek sports car came in sight well down the road, but sports cars rarely stop for hitch-hikers as their drivers are too preoccupied with extracting the last ounce of power from the accelerator to notice a solitary figure standing by the roadside. This one was an exception, and it screeched to a standstill about a hundred yards beyond me. I ran after it, jumped in beside the driver and had hardly got the door closed before the needle was way up into the nineties.

"Isn't there a speed limit on your roads?" I shouted as we broke the century.

"Yeah, sixty," he replied, glancing down at the speedometer, making no attempt to lift his foot off the pedal.

An hour later we pulled up at a glass-built "drive-in" café and I was seventy-five miles nearer Seattle.

"A shake and a hamburger?" he asked.

"Thanks."

When I tackled him again about the speed limit he replied, "If you've got a good car why not go as fast as you can make it?"

Nearly every model produced in the States can clock about a hundred miles an hour. "Damn silly of the manufacturers to make them so fast when they know there are speed limits everywhere. But then we all enjoy power, don't we?" was my driver's attitude. "There's a road sign in this State which says the speed limit is 60 m.p.h. Underneath that it gives the penalty for disobeying the rule, which is a dollar for every mile an hour faster. So, choose a speed you can afford. I don't drive much above a hundred, so my maximum fine is forty dollars. Makes it worth while to me."

He finished his journey at one of the many motels that line the highways, and I picked up my last lift which took me to Seattle. After eighteen hours and five hundred miles of hitch-hiking I was very glad to find a bunk free for the night in the Y.M.C.A. I rolled into it and fell asleep at once.

"Say," came a stranger's voice from the next shower as I was humming a tune. "Are you the English chap who came in late last night?"

"Yes, that's me."

"Saw your name in the registry this morning. Your song gave you away. Going to Vancouver to-day?"

"Yes, hope to start hitch-hiking up there after breakfast."

"Well, I'm the manager of a boy's football team on Vancouver Island and I'm taking the team back there this morning after the game at the Stadium. We'd be glad to have you join us if you don't mind a squeeze. We arranged to meet outside the hostel at one o'clock.

I had been waiting on the kerb for quite a time when cheers and twirling football boots out of the windows of a shooting brake announced the arrival of the rabble. I climbed on to the piles of football jerseys, muddy shorts and boots. A barrage of questions lasted until the Canadian border.

It was continued by an official in the immigration post who kept repeating "This may sound rather pointless to you . . ."

It did. What difference did it make whether I read history, geography or citrus fruit-growing at the university? But it appeared to be a matter of extreme urgency to him.

"Of course as a visitor to Canada you shouldn't compete with Canadians for employment," he reminded me. "You would be taking bread out of Canadian mouths."

A charming, "Oh, no, I shouldn't dream of doing such a thing," seemed the best way to deal with that. I hadn't the slightest intention of taking bread out of anyone's mouth.

"Know anyone in Vancouver?" he asked, sure that I didn't.

"Er, yes," I looked for my address book. "A Mr. MacKenzie at the University, and . . . Mr. H. R. MacMillan."

They were the two Canadians I had met in Peru and on hearing their names the officer's manner was suddenly transformed. He mumbled some sort of apology for having detained me half an hour. Strange what names can do, I mused. Wonder what exactly my two Canadian acquaintances do for a living?

I rejoined the football team who had waited outside for me all this time, and we drove off furiously. The team had to catch the ferry for Victoria Island. We arrived at the quay to find the vessel edging away. Thanks to me and the immigration officer, the boys had to wait for the late night ferry.

Once I was inside the country Canadians did everything to help me. Hospitality first came from Mrs. Crawford who lived in Shaughnessy Heights. I invaded the downtown shipping offices. By the end of my second day every shipping agent in Vancouver knew that I was looking out for an Asia-bound vessel.

I called at the University of British Columbia wondering if the Canadians of the Peruvian fishing expedition would remember me. The University registrar was very helpful.

"Mr. MacKenzie? Now which MacKenzie would that be?"

"I'm afraid I don't know what he does, except that he's on the staff of the University. At least that's what I gathered from our brief meeting in Peru."

"You met him in Peru?" the registrar exclaimed. "You must mean Dr. MacKenzie. He's the President of the University."

I was speechless.

"Shall I take you along to his office?"

I hesitated. "I didn't realize . . . do you think he would mind seeing me now . . . wouldn't he be too busy?"

He wasn't too busy, and wrung my hand vigorously. "You've made it after all." He had wondered only yesterday if they'd ever see me again. Did I have a good trip up from Paita? "Yes, thanks, fine. How did yours go?" "Not so good. The sea was getting a bit rough for our new skipper. We had to leave the boat in San Diego and come on by plane. But the expedition to the Galapagos was worth the effort and we've some fine specimens for the museum. Have you looked up H. R. yet?"

"I've tried. Several people tell me there's a lumber millionaire called MacMillan."

"That's him. Go to MacMillan and Bloedells, Hastings Street. Can't miss the building, or him if he's there."

Before I left, Dr. MacKenzie said, "I suppose you want to earn a few dollars before you disappear across the Pacific? Let's see if we can organise some work for you here."

A temporary job at the University was just what I wanted. Dr. MacKenzie directed me straight away to the buildings and grounds department.

The foreman suggested that I began by helping to clean out the swimming bath. My wage would be one dollar, forty (ten bob) an

8. Eyes glued to the compass on the *Puerto del Sol*, on voyage to California.

9. The ranch whose private airstrip needed weeding. Near San Diego in California.

10. Hitch-hiking on the Redwood Highway in California.

hour. This seemed a lot for a simple enough task, so I grabbed at the offer.

I turned up at the "swimming bath" promptly at eight the next morning. Before me was Canada's Empire Games Pool, fifty yards long, with a fourteen-foot deep end.

Two weeks later we finished chiselling off the weed and collecting the cents and dimes, amounting to three dollars, out of the slime at the deep end.

The swimming bath, clean and shining, impressed the foreman so much that he thought up a series of even more unpleasant jobs.

First I was a road-sweeper, brushing the gutters of mile-long avenues. Next I was a dustman.

One morning I had just returned an empty bin to its corner when the owner of the bungalow stepped out of the back door. "Good heavens, Alistair," he exclaimed. "What on earth are you doing here?" He was an old Oxford friend who had left college to study for a year at U.B.C. I explained hastily that dustbin-cleaning was not my chosen career. He introduced me to his fraternity brothers and later we all roamed round the town looking for entertainment. I deplored the way in which the men and women were carefully segregated in the brightly-lit drinking bars. Unsociable.

Monday, April 30th, was my fourth Monday in Vancouver and I felt I was getting well into the Canadian way of life. I had no immediate financial worries as I was earning £3. 15s. 0d. a day as odd-job man at U.B.C. Another new friend, Mrs. Sloan, was putting me up in her home nearby. Living with a Canadian family was enjoyable. On one particular morning my enjoyment was increased as I had been given a day off.

I would eat a leisurely breakfast; then perhaps have a gentle sniff round the docks. I had all day so there was no need to tear about. Opening the morning newspaper I scanned the "Movement of Shipping" column. There were two Orient-bound vessels listed—the s.s. *Indoran* and the s.s. *Oakhurst*. Both were loading up at the Grain Pool. I had no urgent intention of leaving Canada straight away, feeling too comfortable perhaps, but always somewhere at the back of my mind was the thought that I still had half the world to cover and more, so could not afford to miss any favourable winds that blew up. In a leisurely fashion I dressed and made for the docks, meaning to call on both ships. Quite likely, anyway, they would not be leaving for a week or two.

The captain of the *Indoran* seemed pleased to see me—that was a surprise.

"Let's see now. The mate has a full house on deck but we're short of a few men below. I expect the engineer can use you—go and see him."

That gave me an unpleasant sinking in the tummy as I made my way below. A man who has only worked on deck always feels somewhat daunted at the prospect of becoming a greaser or stoker down in the unknown bowels of the ship.

The chief engineer seemed pleased to see me too. My lucky day—or was it?

"Just the laddie we've been looking for," said he.

"Oh, really?"

"The fifth engineer has just left and we could do with someone to take the eight-to-twelve watch."

"You realise I want to hop off when we get to the other side of the Pacific, sir?" I explained, before showing too much enthusiasm.

"We'll drop you off somewhere in the East at the first opportunity." Sounded too good to be true. I was to be fifth engineer, with fifth engineer's pay. He took me down to the engine room. I began to have doubts as to whether I could cope with the mass of dials and knobs.

"An' she's a real beauty," the chief assured me. I grunted back, praying that her beauty would remain untarnished for the next five thousand miles.

"Have you got an engineer's ticket?" he asked.

"Me? Er . . . no. As a matter of fact ∴ . . well, you see until now I've only worked on deck."

"But you've had some engineering experience before?"

"Well, not exactly."

His face clouded with anger.

"Right up the gangway, boy," he bellowed. "You've no business to waste my time like this."

I raced up the gangway and just had time to wish the captain a brief "cheerio" before the engineer was telling him exactly what he thought of me.

Next I visited the s.s. *Oakhurst*, lying alongside the No. 2 Grain Pool. Perhaps I should have better luck here. The shipping agent whom I had telephoned earlier in the day warned me that she was a Greek tramp, desperately short-handed, and left me to draw my own conclusions. One glimpse of her told me that she must have frightened away most seamen. She was covered in rust from stem to stern.

"Yes, you can sign on as a deckhand by all means," said the captain, amazed and relieved to find somebody who actually wanted to sail on the *Oakhurst*.

"Yes, you can jump off where you like in the east, and we'll pay you a wage of twenty quid a month if that's any incentive."

A passage west and £20 into the bargain. Quite enough incentive for me. Before signing the articles I asked where the *Oakhurst* was sailing.

The captain didn't know. "The orders haven't come through yet. But we'll be bunkering oils in Japan sometime and if all your travel documents are in order you'll be able to hop off there. If not we shall be calling in for a day or so at Hong Kong and Singapore. The mate hasn't found a cook yet, so you can have the cook's cabin."

"Thanks." I decided rapidly. "I'll come along and trust to luck. When do we leave?"

"Midnight to-night."

"To-night?" I was aghast.

"Yes. And if you're not on board by eleven, I'll take it you won't be coming."

It was too good a chance to let slip. I assured the captain that I should be there.

Seven hours to go before leaving North America. What a hectic rush. Oh, hell! I'm supposed to appear on television this evening. Must fit it in somehow.

I tore into the Japanese Consulate to demand a visa from an official who was determined not to part with one.

"I must have confirmation that you have booked a passage out of Japan before I let you in with a visa," he reiterated. "And a letter from someone now residing in the country which guarantees your conduct there."

Naturally, I couldn't comply with either of these requests. Several influential people in Vancouver rang up the consul for me. He moderated his tone a little, but still refused to grant a visa. He was sure that if I asked the authorities in Japan they would be very pleased to grant an entry permit. His attempt to put me off with so feeble an assurance irritated me. In exasperation I paid a rushed visit to the Metropolitan building, where Mr. MacMillan soothed me by saying that he had an ambassador friend in Japan who might be able to help me. He told me to let the ambassador know beforehand by ship's telegraph whereabouts in Japan the *Oakhurst* was bunkering. This seemed far more promising than the consul's trivial assurances.

Then followed ninety minutes of frantic telephone calls cancelling arrangements, and at nine o'clock I was sitting in the C.B.C. Television studios being made up for my travel talk.

"Well, thank you for sparing the time to be with us," the interviewer said at the end of the programme. "When do you plan to leave Canada?"

"I'm off to-night. Midnight."

"Midnight to-night? Oh, well then, it's doubly good of you to come along."

It wasn't good of me, just that another fifteen dollars were most welcome. They brought my total up to a hundred-and-five dollars (about thirty-five pounds). I had done well in Canada.

Mrs. Sloan's chauffeur drove me to the Grain Pool and I was alongside the *Oakhurst* at 10.45 p.m., fifteen minutes before zero hour.

One of the mates greeted me at the top of the gangway.

"Glad you made it. I'll take you to your cabin."

I stumbled along the deck after him, tripping over wire hawsers, ends of rope, wooden hatch-boards and rusty bits of metal.

"You know where we're going, don't you?"

"No, the old man was expecting the sailing orders through some time this evening."

"They've just come through. We're off to Siberia."

"Si . . .?" I choked. "D-did you say Siberia?"

The mate looked at me ruefully and nodded.

From my porthole amidships I saw the friendly lights of Vancouver fade into the distance. Dead beat I climbed into my bunk. The engine-room door was right outside my cabin and I could hear the propeller shafts hammering out its revs—"siberia, siberia, siberia, siber . . . sib . . . si . . ."

7

RUST IN RUSSIA

"*Calimera*," shouted someone outside the door. Then came a bang on it to make sure I awoke. *Calimera?* Where on earth had I got to now? Voices were jabbering away in the corridor in unrecognisable languages. I was aboard a ship. Of course, I was off to Siberia. I looked at the time, 5.30. Should I get up? No, much too early. What about breakfast? I wonder what I'll be set to work at and where I'm going to eat. I suppose the whole crew is foreign. There were a lot of other questions, none of which would be answered while I lay in bed. I peered out of my porthole to see the wooden chalets of Vancouver Island slip by, and wished I was back at Mrs. Crawford's timber house, cosy and warm beneath an eiderdown. It was my birthday, too. Kind of left-handed present, this trip to Siberia. Must get up. Better pull on working clothes just to show I'm willing.

My next thought was for my stomach and I wandered along to the galley.

"*Calimera!*" (Ah, so *calimera* was good morning, was it?) A short weather-beaten Greek beamed as I poked my head through the galley door. "Welcome aboard," he added in English, slapping me heavily on the back. I was glad to find someone who knew a little English, though I could have done without his exaggerated cordiality. The cook was certainly picturesque. His purple corduroy trousers were in keeping with the mop of black hair, oily features and black wire-brush eyebrows. He had a large inanely-grinning mouth which reminded me of the Amazon *paiche* fish.

The breakfast bell sounded in the officers' mess forward. I decided to try my luck there. My sudden appearance in the saloon doorway startled the captain who was already seated at the head of the table. No one else was around, much to my relief. He looked up questioningly as though he had forgotten all about me.

"S-sorry to trouble you, captain," I stammered, "but where would you like me to eat?"

He pointed to the far end of the table, and I sat down. Then he said, "You couldn't live on the Greek food aft. Anyway, you wouldn't understand their talk."

A fried egg all alone on a large white plate was placed before me.

The captain said he would soon find me a job, but I must wait until the mate had sorted out the new rabble that he'd signed on in Vancouver. I was odd man out.

The British officers rolled in to breakfast one by one. First came "Sparks," the radio officer, followed by a bleary-eyed second mate, followed by the first officer; finally the third mate who sat opposite me without saying a single word during the whole meal.

The officers were surprised to see a newcomer at the table after so many months of their own company, but the conversation soon turned to the more usual subject—women. This topic predominated for the rest of the voyage. They all agreed that it was wonderful to be at sea again. As the mate pointed out, "It's the seaman's life cycle. Women, drink and hangovers one week, and work, sea breezes and routine the next." The drain on the pocket after a good night or two ashore increases the urge to escape to the open space of the sea.

Breakfast over I turned to the mate for my instructions.

"Join the other men up forward. Report to the bos'n and tell him I sent you."

The bos'n was a Greek. He ordered me to fall in with the deck-hands in stowing away the six-inch-thick mooring-ropes and the wire hawsers. This was part of battening down, preparing for the bad weather ahead. Tough work coiling up the heavy ropes but the others tackled the job easily enough.

"Right," he yelled, after I had finished with that job. "Now go and put the hatch-cover across the number five."

"Number five" referred to the hold nearest the poop. I ran aft, tripping over a loose wire hawser in my effort to create a good impression. I pulled back the heavy rain-sodden canvas that had been used as a temporary hatch-cover and peered down into the hold, fascinated by the sea of grain below. Must be thousands of tons of grain down there, I reflected. "Ten thousand tons," the mate remarked suddenly from behind as though he had read my thoughts. He never let me out of his sight for a moment. I managed to fit all but two of the hatch-boards into their proper place. The last couple refused to be forced into the space left for them.

"Go on, marry them!" the mate yelled in my ear when he saw me in difficulty.

"Marry?" I wondered, but he stormed off and left me to figure it out for myself.

In the afternoon I was told to clear the decks.

"Throw everything overboard that looks like rubbish," the bos'n said. I regretfully hurled large planks of wood into the Pacific, remnants of the shifting boards which could no longer be used to stop the grain from moving in the hold when the ship starts to roll. There was enough to build a dozen garden sheds, but it was too dangerous to have floating around a deck in high seas.

By four o'clock I had begun glancing at my watch, wondering when five o'clock was coming round. At ten minutes to the hour I was told to go and clean myself up. Dinner started at five-thirty, and was over by five-forty. Afterwards the officers sat round the table and talked. This immobility wasn't due to over-eating, there was just nothing else to do on the *Oakhurst*.

Discussing the cargo with the second mate I asked, "Why are we taking grain to Russia, of all places? I thought that Siberia was the grain basket of the Soviet Union."

"So it is, but the Canadians and Russians signed an agreement for three million bushels of grain earlier in the year. It's a special kind."

Perhaps a frost-resisting strain for replanting in Russia's northern wastelands, I thought. Whatever its final use in Siberia it seemed an excellent way for Canada to dispose of some of her embarrassing grain surplus.

The *Oakhurst* was 10,782 tons deadweight. The Canadians built her as a "liberty ship" in 1942 to carry grain to Europe during the war. Hurriedly knocked together, if she made only her maiden voyage without being sunk, she had paid for the cost of her construction in those desperate days.

And here she was with fourteen colourful years behind her, and still going strong, we hoped.

She boasted her original coat of paint. Until recently she had been manned by a Philippino crew who had obviously never heard of a paint-brush or chipping-hammer.

The pneumatic chipping-hammer and the electric-scaler became my close companions. After eight hours of rust removing my hands were shaking with the reverberation and my ears singing in tune with the high-pitched scream of the scaler. No wonder seven of the previous crew had left the ship at Vancouver. The more pressure I applied the more rust came away and there seemed to be no end to it. One day I was so enthusiastic that I drilled right through the deck plate.

The chief engineer plugged the hole with a bolt that he found lying on deck. "Holes are always appearing on this tub," he said. He left me to imagine the sea pouring into the hold, and the grain swelling and forcing apart the plates. It's happened to other ships. If the hull plates are anything like those on deck, this might well be the *Oakhurst's* last voyage. The history of a ship has to end sometime.

Being a new boy, I tackled the enemy with enthusiasm. My enthusiasm was resented by the Greek crew and I soon learnt to keep to their working tempo or pay the consequences later. And the consequences were unpleasant, shutting you up in the holds or accidentally pushing you overboard in a storm. One of the stewards who was always making himself objectionable narrowly escaped being lost at sea.

The crew thought up every possible excuse to slack off during the day, but on the other hand were very keen to work overtime. The carpenter's advice was, "Work sparingly on duty and generously on overtime." Fortunes were easily accumulated. At the end of six months, everyone had done over three hundred hours' overtime and showed no signs of exhaustion.

The other deckhands regarded me as an untrained apprentice working on deck, not as a globetrotter working my passage. But being English and living with the officers, I was looked upon as a sort of go-between. Any complaints they allowed me to overhear they expected me to pass on tactfully. I was relied upon by the officers and crew alike when difficulties and quarrels arose between them, and these were quite frequent.

News about the Middle East one day threatened to disrupt the *Oakhurst*. The Prime Minister was heard to proclaim over the Radio, "Cyprus has never belonged to the Greeks and it is nonsense to continue talking about it as if it had." The Greek second engineer, who harboured a grudge against the British, saw that this tasty bit of news was conveyed aft to the Greek quarters. Carving-knives disappeared from the galley one by one. I rushed aft to the crew's quarters. The Greeks seemed to be divided into two parties armed with carving-knives. They were startled to see me.

The bosun stepped forward. "We come different islands. We

Greece," he indicated the little band around him. "They Turkey," and he spat in the direction of the other group. They were all Greeks really, but one group belonged to an island with Turkish sympathies. If I had known it was only a private feud, I mightn't have interfered. However, now that I was here they would expect me to settle the dispute. Most seafaring Greeks would probably love the sound of their own voices. So I gradually worked them round to a sing-song, and within a few minutes they were bawling out, "She'll be coming round the mountain . . ." To my surprise the two islands were on the best of terms by the time they went to bed. Later all the carving-knives reappeared in their drawers in the galley as mysteriously as they had gone. How long they would stay there depended on our Prime Minister.

The captain chose the northerly route to Siberia, open only in the summer months of the year. This took us into the cold grey expanse of the Bering Sea where the Pacific meets the Arctic. The Aleutian Islands were now to the south-west of us, and we had no protection from the northerly gales. The fore and aft masts became clothed in white, but their moment of beauty was short-lived. The vibration of the pneumatic hammer kept the blood circulating in my fingers, but my toes grew numb early in the morning and stayed that way until evening. They thawed out painfully through dinner.

When it grew too dangerous to chip rust from a bos'n's chair swinging in the wind fifty feet up the main mast, and too cold to work on deck, we started on interior decorating. The crew's accommodation was grimy, but so were its occupants who turned in happily without washing or changing their clothes. A paint-brush covered up most of the dirt.

Once past the Kamchatka peninsula of Eastern Siberia, the *Oakhurst* steamed into quieter waters and warmer weather, although there were still a number of iceberg stragglers floating around. I remembered the Sea of Okhotsk on the class-room map at school and it seemed strange to be sailing its waters now. It was just like any other sea, which was a little disappointing.

Everyone assumed we were bound for Vladivostock. On May the 15th, during the mid-morning coffee break, Sparks received a radio message.

"Hi, chaps," he called out from the bridge, "we're not going to Vladivostock after all."

"Rubbish!" retorted the third mate, who was lying on the hatch-boards like the rest of us. "Where else could we be going?"

"Little place called Nakhodka. The second mate says it's about a hundred miles from Vladivostock, but he can't find its position on the chart." The third and I raced up to the bridge and joined the second, who was now poring over the pilot instructions for East Pacific coast ports. "Nakhodka is a small fishing village of under 2,000 people, Lat. 40° 40', Long. 132° 50'," he read out. We looked at the chart but the place was too small to be marked.

The third mate suggested we made for the readings and see where we landed up, and the captain agreed we hadn't any alternative.

For the next few days we heard no more about our destination. If Sparks did receive any more messages, like all good radio officers he would not divulge them without the captain's permission. But the day before we were scheduled to arrive in Nakhodka, the captain received fresh instructions for our destination after Siberia. He called me to his cabin, as they affected me.

"When I signed you on in Vancouver, the Company wanted us back in England by August," he said. "They've changed their minds. We're not going on to Hong Kong and Singapore after all. It's back to North America for another load of grain."

"Back to North America? Oh no!"

"Hold on. We have to bunker oil in Aomori on our way back. That's in North Japan, so you can hop off there. Trouble is if you haven't got a visa, the authorities won't be too keen on letting you land. Do my best for you the moment we get there, but no promises."

"Oh well, thanks for telling me anyway." I tried to hold back my exasperation. I mustn't give way to it and worry unduly. I'd be able to jump off in Japan, visa or no visa. I must telegraph Mr. MacMillan's ambassador friend in Tokyo.

The captain told me to do it quickly. "Once we arrive at Nakhodka the radio room will be locked," he explained. "Russian regulations."

I drafted a message: "Bunkering at Aomori in transit. Must land," and hoped that something would come of it. I tried to take comfort in the assurances, thin though they were, of the Japanese consul in Vancouver.

The feeling of elated expectancy on nearing a strange port dispelled my worries for a while. In a few hours we should be in Nakhodka, Siberia! The name gave me a shiver of excitement.

The mate was having difficulty in plotting our position by the stars. We had run into dense fog. There were no radio direction finders on the Siberian coastline to aid navigation, so no one knew which headland was hiding elusive little Nakhodka. Our progress was spasmodic. We would slacken speed when the officers disagreed over our position and then go full steam ahead when they all thought we were moving in roughly the right direction.

The fog suddenly lifted. Everyone, including the navigation officers, was amazed to see the lights of Nakhodka twinkling about three miles dead ahead. They made a far more spectacular display than we expected from a mere fishing village, and for a minute I wondered if we had made Vladivostock after all. Astern I could just see the dim silhouette of a gunboat without any navigation lights. It appeared to be trailing us. Russia was running true to form in providing an escort to keep us out of mischief. I felt slightly annoyed.

A pilot boat came towards us. "Stop the engines," the captain ordered. "Stand by with Jacob." Jacob was the rope ladder.

Everyone leant over the port rail to catch his first glimpse of the Russian officials. They scrambled aboard, impeccably dressed in their grey overcoats. The Russian pilot greeted the officers on the bridge with a brief nod. Someone asked him if this really was Nakhodka, and was given a dirty look for his impertinence.

Instead of easing the *Oakhurst* alongside nicely, the pilot brought her to a full stop several yards from the quay and at right angles to it. Fifteen dockers on the quay waited to catch our two heaving-lines but in the scuffle to grab they all missed. The captain suggested to the pilot that it might be easier if he brought the *Oakhurst* nearer the quay. When she was at last happily secured, the mate asked why he took the ship into the quay bow first. The pilot replied, in quite good English, "We do it this way in mid-winter to break the ice that collects in the harbour, otherwise we could not bring the ship right alongside." This sounded a reasonable explanation, except that it happened to be mid-summer and there was no ice to be seen anywhere.

Waking up on my first morning in Russia didn't seem very different from the same process anywhere else in the world. I peered out of my porthole. The *Oakhurst*'s book of pilot instructions was obviously out of date. Nakhodka was no fishing village, it was a large flourishing port. Later we learned that the population was at least 25,000. That was our first surprise. The second was Alvira. Alvira was one of the interpreters who had come the 5,000 miles over the Trans-Siberian Railway from Leningrad University to act as hostess while the *Oakhurst* was in port. She spoke English very well with a remarkably good accent, but when the conversation drifted onto political topics, her understanding of English was not so good. Alvira was a Party Member (under 25% of the population are members of the Communist Party). Although well educated by European standards, with a University degree, she had no idea of what was happening outside the world of Russia. When tackled about the Iron Curtain, she retorted, "It is not *our* iron curtain, but an area patrolled by British and American forces to prevent the exchange of people and ideas between the Communist world and the West. Look at the large number of refugees pouring over the border from West to East Germany! The progressive peoples of the world," she continued hastily, before the fiery third mate had time to explode, "realise that a communist world is inevitable. We envisage a world without money and. . . ." At this point the third mate stormed out of the room in disgust saying that she ought to get bloody well educated before she started to spout propaganda. But to Alvira this was education, and she continued to propound her faith staunchly in spite of more noisy and rude interruptions. "Peaceful co-existence is only a shield; the Bible a stupid fairy tale."

"What about Stalin?" I put in.

"That was all a big mistake."

But as the Party still hadn't finally decided what line to pursue after denouncing Stalinism, Alvira was understandably reluctant to enlarge on the subject.

That evening a notice appeared on the ship's board cordially inviting everyone to spend the evening at the "Hall of Culture."

"If you're all that damn progressive," the third mate jeered, "you'd lay on a free coach to take us there." They did.

The officers dressed in their most British-looking clothes, blazer, flannels and striped tie; to allay any suspicions, I became the supernumerary fourth officer.

We found the security precautions less strict than expected. Once past the guard at the foot of the gang-plank there was one other barrier to pass through. No one halted us after that.

Everywhere were signs of the recent expansion that promises Nakhodka a leading place among the townships springing up in Siberia. Alvira hinted that it might become a larger mercantile port than Vladivostock. I didn't see any shops in the town but perhaps they were included in the next five-year plan. Nearly all the buildings were symmetrical apartment houses five floors high with twelve flats to each block. They were all a sickly ice-cream pink. Perhaps the party colour had faded.

The Hall of Culture stood on a prominent knoll to the south of the town. It was a clumsy excursion into architecture, a monstrosity, cold, bleak, forbidding. Inside, the mural decorations consisted of a few extensive canvasses of the "Glorious Campaigns of 1812 and 1945" and several musty portraits of past and present political figures. On one wall there was a clean patch. De-Stalinism had reached Siberia. Upstairs were the library and reading room. The magazines on show were printed in English. They gave information about the great advance of Soviet Industry, comparing it with industry in Europe and the United States. In every graph, diagram or list of figures, Russian production far outstripped that of all the other countries put together.

"Let us go dancing," Alvira proposed when someone remarked on the music coming from below. It was her best suggestion yet. The Saturday night "Social" was well under way. A hundred couples collided with each other whilst a brass band thumped out Viennese waltzes from the minstrels' gallery.

"Strike me pink," exclaimed the third mate, "did you ever see such a crowd of gawks?" Siberian girls appeared to scorn make-up. Perhaps it is an evil of the capitalist world. There were no stockings and the clothes were deplorable, but that probably wasn't the girls' fault. The State issues mass-produced, printed-cotton skirts which are drab and shapeless. "Look as if they've just come from a January Sale in the 1920's," the mate observed.

The waltz was followed by a quickstep, but as the band played all tunes with heavy military precision, the change was hardly perceptible. The dancers took their cue from the band and swept across the floor with vast strides. They seemed to be enjoying themselves.

"Come on," insisted the second mate, "it's time we broke this up and showed them how to dance," and charging in we grabbed partners for the evening. In spite of the drab background these Russians seemed to retain their great sense of humour. They were gay and friendly, much to the annoyance of Alvira whose duty it was to break up any attempts at liaison between East and West.

"Eden—Bulganin," a Russian sailor toasted as we swallowed vodka in the Hall bar. The recent visit of Russian leaders to

Britain had been favourably reported in the press, and it helped to establish a temporary entente-cordiale between us. After the vodka they gave us beer, which we all agreed came closer to our own than any we had tasted elsewhere.

Our money didn't go far in Russia. A bottle of vodka cost thirty-three roubles (about three pounds) so it was difficult to return the hospitality of those who forced drinks upon us. The second offered some cigarettes instead, which were eagerly accepted by the Russian sailors. But when they saw "made in U.S.A." they refused to smoke them, because as Alvira explained, it would stimulate production inside a capitalist country. For some obscure reason, they saw no objection to smoking British cigarettes. Evidently we were not so capitalistic now that B. & K. had visited Britain.

We were offered Russian cigarettes. Their manufacture seemed to be governed by economy. Only one half of the cigarette was filled with tobacco, the rest was hollow cardboard which you could mould to fit your mouth. When the second brought out his lighter, the Russians were very intrigued, never having seen one before.

The chief mate sat at a separate table in the bar engrossed in a conversation of which, he later admitted, he didn't understand a single word. He was smoking his old briar pipe. Every time he drew a puff, a round of laughter and applause went up from his Russian companions. They hadn't seen anything like that before either. "Please may I try?" one of them asked. The mate's hackles rose at once, but not wishing to cause any ill feeling, he handed the pipe over. Instead of returning it, the Russian passed it around the table for everyone else to smell and take a draw. When it finally got back to him the mate was furious—any pipe owner would have been—and when one of them asked to have it for a memento, he had a struggle not to explode.

"Can't," he said very gruffly, and raising his voice to make sure the rest of us could hear, "it's been in the family for years and I'm not parting with it for anyone, not even for a ruddy Russian."

The Russian wouldn't take "no" for an answer and offered him his own cigarette case in exchange. Fortunately, this made the mate quite inarticulate and the second rushed over in an attempt to save the situation. He explained, with Alvira interpreting, what a treasure the old pipe was, and that it was a family heirloom which was handed on from one generation to the next. But the Russian was obviously still puzzled that a straight swap could not be made.

No effort was spared to convince the crew of the *Oakhurst* that Russia was the finest country in the world. One evening the Hall of Culture showed us a film on farming—collectivisation versus private ownership. This was not only for our benefit. The populace of Nakhodka were becoming sceptical over the farming returns in Siberia. Collectivisation hadn't been quite so successful as the Party made out. The theme of the highly coloured film was the might of the state, with its superior equipment of combine harvesters and tractors in contrast to the poor and useless tools of the private farmer. Alvira was bursting with pride. "You see what tremendous strides Russia has made with her new farming methods," she exclaimed, "that's what Communism does for us."

"Yes, amazing," I said. "I wonder where that picture was made. The parts about Britain are quite untrue, or else I didn't realise that we still use wooden ploughs." Alvira merely changed the subject.

From the *Oakhurst* we could see quite a lot of Russian life. More striking than anything else was the "equality of men and women" which was obviously taken literally. Great beefy women could be seen working as stevedores, sweeping up the grain between the railway lines on the quay, and operating the enormous cranes handling our grain. These cranes, ten in all, spanning four tracks of rails, had only recently been installed in Nakhodka. Beneath them, ancient puffing-billies shunted the grain trucks in a disorganised way. It was not what I had expected to find in the "Efficient Russia" that we had all read about at the Hall of Culture.

Automobiles were a rare sight in Nakhodka. If anything you had a Zis or a Zim. There were no roads to speak of. Alvira told us that they were next on the construction list, but if my nose isn't mistaken, the sewerage needs attention first.

On our last evening ashore we decided to walk back to the ship in feminine company, rather than take the bus as Alvira wanted. Some of the sailors had struck up quite a friendship with the girls. When sailing day came, a week after our arrival, we were all sorry.

Two hours before we were due to leave, the Russians toothcombed the ship for stowaways. After finishing their rounds they dropped a few remarks about the disgraceful condition of the crew's quarters. Certainly in her present state the *Oakhurst* was a poor advertisement for the British merchant fleet and fine propaganda material for the Russians.

The chief impression left by this brief encounter with the Siberians was that the ordinary non-party people of Nakhodka wanted to give us a genuine welcome without any attempt at indoctrination. Not so Alvira and her fellow party members who siezed every opportunity to impress us with the great benefits brought by Communism. Admittedly "Russia's Far East" is developing rapidly. Every step is hailed as benevolent largesse from the omnipotent hand of Communism. But we wondered how much more the people might have progressed had they been allowed to develop on the pattern of the free world? Their thoughts and actions are still dictated. Beria's police state may have disappeared but the limited outlook continues. Even the party members appeared ignorant of what Communism really meant or where it was leading them, or how it was trying to obtain its objectives.

Just as Alvira was saying goodbye to us she caught sight of an American magazine with its brilliantly-coloured cover. She gasped. "Do you think I could have that?" she said in a meek little voice, quite unlike the Alvira we had become accustomed to.

"Why, of course." The mate handed it to her.

"I've never seen such gay pictures before," she admitted. That summed up the drabness of Soviet life.

We steamed slowly out of Nakhodka Bay and soon Russia's coast-line was a blur on the horizon.

Life had been so hectic in Nakhodka I hadn't pondered over my next move. Now that we were at sea again, I suddenly realised that the forthcoming tussle with the immigration authorities was but two days away. I packed my bags in readiness and felt childishly excited at the thought of entering a country where the people and customs are so very different from anything I had yet seen.

The captain came along to my cabin and handed me a bundle of pound notes. "Here's twenty quid, your overtime and wages."

I thanked him and asked what time we bunkered in Aomori.

"About six o'clock in the morning. We'll anchor off shore as there's no water alongside. Have to take a few stores as well, so we should be there most of the day. I hope the immigration chaps are a nice bunch. Humour them first before you do the asking."

A frantic shuddering awoke the entire crew at five-thirty. I dressed hurriedly and clambered on deck to see what had happened.

"It's all right," the mate yelled on seeing me appear at the foot of the bridge. "Just putting her into reverse to avoid ramming that

11. A haircut on the *Oakhurst* in the Pacific by Chippy, the ship's carpenter.

12. "Pusan's streets were thronged with people bustling in all directions." South Korea.

13. The inn-keeper's daughters wore Western clothes during the day. In Kyoto, Japan.

14. The Kinkajuji temple in Kyoto, painted entirely in gold.

thing." A large passenger ferry, with funnels placed like a four-poster bed, had cut straight across our bows and was disappearing into the mist. At the same time a vintage four-poster, belching clouds of dense black smoke, steamed at full speed across our stern. The accident rate is high on the ferries that ply between Hokkaido and the main island.

The captain dropped anchor in the roads. Within a minute of the hook finding rock-bed, the Japanese bunkering-barge was alongside. From another barge twenty pairs of hands shovelled coal for the galley. Speed and efficiency seemed to be the watchwords. At this rate the *Oakhurst* would be ready and away in a few hours. At last the agent and the immigration authorities manœuvred alongside in a smart pinnace. The agent presented me with a letter from His Excellency, Mr. MacMillan's ambassador friend in Tokyo. So my telegram had reached him. I should be all right now. I tore open the envelope. There were many difficulties over landing, said the ambassador, and I must telephone him at the first opportunity. For that I should have to wait until we went ashore.

As I had finished reading it through a second time, the immigration officer asked to see me in the saloon. I followed him in and was waved to a seat in front of three Lilliputians.

"You wish to sign off the ship here?" one of them asked in a clipped, high-pitched voice.

"Yes, that's right." I produced a host of documents to convince him that I was a most desirable person to have visiting his country. Some of the papers were quite irrelevant but looked impressive. He seemed much taken with the array.

"How long do you wish to spend in Japan, Mr. Boyd?"

"About two weeks."

"And if I let you into the country, how do you propose to get out?"

"If I can't work my passage out, I've enough money to buy a passage from Yokohama to Hong Kong. The captain has just paid me off."

"I understand that the objection to your landing is that you have no visa in your passport. Why didn't you ask for one in Vancouver before boarding the *Oakhurst*?"

"I did my best in the short time I had," and I gave a brief résumé of the assurances I had had from their representative in Vancouver. A long pause followed while my questioner leant across the table to confer with his fellow officers. At last they appeared to have agreed upon some action.

"Mr. Boyd. We must present your case to higher authority. We wish to talk with your friend in Tokyo. Please give me his telephone number." I handed over the ambassador's letter. "After lunch we shall return with the decision."

The white pinnace shot away from the *Oakhurst* and with it went my passport, papers, medical certificates and my prayers.

I didn't feel like eating. I spent the lunch hour brooding over my prospects of landing. The second officer joined me on the bridge.

"You were quite a time with those fellows. How did it all go?"

"Seemed to pass off all right, but you can never tell which way the wind is blowing with these chaps."

"Yes, that's true enough," he agreed. "In a few minutes you may be ashore, speeding south to Tokyo, but you might equally be chipping more rust off the *Oakhurst* for weeks to come. If the balance tips the wrong way, you're in for a rough time, ten thousand miles of ocean, eight more weeks wasted on the Pacific. That's a damn high price to pay for failing to produce one tiny little stamp."

This issue was the most vital of my voyage so far. I had done everything in my power to effect this Japanese landing.

Having got this far I couldn't contemplate turning back.

The second and I gazed in silence towards the shore. At last we saw the white pinnace leave the quay. As it drew near I wondered if my fate had been sealed the day I left Vancouver, or had the authorities in Tokyo reasoned the thing out? The whole crew were awaiting the answer as if they too were concerned about my future. The launch was almost alongside.

8

H-BOMB IN THE LAUNDRY

Back across the Pacific. Back by five thousand miles to where I was in April. This is the end. The endless circles of red tape have strangled my adventure: I shall have to slink home, the royal challenge lost.

Before the shipping agent opened his mouth I had guessed that I was to serve a longer period on the *Oakhurst*. He looked as unhappy as the rest of us while he read out the decision of the immigration officers.

"We regret we cannot grant you permission to land without a passport properly visaed by a consular authority outside Japan."

"We regret!" I boiled. But it was pointless to turn on the unfortunate messenger.

The captain was taken aback by the news. "Rotten luck," he commiserated. "But don't lose heart and give up. You'll get another chance, I'm sure of it."

But nothing he could say would convince me that I had any chance now of meeting the royal challenge. In Brazil the officials had ordered me back home, in Bolivia they had refused me a visa. The law had nearly caught up with me in Peru. But all along I had just managed to steer clear of serious trouble and press on. Now I was checkmated at the half-way mark, and everything that I had accomplished seemed worthless in the face of this defeat.

My frustration choked me. It was all wrong, preposterous. Why couldn't there be freedom from bureaucracy for all mankind? Was I to return home a disillusioned young man?

The press at Aomori got to hear of my arrival and departure. Hungry for a story, the Yumiari and Mainichi journalists swarmed aboard before the captain had time to pull up the hook. After a hasty interview they hurried back to write up Mr. Boyd's impressions of the Japanese. Just now they weren't very favourable.

The *Oakhurst* was away at dusk. Billows of black smoke belched

131

from two more ugly four-funnel ferry boats and drifted up lazily, forming clouds etched vividly against the falling sun. This was a perfect Japanese evening. But somehow I couldn't appreciate it.

I gazed seawards, well into the night. I had plenty of time to waste now. There were many similar evenings ahead. Steaming through the straits of Tsugaru, the narrow stretch of water that separates Hokkaido from Honshu, the *Oakhurst* threaded her way past a myriad of lights shining from the mast-heads of swarms of little fishing boats. They seemed unimpressed by the passing of a 450-foot freighter, but scraping sounds from our hull meant that some of the craft without lights were running serious risks.

Still gazing seawards I prayed for a miracle. Perhaps I was dreaming and I should wake up in Japan after all. But it was no use, I had to face reality.

The *Oakhurst* rolled unmercifully as she began her five-thousand-mile trek back across the Pacific. She was high in the water now that her ten thousand tons of grain was discharged, and travelling in ballast is always uncomfortable.

The captain went down with an acute attack of 'flu the morning after Aomori and stayed in his room all day. I tackled the fried egg alone that morning without enthusiasm. Sparks joined me in the saloon before I had finished eating. He looked exhausted as he always did even from a ten-hour sleep, and spent the rest of the meal commiserating over my bad luck. Sparks was a Scottish lad from Kirkcudbrightshire. He told us all that he was only seventeen, though he looked nearer twenty-one. His most prominent feature was a shock of untamed black hair which jutted out from his forehead by several inches. His cheeks, normally pink, would change to deep maroon after the frequent sharp reproofs on his table manners. It was pointless to argue about anything with Sparks as he would fly into a rage, airing his large and vivid vocabulary. Yet, of all the officers, Sparks was the most liked by the crew, perhaps because he was the only person whose duties did not necessitate talking to them. According to the other officers, he had been gently introduced to the bottle, but in spite of a careful apprenticeship, he was still unable to sink a glass of neat whisky.

The second mate tramped in after his night watch. During his twenty-seven years he had miraculously remained single, though he confided in most of us that he had often been on the verge of holding an international marriage certificate. He entertained us at meal-times with many vivid accounts of his past romances.

After breakfast the second handed me a pair of goggles and a nose-mask. "You're going down below this morning," he told me.

Down, down, down the rope ladder I climbed to the bottom of the immense cargo-hold. This was another world, a world of steel plates, girders and cross beams, the ancient vessel's bones. Far above was a tiny patch of blue where the hatch-covers had been drawn back for some light. It was eerie down here. The thump of someone walking on the deck plates or the clang of a dropped shackle magnified into a deafening echo. When the chipping-hammers started I was gripped with panic. I must get out, I must get out . . . . And to think that I might have been sight-seeing in Tokyo this morning. I pulled myself together. I was on the *Oakhurst*, and, as the mate was continually reminding me, here to work.

One by one the rest of the deckhands joined me below. Around us lay the residue of the grain cargo, fine grey powder, inches deep, every bit of which had to be cleared out before the next load could be admittted.

"Right, lads," roared the bos'n. "Up the ceiling-boards and start dusting down from the top!" With four Greeks I scaled the boards that stretched horizontally up the sides of the hold. We clung on while the *Oakhurst* rolled, and began to brush off the loose grain sticking to the dank plates of the hull. The fine dust choked me and parched my throat, but there was no relief. Sheets of rust were dislodged as well and landed on the bilges where they would probably remain until the *Oakhurst* fell to pieces.

Ceiling-boards are not the best place to start an argument. They are precariously wedged and liable to jump out of their slots at the slightest provocation. But that was of no concern to the crew. A particularly loud-mouthed Greek called Agentacis was always ready to start quarrels with anyone, backed by his superior physique. He weighed sixteen stone. One day a load of rust accidentally dropped on his head. He instantly assumed this to be deliberate. Bent on revenge he lashed out at the Greek above him, missed his foothold and crashed into the bilge-boards fourteen feet below. Fortunately, his sixteen stone landed in a pile of grain that the carpenter had taken an hour or so to get together. This was now scattered all over the place again, but Agentacis's bones were saved. Everyone laughed, but when he rose rubbing his backside and yelling vengeance, doubtless some wished that a few of his aggressive limbs *had* been broken.

The deckhands worked below for a week, clearing out deep tanks, sweeping 'tween decks, stacking shifting-boards. The grain-dust penetrated every piece of clothing and wormed its way behind goggles and nose protector. At the end of each day we emerged from the holds grey, haggard, ghostly. The fresh air smelt good.

Food on the *Oakhurst* was plentiful but unappetising. It had been a subject of controversy for a long time. The catering staff, a chief steward and two cooks, were all Greeks whose ideas on preparing food for the English were strictly limited. The chief steward had suddenly discovered fish and chips in Newcastle and these had filled the imagination of the two cooks as well. Exhausted-looking fish buried in cold chips became the basis of the *Oakhurst* menu. "But that is your English diet," replied the chief steward when I asked him whether we could have a change.

But if our meals were monotonous, the Greek diet looked even more so. Day after day we saw the crew hurrying aft with mountains of macaroni on their plates, fingers plunged well into the melange long before they reached the mess. Some never tried to reach it, mopping up their portion while still on deck so as to be on the spot for the second, third and fourth helpings.

The fatal day came. The purple-trousered second cook, who had forced his amiability on me at the beginning of the voyage, was unable to stand up to his own cooking any longer. The captain packed him off to his bunk. Chef Boyd was ordered to the galley.

"Sorry to have to ask you to do this," apologised the captain, "but I daren't trust any of the other crew in the galley. Might be getting fried toe-nails next."

The food couldn't have been much worse than before and there was a chance I might produce something a little better.

"Omelettes for breakfast," I cried, waving a giant-sized frying pan before the astonished eyes of the chief steward. He was most unco-operative, still resenting my intrusion which upset his lazy routine. The memory of those omelettes lived for a long time. They were hot, and with three eggs each they covered the white plates entirely. After the meal, a smug-faced chief steward came up to me and hissed, "You use a hundred and fifty eggs this morning. No more left in the freezer." I told him it was his own fault as he was supposed to control supplies. After what he had said, I was rather surprised to find a nest of eggs in the storeroom, but I said nothing. Just enough eggs, I thought, to make some pancakes, but my scanty knowledge of culinary matters did not stretch to the recipe for these.

I borrowed a *Pears Cyclopaedia* from the Chief Engineer and thumbing through the pages found "Recipes for miscellaneous dishes". The pancake *á la Pears* turned out better than I or the officers had thought possible, though the chief steward couldn't distinguish between it and an omelette, and he promptly announced it on the menu as 'grand omelet'.

I had one failure as cook—an attempt at rock buns. They were doomed from the start when I mixed the flour with hot water. An hour later than intended I hauled little lumps of charcoal from a seven-hundred-degrees oven. They vanished over the gunwale.

Then came bad weather. It had to come sometime and we were lucky to have escaped it so far. The galley was on deck, open at both ends, so if we forgot to close the iron doors, the Pacific would roar through carrying everything away with it. Utensils hanging on the bulkheads swung in unison with the *Oakhurst*'s roll; a dozen times I chased the pot of macaroni as it gathered momentum across the stove and just stopped it dropping off the edge. The crew, soaked to the skin with sea-spray, poured in, demanding grub. There was no time to use the ladle; one hand gripped the pot and the other scooped out macaroni and dropped it into their plates. A giant wave swept through the galley removing the broom, mop and wooden ladle.

In spite of her age the *Oakhurst* reached a speed that surprised even the engineer. When the full force of the Kuro Siwo current was behind her she averaged about two hundred and seventy-eight miles a day, a speed of 11.6 knots. But the return voyage to North America dragged depressingly. For me, that was only to be expected. Every mile seemed a further step in the wrong direction.

After dinner in the evenings there was a game of bridge, or cricket on deck with home-made balls which always disappeared over the side. Sometimes we just talked until the second mate decided to turn in for a few hours' sleep before his midnight watch. Peace descended after that except for faint strains of Greek chants from the crew's quarters aft when the wind happened to be blowing from astern. At six o'clock the clattering of crockery informed us that the stewards were awake and breaking cups and saucers in their effort to produce a drinkable early morning cup of tea.

There must have been even more boredom in the crew's quarters. They read nothing, wrote precious little, but talked their heads off as though they were all deaf. They thought themselves very overworked and always expected applause for the slightest effort.

For security reasons which weren't quite clear to us, our exact destination in North America had not been disclosed by the agent in Japan. When Sparks received the fresh orders they circulated rapidly round the ship. The third mate broke the news to me when I was at the wheel.

"We're bound for the States—Portland, Oregon—to collect more grain. Don't suppose it matters much to, you where we go. Got any plans?" "None. I suppose I could hop off and hitch-hike back across the States."

Our reception at this back door of the United States was most unusual for the kind of ship we were. The *Oakhurst* seemed to have become a sort of V.I.P. in reverse. Military aircraft met the ship a hundred miles off shore and escorted her all the way to the Columbia River estuary. Then motor torpedo boats, manned by armed coastguards, kept tearing around us at dizzy speeds, kicking up a racket from their racing engines from which, apparently, the, silencers had been removed. We dropped anchor off Astoria and prepared to face the music.

"Ship arrives in Columbia Estuary from Russia", Oregon newspapers blazoned us in headlines. We were the first since the shipment of arms between war-time allies had ended. Taking no chances, Washington had us black-listed and under observation until we were proved innocent.

Early next day units of the U.S. Airforce arrived on foot, armed with geiger counters. They began a most thorough search for possible plutonium or uranium bombs that might have been hidden aboard by anti-capitalists while the ship was in a Russian port. Some of the searchers looked all ready to jump overboard the moment they heard the tell-tale tick. They realised, of course, that the *Oakhurst* was anchored out here so that if she did blow up not much harm would be done—except to them. And to the crew—us. For two hours they patiently poked their machines into every nook and cranny. The only explosion was one from the second mate when he witnessed a geiger counter being plunged into the straw protecting a precious tea-set he was bringing home from Japan.

There might have been another, we heard afterwards, from the chief engineer. He was asleep when they came to search his cabin. The first he knew was a shadow sweeping across his face. "Woke up in a hell of a fright," he said, "with this bloody machine inches from my nose. But I made that bloke shift quick when I pointed to the air compressor from the frig. and told him it was a special radium plant. He rushed his geiger over and swept all round it, looking like a clock just going to strike until he tumbled to what it really was."

Well, O.K. was the verdict. We were clean; we could move on. Ninety miles up river we drew into the Portland grain pool. And here awaiting us were the coastguards with *their* geiger counters. Even the ship's laundry didn't escape a go-through from the inquisitive machines. So far the immigration officers wouldn't let any of our crew ashore. A wily hint that we might have information about recent installations at Nakhodoka for the State Department soon changed their minds.

The captain had some startling news to deliver at breakfast next morning. The *Oakhurst* was re-crossing the Pacific. He turned to me.

"We're calling in for some bunkers at Moji, Japan, on our way to Korea. Want to try your luck again? I've found out that there's a Jap consulate here, so I hope you can lay your hands on a visa this time."

So the *Oakhurst* was returning to the Orient. The captain had been right, I mustn't give up, there would be another chance. This was it.

"Can I take the morning off to get everything fixed up?" I asked. He gave me a day.

I went ashore wondering who on earth could help me to get that visa.

Of course! The third member of the fishing trio I had met in Peru, Mr. Bates, was a Portlander. So I hunted out the address, and made straight for his down-town office.

He was astonished to see me, having just heard from MacMillan that I was about to land in Japan.

I told him the story.

"That's bad. What's next on the agenda? Suppose you've got ideas about recrossing the Pacific."

"Yes. I can't give up yet. Matter of fact, I've come to ask you a favour."

"Well, so long as it isn't illegal or immoral."

"The *Oakhurst* sails for the East again in a couple of days. I still want to hop off in Japan. Can't afford to make another mistake with my visa. Any more Pacific crossings would just about finish me. I'm wondering whether the consul will want someone to say that I'm a bona fide chap and . . ."

"You hoped that Mr. Bates would do his stuff. Well, you are a lucky fellow. I know the consul quite well, I'll call him up just before you go there and tell him all the facts. When's your appointment?"

"Midday."

"I'll give him a tinkle just before. Good luck, and I hope you get the visa."

At two minutes to twelve I walked into the Japanese Consulate and asked the receptionist if I could see the consul. At twelve-thirty I stepped jauntily out of the Consulate. Mr. Bates was delighted to hear that the elusive visa had at last been stamped in my passport. As for me, I celebrated the event with a large steak, a luxury I could afford after two months on the *Oakhurst*.

Before the *Oakhurst* sailed, Mr. Bates came down to the ship to wish me *bon voyage*, with an enormous box of candies and a jar of vitamin tablets, a kindness typical of American generosity.

The anchor was weighed at midday, and soon the *Oakhurst* was gliding down the Columbia River heading for the open sea. Her bows lifted to the gentle off-shore swell as she struck west. We were sailing the mighty Pacific again and I prayed it would be my last crossing.

Last time the captain had taken the Great Circle route to the Far East but now he chose a more southerly course. This way we escaped the bad weather, he explained. "With any luck we can get on with some painting."

For a week we steamed through low-lying mist and thin driving rain which prevented any kind of work on deck.

The chief engineer came to breakfast on our second day out, dishevelled and unshaven. It was his first appearance at breakfast since I had joined the ship. He was a north-countryman, short, square, broad-shouldered—I think he had taken a weight-lifting course in his twenties. He was a brilliant engineer, usually immersed in grease and oil through doing engineering repairs of which he considered his subordinates incapable. His work took place in the evening and night. "Work until two o'clock in the morning," he always boasted. Most mornings found him stretched out on his chaise-longue, from which he graduated to an easy chair. The lunch bell had usually sounded before he rose to a vertical position. On this particular morning, however, he was turned out of his cabin by the boy who had been trying in vain for half a year to tackle the dirt. A chief engineer is often confined to paper work, but our chief had more manual jobs aboard the *Oakhurst* than ever he had as "second" on other ships. Couldn't trust these Greek engineers, he complained; whenever something went wrong down below all they did was roar with laughter, shrug their shoulders, and call for the chief.

Once clear of the mist and rain we began to paint, first a coat of yellow to stop the rust forming again, then one of red lead, and after that a garish pink. "You can put the pink on with this." The mate handed me a roller. "Gets the job done much quicker than a paint-brush." At first the bos'n didn't agree. "You can't get round the rivets as well as you can with a brush," he grumbled. This was true but the roller boosted my morale and by the end of the day I felt as though I had accomplished a huge task.

A week later the rust was with us again.

Japan is a country of over two thousand islands. There are four mainlands and Moji harbour lies on the straits that separate two of them. About a hundred miles east of Moji the straits are crowded with little islands which make navigation very dangerous, especially as many of them show no warning lights. To add to the difficulties we ran into a thick fog. The *Oakhurst* had no radar, so the mates had every reason to be anxious when the Old Man decided to charge on at half-speed, giving intermittent blasts on the whistle to warn anyone else cruising in the same waters. The skipper relied on "commonsense navigation". It carried us through Japan's territorial waters without mishap until three in the morning. Then suddenly a flash of yellow lights broke the misty blackness ahead. "Hard starboard!" yelled the mate on watch. The *Oakhurst* changed course, missing an anchored freighter by inches. The fog patch ended abruptly.

A shriek from the mate on the deck above was followed by a violent jingle on the telegraph. The vessel shuddered from stem to stern as the engines now rammed into full reverse, forcing her to a grinding halt. I shoved a jacket over my pyjamas and tore up the bridge gangway. "Look!" the mate pointed to a light shining out two hundred feet above us. I stared.

"A bloody lighthouse."

By this time everyone was on the bridge.

"Cripes," gasped the third mate, in his underpants and maroon silk dressing gown. We were no more than a few yards off shore.

"Quiet," hissed Sparks, "they're signalling to us." He decoded for the captain, and read out, "AWAIT PILOT". We waited.

In a few minutes the coastguard launch came out with a Japanese pilot. He tore up our ship ladder shouting.

"Hard astern, captain. You're almost on the beach." Just as he was shaking hands on the bridge there was a shattering sound. "Stop engines!" yelled the captain. Then followed an agonising silence which no one but the Old Man cared to break.

"Pilot," he said in quiet accusing tones, "we're on the putty." The pilot was all apologies but could do nothing to alter the fact that our 17,000 tons were now aground. The captain exploded.

"What's the ruddy use of having a pilot, eh?"

"I am sorry, captain," mumbled the pilot, "you must wait until the high water."

"When the hell's that?"

"Midday, tomorrow."

When the captain had stamped off to his cabin I asked the pilot if we'd still get to Moji tomorrow.

"About four o'clock," he nodded. "Why? You leave the ship there?"

"Tomorrow night I hope to be sleeping on Japanese soil for the first time. I'm looking forward to a week or two in your country."

Thinking back to the day at Aomori when I had been turned away from Japan, it didn't seem so very long ago. Crossing the Pacific again hadn't ruined my journey after all. I had learned even more about life on a tramp and I was thirty pounds the richer.

Sparks was already down when I waltzed into breakfast on my last morning aboard the *Oakhurst*. I was supremely happy; on top of the world and journey-proud, even after thirty thousand miles.

"You've heard the latest, I suppose," said Sparks, helping himself to a leathery egg. I looked up expectantly.

"We're not calling in at Moji for bunkers."

"That's a pretty feeble joke," I laughed.

Just then the second appeared. "Well, what do you think of the news?"

"The news?"

"Yes, surely Sparks has told you. Or has he been keeping to his usual reticence? We've been ordered straight through to Pusan." I just couldn't believe it. There must be some mistake.

Three hours after the *Oakhurst* left her mud berth she passed within a hundred yards of the quay at Moji. She didn't stop.

It was unfair, unreasonable, damnable—I very nearly jumped over the rail and swam ashore.

Pusan, at the southern tip of the Korean peninsula, is only a hundred and fifty miles away from Moji. Sparks assured me that we should be there in the early morning. But of course we weren't. The *Oakhurst* was re-directed to Inchon, four hundred miles up the west coast of Korea.

As far as I was concerned, it didn't matter in the slightest where we were going. The plaything of fate, I had completely given up hope of making a landing in the East.

In the middle of the third watch another urgent message came through, ordering us to proceed to Pusan. About turn, and the *Oakhurst* ran slap into another fog blanket. We anchored at five in the morning then again at ten and at midday, and by the afternoon our whereabouts had become a guessing game. According to the log, we should have been off Pusan harbour entrance, but Sparks was unable to confirm this by radio direction finder.

Standing back from a bulkhead to admire my paint-work I heard the sound of a train-whistle. I wiped a few careless drips from the rivets. There was the whistle again. *Train!* I suddenly realised the significance and rushed to the rail to peer into the fog.

"Cripes," gasped the third mate, "nearly on the ruddy beach again." He disappeared up the main mast into the mist. A minute later he was down again.

"Know what?" He grinned. "We're anchored in a bay. Mountains all round. We'll have to get out the same way we came in." When our position was pin-pointed on the map we found we had overshot Pusan by seven miles.

We reached Pusan next morning and a pilot anchored us in the roads. "There is no room alongside," he explained. Lighter barges would take off our cargo. We were only too thankful. The smell of Pusan was billowing from the shore. A launch took us to the quay.

Pusan's streets were thronged with people bustling in all directions. After a sudden rainstorm the women dashed out of their huts to scoop up the water lying in puddles on the pavements. Children used these puddles as wash-basins, street beggars cupped their hands to take a drink. Running water was a luxury in Korea.

The *Oakhurst* stayed at anchor in the outer harbour. Lighter barges with a carrying capacity of about three hundred tons came and took away her cargo to grain elevators up river. But as the *Oakhurst*'s derricks transferred each load into these barges a large proportion disappeared. Small Korean boys were making well-planned assaults, the result of much experience. They paddled up to a lighter, nipped aboard the stern and filled a bucket with grain when the barge hand was at the other end. As soon as the bargee ran aft to throw them off, a second lot of boys leapt up the bows and harvested another bucket or two. There were complaints of serious underweight from the buyer.

The cargo wasn't the only thing to vanish. Two shirts left hanging in the mate's cabin were stolen by a porthole climber, and Sparks came down to breakfast one morning swearing his head off. Someone had stolen his ruddy pants from the bloody drying room. And one day all the soap disappeared from the bathrooms.

"But you must hire our police guards," a fussy little Korean insisted when he heard of the robberies, "otherwise you will lose many more things." The captain wasn't very taken with the idea but under pressure from the officers he consented to have three police guards on the ship. They were stationed at the head of the gangway to prevent any unauthorised person from coming aboard after dusk. The mates could now enjoy a night's sleep without interruption, a welcome luxury on the *Oakhurst* when in port.

One night the third mate woke up with a hunch. He went out on deck. There were the police guards, removing all the grain-shifting boards from the holds and flogging them over the ship's side.

Every time I opened up the paint-store cupboard, Korean stevedores milled round me with their little jam jars hoping that I should let a tin slip. "Please, I have a wardrobe . . ." "My table needs . . ." They watched and waited. They saw gallons of paint in the store, the paint-scrapers, brushes, rollers and chipping-hammers, and I could feel the intensity of their hopes that I should forget to lock up. They hoped in vain. As it was, by the end of the week the *Oakhurst* looked well-stripped without anyone giving presents away.

One morning a mob of Koreans swarmed up the gangway, chipping-hammers in hand. They set to work on the outside of the hull. Within three days most of the rust was off, and what remained was quickly covered with red lead before anyone was the wiser. A coat of black paint was slapped on top. The transformation seemed a miracle, though just how long it would last was anybody's guess. One needn't feel quite so ashamed of the *Oakhurst* now with her new look. It was a great pity she hadn't had it for her visit to Russia.

It was our last day in Pusan and the captain was in a lively mood, even at the breakfast table.

"We're going to Australia," he announced, "calling in for bunkers and a few stores at Moji on the way. Should think you'll want to have a shot at hopping off, eh, Boyd? We'll be there early tomorrow."

I grinned back at him. "I've got a Jap visa so there shouldn't be any trouble this time. When do we leave here?"

"Just as soon as the chief has got up steam—in about two hours."

Just then one of the Korean boys poked his olive-brown face through the saloon doorway asking in a precise little voice, "Captain, who is Mr. Boyd?"

The old man pointed to me, the boy handed over a note, grinning mischievously. Unfolding it I read: "Please bring twenty-five dollars to the Hotel Majestic and bale us out before the *Oakhurst* leaves. PLEASE. J. & H." A mate and an engineer, who had gone ashore two days before, were in trouble. Doubtless they were in feminine company. They knew I was the only one who would have any dollars left, because of my special need to hoard. That need was still very much with me. However, there was nothing for it but to get them out somehow. I left the breakfast table in a hurry.

"You take me to Hotel Majestic?" I asked the Korean lad on deck. One soon picks up pidgin English. Out shot his hand, and he wouldn't budge an inch nearer the gangway until a crisp thousand *hwan* note (fifteen shillings) was placed in it.

"O.K. I take you, mister."

The hotel lay in a respectable quarter of town, catered for the wealthy and was, as I suspected, a brothel. The mate and the engineer were both thankful to see me. Not so the two exquisitely enticing, lightly-clad Korean girls who lay stretched out on the beds.

"Thank goodness you've come," the mate muttered. "We've run up a hell of a bill, what with all the whiskies and the like. Somskie here cost me five thousand to hire from mamousette up the road. . . . Well worth it," he added, smiling at his girl on the bed. "But this hotel's too damned expensive. When we couldn't pay the bill the manager refused to let us out." He disappeared through a doorway and Somskie, sensing that the moment of parting was at hand, stirred from the bed. She squinted at me through those alluring bedroom eyes as if to say "Please" and followed her customer through.

"You'd better hurry up," I shouted after them, "the *Oakhurst* leaves in a couple of hours."

The engineer laughed. "That's the bathroom in there. And baths in Korea are communal." After so many months on the *Oakhurst* I had lapsed into indifference about these sailors' attitude to sex.

I wrote in my diary on July 26th:

"This is my last day aboard the *Oakhurst*. Tomorrow I shall be in Moji."

Three months ago I stood on the doorstep of Japan and was shut out. Sixteen thousand miles have passed since then. Once again I stand on the doorstep of a country whose fascination has twice lured me across the Pacific; there must be no Mistake this time. The door must open.

9

CHOPSTICKS LET LOOSE

Once again my documents were scrutinised by the immaculate immigration officers in spotless grey trousers, white gloves, belts, cap bands and watch straps. The watches looked enormous on their thin wrists. I felt rather a contrast with my squashed panama hat and shoes that had carried me thirty thousand miles and looked like giving up at any moment.

"Tourista?" the officer grinned.

"Student."

"University?"

"Oxford."

"Oxford ver' good. Me, Kyoto," he replied with pride.

I had never heard of it, but had to say, "Kyoto ver' good too." He was so gratified by this remark that page thirteen of my passport was instantly decorated with stamps and signatures.

Another officer flipped through my medical certificates while a third recited the local currency regulations.

"Under the status of a tourist you are not allowed to earn any money in Japan; you may not take any money out of the country."

I smiled back at him, I was perfectly aware of the regulations. It was the same old story all over the world. Regulations I had to disobey. To make sure the officials wouldn't change their minds about letting me land, I produced a number of newspaper cuttings. They were very impressed.

At last I could land in Japan. After fifteen thousand miles of the Pacific, three months of the *Oakhurst*, this was a turning point to remember. I wished the captain, mates and crew a long "cheerio" and hopped into the waiting launch with a little pang of regret.

"I take you to British Consul," came the clipped voice of the launch helmsman as we drew alongside the customs quay. The consular agent had received a string of letters from me during the last six weeks, so that by the time I stepped into his office he knew all about my travels.

"Hallo, Boyd, so you've made it," he greeted me at the door. "Been expecting you for some time here."

"Sorry to have kept you waiting so long," I laughed.

"I've fixed up a bed for you in my house so you needn't worry about tramping round the town for lodging." This generosity was particularly welcome.

My first evening ashore, Fusai Saito, the secretary of the local Y.M.C.A., invited me to dinner. His house was a frail wooden building in the centre of town. He greeted me at the door and asked me to remove my shoes before entering the house. He led me upstairs and into a room floored with raffia matting (*tatami* mats), where we sat down on red silk cushions arranged around a low table. He handed me a glass of yellowish green liquid.

"Do you like our wine?" asked Saito's father, using Saito as an interpreter.

"Very much. Is it *sake*?"

"No. It is *ume-shu*, made from gin and plums which are left to stand for several years. We keep it for special guests," he explained.

Then the meal was brought in. The main dish was a Japanese delicacy called *sashimi*, raw fish sliced up, but I could swear the fish wriggled in its pot and that ruined the whole meal for me. I found it hard going with the chopsticks.

The consular agent's calendar reminded me that we were now in August. He said I mustn't miss seeing some of Japan's ancient cities, so I decided to set out for Kyoto.

The train fare for the four hundred mile trip was two pounds ten. There were three classes of travel on Japanese railways. Second class was twice the price of third class, and first class, with its air-conditioning and luxury armchairs came to twice as much again. Prices are scaled according to whether the train was a local, semi-express, limited express or express.

Some British officials could learn a great deal from the polite manners of Japanese porters who not only show you to your seat but sometimes bow to you from the platform as the train leaves the station. Travellers received excellent service without having to grease any palms with coins. Tipping, an unnecessary invention, was virtually unknown. I was annoyed to see one foreigner pressing a one hundred *yen* note upon a Japanese porter who refused it twice. The Japanese seemed to dislike wealthy tourists, especially when they started to throw large sums of money about.

The seats all faced the same way down open coaches. The only complaint I had was the lack of leg room. The passenger in front of me, however, suffered more through my discomfiture than I did. He tolerated the gentle prod of my knees in his back for fully half an hour before turning round to investigate the cause. His pained expression changed into a sheepish grin when he saw it was a foreigner giving him all the trouble. He commiserated with me over my discomfort, but pointed out that "Japanese railway carriage manufacturers couldn't be expected to make allowance for long-legged westerners."

The train roared through vivid countryside, its travellers putting up smoke windows on entering tunnels, pulling them down again and propping up sunshades as the temperature soared into the nineties.

Over half the working population in Japan (compared with one twenty-fifth in England) is engaged in agriculture. In every field we passed there were crowds of women planting paddy rice. Occasionally a group of labourers with their *sugegasa* triangular-hats looked up to watch the Kyoto Express charge through their little world.

Today there are over ninety million people in Japan. In a few years, the number will rise to one hundred million. The Japanese work desperately hard to feed themselves, but very soon there will be ten million more hungry mouths demanding a fair share of the nation's rice. Living in Japan is like being inside a gigantic sardine tin—without an opener. International immigration laws prevent her from spreading her surplus population to other countries, so it is no wonder the Japanese have made several attempts to violate other countries in her efforts to secure *lebensraum*.

A chorus of voices greeted the train's arrival at every station. "*Bento! Bento!*" That was the loudest cry and passengers scrambled to get hold of a *bento* box. They were one hundred *yen* each, no bargaining. My neighbour leant out of the window and bought two.

"Please try one." He handed me a neatly-tied cardboard box. Two chopsticks lay on top and that meant I wasn't going to enjoy whatever was inside with the whole coach looking on. Rice occupied half the box, baked fish, ginger, pickled vegetables and peppers were separated into smaller compartments. The *bento* box was a much better idea, if one could stomach the contents, than the messy lunch dug surreptitiously from a rustling paper bag. My only trouble was that half the meal found its way on to the floor. Little clay teapots could also be bought for a handful of *yen* at the stations, holding one mouthful of tepid green tea. They could be refilled for about four yen (1d.) from an urn standing on the platform. "Refreshing?" My neighbour smiled. After a number of refills I agreed.

Tea cultivation requires heavy moisture, well drained soil, and a large labour force to harvest the crop. The terraces on Japan's steep hillsides are highly suitable and there is always an abundance of leaf-pickers. The standard Japanese teas are green. In the countryside they are still prepared by hand and sometimes each leaf is rolled separately.

That a foreigner could outdo the Japanese at tea drinking interested most people in the carriage; there were raised eyebrows at the way I gulped down the national beverage.

Thick black smoke belched from many chimney stacks as we entered the industrial area of Kobe and Osaka, a "black country" which both in appearance and industrial potential rivals our own. My neighbour summed up the way to succeed in competition. "Lower standard of living, lower wages, cheaper prices." Goods made in Japan find their way into every corner of the earth. Immediately after the war, the Japanese started with textiles. They have now moved on to compete in shipbuilding and in a great variety of light industrial goods, cameras, radios, chinaware and complicated mechanical toys.

Fusai Saito said he would arrange for someone to meet me off the train at Kyoto. But all the faces on the platform looked identical to me. The crowd whittled down to a handful of people, at last a young man approached me. He bowed low. "Mr. Boyd?" I nodded. "Come, I take you to an inn where you will be ver' comfortable."

We set off at a brisk pace along Kyoto's narrow streets, then down a succession of dimly-lit alleyways. At last we stopped in front of a frail doorway flanked by climbing shrubbery, hanging lanterns. My guide pushed open the rice paper door and I followed him in. The proprietor greeted me in Japanese. Neither of us could speak the other's language, so we laughed as orientals always do on such occasions and bowed profusely.

The guide explained I wanted bed and breakfast, and left me

with assurances that he would be back in the morning to see how I had fared.

As soon as he left, a most exquisite Japanese girl floated across the hall towards me, in a flower-patterned kimono. Her black hair, shoulder length, surrounded a dainty face and her waist was girdled with an ample *obi*, the Japanese cummerbund. My hostess fell on her knees, rose and summoned another dainty creature to take off my shoes. Supple fingers gently untied the laces. The girl held my shoes in her hand as if she were weighing them, and began to giggle over their heaviness. While the other girls hovering in attendance were laughing at the shoes, I tried to cover up a large hole in my sock.

My hostess and her retinue led me upstairs and into a room through a sliding door. The guide had asked for a "bed-sitter", but there was no sign of a bed. "Where do I sleep?" They stood motionless as dolls. Smiling back, I wondered what to do next and gazed at the elaborately decorated room hoping for inspiration. The wall opposite had two alcoves; in one hung an intricately patterned scroll depicting a traditional country scene; in the other sat the impassive image of Buddha, mottled green. Two of the "walls" were rice-paper panels that could be slid along grooves to give varying lighting effects. The others were made of light wood and could also move to increase the room to twice its present size. The ceiling was low, the table only two feet and the standard lamp three feet high. Both the furnishings and the girls made me feel like a giant. Everything about the room seemed fragile, but then the whole inn looked as though I could have run right through it leaving a wreck behind.

Four pairs of eyes awaited my next move. I returned to the bed problem and tested the *tatami* mats which could be fairly comfortable. Perhaps something better would turn up later. In the meantime I decided I'd like a bath. I had forgotten the Japanese for "bath" and I acted a dumb charade, going through the motions of turning on and off a tap. One of the girls disappeared and returned with a glass of bubbling water. Japanese baths have no taps—perhaps it might be unwise to search the inn for the bathroom, as there were so many sliding doors that could lead either to the elusive room or anywhere but. Also I hadn't yet decided whether the red lantern swinging over the door of the inn was just part of Japanese gaiety.

A piece of soap eventually saved the day.

"Sir wants to take a *furo*?" I nodded vigorously and followed up the rear of the procession downstairs to the bathroom. Having shown me where it was, they hadn't any intention of leaving, however. Close by I heard panels sliding to and fro and I imagined that the front stalls lay right behind the rice-paper partition before me. At what point I wondered, did the curtain rise for Act I? The bath was a square wooden tub, sunk in the centre of a tiled floor. Bathing in Japanese style tests one's powers of restraint, for it is the custom to wash outside the tub before you get into it. This done I looked forward to a good soak.

My toes met water near boiling-point, I yelled "HELP!" and was rather surprised to see that the outburst hadn't shattered the inn to little pieces. It froze into silence. Then came a soft pitter-patter of footsteps down the passage-way. They stopped outside the flimsy door. A panel slithered noiselessly aside and a tiny voice said, "You wanta me?"

Returning from this excursion I was relieved to find a floor bed made up for me on the *tatami* mats. In a tray by the door lay a neatly folded kimono. Pyjamas or dressing gown? I wondered. Anyway it felt unbearably scratchy and I discarded it in favour of my own pyjamas. The floor bed was hard; I soon became accustomed to that but there can be no worse sedative than a bean-filled pillow. I hopped into bed under an eiderdown-cum-sheet, after a voice from outside the door had sharply reprimanded me for walking into the room with my slippers on.

When morning arrived, the room had grown larger; there were windows at both ends. One of the walls had been pulled aside during the night to give me more ventilation. Instead of the early cup of tea, a small tooth-brush and minute tube of toothpaste were brought in on a tray. Putting on the kimono, I slipped out quietly to the bathroom. When I came back the bed had gone. In its place were two silk cushions. On the low table stood a wooden basket brimful of rice, enough for a regiment, next to it an exhausted fish two inches long, and more formidable still, an earthenware pot with a raw egg floating round. Breakfast was served.

I was about to start when a petite girl of about twenty crept in, clapped her hands, and sat on the cushion opposite. She produced a fan and set to work, barely moving her wrists. I would have appreciated it had I not been trying to lift the floating egg-yolk with chopsticks. The more vigorously she fanned, the hotter I became.

My faithful guide returned from the Y.M.C.A. after breakfast. "I defy anyone to lift an egg-yolk on the end of two six-inch sticks without asking for trouble," I remarked when he asked how I had fared.

"You will succeed with experience," he assured me. "How did you manage this time?"

"I sent the girl away for some more tea and used my hands. The whole egg was well on the way down when she came back. Her eyes had widened in surprise, but of course she knew all right. The fanning became more vigorous and we just looked at each other in embarrassed silence."

"Expect you missed that phrase book." I ignored the comment.

It was Sunday morning and for the first time in months I became a Tourist. But I avoided the dollar-trap of a guided tour. My own guide-book was quite good enough. "In all Japan, in all the world, there is no city like Kyoto. Ever since its foundation in 794 A.D. it has been the leading artistic and religious centre, and until 1868 was the administrative capital of the Japanese Empire as well," I read. A tax dispute over the entrance fee into some of the temples had closed their doors to the visitor, but there were plenty of others to keep me going for the day. Most of them were filled with Buddha statues. The Sanjusangedo temple, built seven hundred years ago, houses 1,001 images of the Goddess Kannon, in gold leaf.

"The extra one over the thousand," I overheard a guide say, "denotes infinity."

"Infinity of what?" someone asked.

"Of the money spent in building them all," came an American voice. The little party moved on to examine the curious natural curve of the temple roofs, just as they had done in all the other temples, judging by the boredom on their faces. The interminable clicking of camera-shutters promised many evenings at home of comparing oriental tours. They passed on out of sight. I was glad to be on my own.

In another temple, the Higashi-Hongangi, a crowd of people gaped at a three-inch-thick rope in a glass case. The guide asked them to guess the material from which it was made. They suggested sisal, goat, llama and cat, and after further efforts he recited with the tone of one who has played the same game for the last decade, "It is human hair, contributed by the women of Kyoto, to raise the beams of a new temple into place after the old one was burnt down in 1895."

"Isn't that just fascinating?" came from the little group of spectators. As they left the temple they were asked to notice the curious curve in the cedar roofs.

In the magnificent Nijo Castle of the Shogun Tokugawa the floors squeaked under my feet. Bad joinery, I thought. But I was wrong. It was a little device of the Shogun's to warn him of the approach of any possible assassin. The Shogun, feudal lord of the Kyoto district, once had a large number of visitors. There were many waiting-rooms and grand audience halls, whose painting, frescoes and screenwork indicated their functions. The lesser chiefs liked to be received in rooms where bold pictures of lions and eagles depicted the power they wielded over their subjects.

Kyoto has always been a centre of traditional handicrafts. Delicate cloisonné and Satsuma pottery portray the unbelievable patience of the Japanese. Some sets have been worked on for twelve years before they are displayed, and many a dinner service stands incomplete owing to the death of its designer or painter. Many are sold for as much as two hundred pounds.

I walked over to the Nishimura lacquer factory. Here again time means little in the processes of polishing the cypress wood or burnishing gold dust for the relief of a Japanese scene. Modern industry in Japan has inherited the ingenuity and the high quality workmanship of the ancient craftsmen.

It will be interesting to see how long these handicrafts can survive mechanisation and whether the arts and skills handed down through family generations will be swamped. Already they are diminishing; they might have faded altogether but for the tourist trade.

When I praised the meticulous work that must have gone into a delicate lacquer cabinet, every shop assistant and workman put down what he was doing hoping to see yet another customer take away one of the masterpieces. The salesman-in-chief advanced towards me and quoted 250,000 yen—£250. I made a pretence of feeling in my pocket, mumbled something about it being a little expensive and hurried out.

The click, clack, clock of the wooden *geta* (sandals) echoed the passing of a thousand feet down Sanjo street for the evening market. It sounded more intimate than the voice of any other street. People from all walks of life intermingled in the arcade beneath the swinging lanterns and gay bunting. I heard the swell of a Brahms concerto and the throb of a jazz number clashing with the high-pitched wailing of a Japanese traditional. Modern culture in

Japan blends west with east, accepting the new but preserving the old.

When I returned to the inn a crowd of people was sitting round the television set in the entrance hall. There was a good chance that I could slip up to my room unnoticed. But ten pairs of eyes found the programme less absorbing than I had supposed and I became the centre of a huge joke. Again I had forgotten to remove my shoes. . . . More waist-deep bows and laughter.

Next morning I joined a crocodile of tourists in the grounds of the Imperial Palace. Just ahead of me there were two women visitors doing the rounds with a chauffeur and a private guide in tow. The guide had been bombarding them for some time with hundreds of irrelevant details about the Palace, until they were on the verge of screaming. Both women were utterly bored with Buddhas, cedar roofs, temples, and the guide who couldn't pronounce his f's and l's. One began to complain of sprained ankles, the other of pinching shoes, but their cicerone was determined to show the foreigners one last temple—the pride of the city, the jewel of Kyoto.

Globetrotters often arouse sympathy in a big-hearted tourist, especially if they look under-nourished. The one with horn-rimmed diamond-studded sun-glasses approached me. "Say, do come along with us, Alma and I should be delighted." I thanked her very much and remarked that it was good to be amongst English speaking people again. From that moment Alma and Mamie were absorbed in my adventures, and Kyoto history slipped into the background. We got into their car and were driven to the next tourist 'must'. The couple paid no attention to the guide when he announced for the second time that we had arrived at the Kinkakuji temple.

He became extremely angry at my intrusion into the smooth running of things and in vain sought an opening to tell Alma and Mamie that they were standing before the Gold Pavilion. They weren't even looking at it.

"Do the *piranha* fish really eat human beings?" Mamie pressed for more details of blood-thirsty habits.

"If you are silly enough to tempt them, they could tear you to pieces in five minutes."

"Built in 1397," interjected the guide.

Alma was concentrating on one of her fellow-countrymen with three cameras draped round his neck. The guide pointed desperately to the Kinkakuji temple.

"It's gold, gold, GOLD." His eyes glistened. After hearing the magical word pronounced the third time, Alma and Mamie at last turned toward the spectacle. Something valuable as well as historical was worth looking at.

"Real gold," the driver emphasized.

"Leaf," Mamie concluded with a sigh. "Oh, well, its still quite valuable." Alma tried to think up some suitable description of it but only managed, "Lovely pagoda."

"Pavilion," the guide corrected her. He then traced its six hundred years of history with meticulous detail, neglecting to mention that the whole structure had been destroyed by fire in 1950 and rebuilt in 1955.

After the pavilion we went to the Oridono Textile Gallery to order yards and yards of material for all their relatives who must each have a tiny souvenir.

"Say, don't you think this is Kitty all over?" Alma exclaimed, opening and closing a brocade evening bag a hundred times. Then her eyes caught something that glittered still more. This could go on indefinitely; I must leave them as tactfully as possible. But Alma bore down on me with another prize. "Isn't this just an exquisite stole?"

"Yes, yes," I mustered enthusiasm for the last time, "it's lovely."

Mamie was wrapping herself in one kimono after another, glancing in the mirror wondering at what stage the customs officials might start to suspect her bulk. Hearing that lunch was next on the schedule I decided to see the shopping through to the end, and was rewarded by a superb meal in the hotel.

Sometime later I felt in my hip pocket for my wallet. It had gone. . . . Stolen, I suppose.

"How much was in it?" Alma asked.

"Ten thousand *yen*—ten pounds."

We looked everywhere, the car and the silkstore, the Gold Pavilion, but returned empty-handed to the hotel. I was really shaken by this disaster. Then to my intense relief the manager approached us holding up the wallet, complete with the 10,000 *yen*. I had left it in the restaurant. We were very impressed by this honesty, but I resolved to be more careful in future and to keep all my cash in the pouch under my belt. I could hardly believe now that in my circumstances I could have been so careless as to *lose* money.

I thanked Alma and Mamie for all their kindness and boarded the train for Tokyo.

The third class was overflowing with Tokyo-bound holiday makers who sprawled in every possible direction over the carriage seats. Following their example, I removed my socks with relief, but not my trousers as my underpants were a different style from their long cotton ones. We reached Tokyo early next morning.

After an English breakfast at the station I started looking for accommodation—my ever-present problem. I was in the centre of a vast strange city, knowing nobody, unable to speak the language. Tokyo was hard and forbidding. For four hours I walked along the streets, calling in at a large number of shipping agents. I finally landed up at the British Embassy, where I discovered a fellow graduate of Wadham, who invited me to stay. Tokyo was suddenly a friendly, welcoming city.

Greater Tokyo has a population almost the size of Greater London. Most of her eight million people are pedestrians who assume right of way. Unfortunately motorists are not ready to concede and there are arguments on points of law at every road crossing. I found it quicker to travel by rickshaw in the end. Rickshaws were just as expensive as taxis, because at the end of your journey you felt so sorry for the sweating rickshawist that you tipped him fifty cents—the price of a short taxi ride. Motor travel was no pleasure on Japan's pot-holed roads. Few people possessed private cars.

Tackling the city railway system in Tokyo was a nightmare. I wanted to get to a station called Asaksa, and tried to compare the signs on the train indicators with what was scribbled down on my card. I thought I found something that matched. Then I noticed an extra little squiggle on the corner of one of the characters and that ruined the whole puzzle. After half-an-hour, I emerged defeated. I would rely on my feet in future.

It was early August and the Suez crisis was having repercussions as far away as Tokyo, where university students discussed its implications at length and with great eloquence. What was my opinion on Suez? I was asked time and time again. Abroad one tends to support the decisions of the home government whatever one's personal feelings. Foreigners expect it of you. But presently the East-West Club found time to talk about something else, and became absorbed in first-hand stories of South America.

I spent the rest of my stay in Tokyo curtailing my expenditure and trying to find a way out of the country. Since leaving Moji I had been spending money at a rate that would soon dissipate the hard-earned cash I had worked for on the *Oakhurst*. A newspaper correspondent made a suggestion which considerably brightened my prospects.

"Ever tried scribbling a few lines for a newspaper?"

"Try anything once," I said, and the very next day I was struggling behind a typewriter pouring out my story for the local press.

Working a passage on a ship out of Japan seemed impossible. Once again, there were regulations and unions to comply with—Japanese this time. One of the shipping agents in Yokohama told me that no foreigner could work as a deckhand on a Japanese vessel. But past experience had shown me that there was often a loophole in this kind of regulation. A personal introduction to a shipping manager would be a help. Mr. MacMillan's ambassador friend in Tokyo put me in touch with the Hong Kong and Far Eastern Shipping Company, who in turn knew of a Japanese managing director of a company which might be able to help me. An hour later I was relating my travels to Mr. Onemoto, shipping operator of the Mitsui Line.

"Ver' interesting. We like to do something for you. Let me see your passport and papers." Things were turning out better than I could have hoped.

"That's very good of you."

"No, no," he interrupted. "No trouble. We like to assist. You wish to reach Singapore? Our ship the *Yoneyama Maru*, is in port now. She leaves for Dungun, an east coast port in Malaya, next Tuesday. Can you go so soon?"

"Suits me fine. I can work at anything—painting, helming, clerking . . ."

Mr. Onemoto waved aside these suggestions.

"The company wishes its men to know English," he explained. "Captain of the *Yoneyama* speaks well but the other officers ver' little. You will do us a great favour by giving conversation lessons."

I was doing them a favour! Such an easy way of earning my passage was laughable after all the other shipping companies' pessimism.

The Mitsui managers prepared documents for my departure on Tuesday.

"Tokyo sweltering under heatwave of century for sixth successive day," said the evening newspaper. The weather man promised 96 degrees. Any suggestion for getting away from this heat was welcome and at the invitation of some newly-made friends, I spent the weekend at their summer resort on the shores of Lake Chuzenji. I completed all but one of my articles for the press before returning to Tokyo late on Sunday night. My host was relieved to see me. He had received a message for me that morning, marked "important". It read, "E.T.D. *Yoneyama Maru* forwarded to 12.00 hours August 6th." "Tomorrow morning," I groaned, and set to work on the last article.

Monday came with the usual rush. Even in Japan Monday morning is unwelcome. I got up at six, fell into the newspaper offices and dumped four thousand words on the editor's desk. Messy ink corrections made the typing almost illegible, but I managed to sooth the editor by telling him how wonderful the Japanese had been to me. I noticed a bundle of *yen* waiting for me on the table and continued to pour out compliments about the Japanese until it was safely tucked away in my pocket.

Last minute help came from the Hong Kong and Far Eastern Company who lent me their car and chauffeur. They had also co-operated for the past hour by telling the Mitsui Line office, round the corner, that I was just on the way. Now I really was under way. The chauffeur stopped at Mitsui's to pick up the shipping agent. The mad rush to reach the vessel in time was checked by the emigration authorities who rummaged through the chocolate-box containing my medical certificates. The cholera certificate was out of date. We went back to Tokyo and bribed a doctor to inoculate me at once. When the car finally drew alongside the quay it was two hours late. The *Yoneyama Maru* hadn't sailed. The officers must have been more enthusiastic about those English lessons than I had supposed.

The captain greeted me at the top of the gang plank. "You are just in time. The tide has not turned." The *Yoneyama* belched three blasts on her whistle and a minute later she slipped away from the quayside to the tune of "Auld Lang Syne" played over the dockside amplifiers.

It was a strange but apt conclusion to two unforgettable weeks in Japan. The last hectic rush was behind me. Here was leisure and tranquillity. All my worries seemed to drop away. I was on the mighty Pacific again and it felt good to be back at sea.

The *Yoneyama* was no speed merchant. Her maximum was nine knots. She was a welded ship built in 1944, like the Canadian Liberty vessels. Her lines were ugly with a beam of seventy feet, unusually wide for a vessel four hundred and thirty feet long, a very fine sheer to her bows and a tall chimney-shaped funnel in the stern.

The captain took me along to my cabin, the vessel's one and only stateroom, on the captain's deck.

The stateroom deck was wooden and long lines of black Bostik glue oozed up between the planks for the unwary to stub his toe on. My only complaint about the bunk was that it wasn't twice as long and half as wide again.

"You wash below," said the captain. "Remember that you are in an old Japanese lady. You will soon like the wooden tub down there, but I am so sorry no geisha girls." He chuckled to himself.

The Mitsui management had been concerned about my adaptability to the food aboard. The captain seemed equally anxious.

"You think you can eat Japanese food?"

"Of course," I assured him. "Glad to try it."

Meal-time with the senior officers was a very noisy affair. The louder the sounds you make while eating the more you are supposed to be enjoying it. The captain assured me I should get used to rice, *sashimi* and *miso* soup.

The last of these was a nondescript melange of vegetable and fish soup, served with a bowlful of very small shells. My stomach always turned over, but somehow managed to hold out. By the time we reached Dungun I could perform the customary waist-bow without too much embarrassment.

The English lessons began on the second day, with individual tuition in the morning and a collective class in the evening. Some of the officers might be able to join two English phrases together before I left the ship. They asked if I would teach in Japanese, but I thought it better practice for them if we kept to English.

The lessons finished in roars of laughter, though I admired the way they all struggled with the th's, f's, w's and r's. They read from scripts which I had typed out on the subjects well known to all seamen. The chief radio officer was the only one who failed to complete the course. His enthusiasm soon waned and he usually contrived a haircut, radio fault, or weather forecast at the beginning of each lesson.

"Chief steward say he give you egg every day," the second mate managed to recite when I came down to an almost English meal one morning. It was a welcome change in a menu without bread, butter, jam, or potatoes. At lunch-time that day I disgraced myself by enptying a tin of Nestlé's milk onto the bowl of dry rice. Looks of horror greeted this barbarism. "Rice pudding!" I grinned at them, setting to with a spoon. But with such disapproving onlookers it wasn't half as enjoyable as it should have been. Somehow it didn't taste like our rice puddings.

Before dinner at six o'clock, I had to study the weather charts. The reports came over the air in English from the weather station at Okinawa. The captain was an excellent meteorologist and glad to find an enthusiastic listener.

"Come, see the chart," he yelled down the gangway one evening. "Weather man is working ver' hard." Something must be up for the old man had never been so excited over cyclones and anti-cyclones. A minute later I was studying the movement of a tropical storm hanging around latitude 24 degrees north. It was some two hundred miles ahead, proceeding in a north-westerly direction at the rate of fifteen knots.

"Ver' bad weather tonight. We change course," said the captain. As the evening drew on the sea started to pile up and the storm centre deepened. The captain swung the *Yoneyama* round 20°. Sparks was busy tapping out his weather reports and receiving the area forecasts from the American radio station at Okinawa. The first bulletin read—"Very strong winds; seas high; visibility 200 yards."

Four hours later—"Gale force winds; heavy seas; very poor visibility." Whichever way we turned the cyclone appeared to be chasing us in a nightmarish way.

It was midnight. The bows of the ship lifted high above one huge wave and fell with a reverberating shudder on the following wave-crest. The *Yoneyama* shook from stern to stern in bitter complaint.

Forecast for next few hours—"Typhoon Babs is born. Wind force 75 knots; seas mountainous, becoming momentous." Flying spray reduced visibility to zero. Our speed was nil. The barometer needle had fallen almost beyond the lowest millibar. Steel and water collided with shattering violence and the *Yoneyama* must have been near to breaking her back.

Six a.m. "Babs" was screaming past the *Yoneyama's* halyards and derrick wires, hammering on the ports, cutting through every chink in the wheelhouse. We are all in the radio room listening in, tense with excitement, fear and awe, at this manifestation of nature. The last weather forecast over—"Typhoon Babs; winds 100 knots ... seas ... p h e n o m e n a l!" A sheet of water cracked against the bridge window, a door slammed, and we all agreed with the meteorological station. After that announcement Okinawa closed down. The range of superlative adjectives was exhausted. Further speculations on the weather seemed pointless anyway.

We lay head to wind, steaming ahead at four knots, being blown back at six. The captain looked anxious. "We keep her head to wind; a wave on the beam would roll her over." He turned to me. "How does your stomach like this sea?"

After *miso* soup, octopus and squid my stomach could take almost anything. Not so Sparks, the youngest aboard. This was his second voyage at sea, and he was suffering badly over the lee-rail.

"Today no food, no work, no lessons," the operator remarked, thankful he hadn't got to search for an excuse to be absent. Instead he ushered me into his cabin, unfastened a chest under his bunk and pulled out a bottle of whisky. "Please take. Best Nippon."

I thanked him for the gift and promised not to tell anyone.

Back in my cabin I was about to pour out a tumblerful when someone knocked on the door. I hid the bottle under the bed-clothes. It was the mate.

"Hallo, Mr. Boyd, you not feel well, no? I bring you this." He withdrew a hand from his coat, and presented me with a replica of the gift hidden just next to him.

"I won't say a word to the others," I forestalled, and he flashed a grateful smile.

Before dinner that evening the captain invited me up to his cabin for a drink. "You have tasted Suntory, our rare old whisky?"

"Rare old whisky? Never." The other two bottles must be a less expensive brand, then.

"Take this bottle. But say nothing to the mates."

At dinner the *sukiyaki* rolled across the table as the vessel heeled to thirty degrees. Three faces opposite me waited to catch my eye hoping I should acknowledge their little gestures with a special smile. I smiled for most of the meal.

The mate tried out his English on the captain. "Our cargo of dynamite is O.K., yes?" My chop-sticks clattered to the deck. "We're not carrying dynamite?" I spluttered.

"Under there." The captain pointed to the deck under my chair. "But please do not excite yourself. There has been so far no trouble."

"You wish to move to quarters aft?" taunted the mate.

Typhoon and dynamite! We were sitting on top of a potential volcano. The sooner we got to Dungun the better.

Sparks rushed into the room and announced that there had been an S O S signal from a vessel 200 miles ahead. There was a man overboard and would we look out for him.

"Double the watch and see the searchlights are in order." Then the captain turned towards me and said slowly, quietly, "Man lost at sea in typhoon. No chance in the world."

I couldn't stop thinking about that dynamite.

10

HITCH-HIKING IN MALAYA

She was crying bitterly. Great white tears rolled down her wrinkled cheeks, gathered into enormous drops and plopped onto the sand. I felt distressed but there was nothing I could do to help. I just stood watching as she scooped out a hole in the sand. The strangest reptile I had ever seen was preparing a nest for her young.

The *Yoneyama* had been anchored for eight hours in Dungun, a small port on the east coast of Malaya. I went ashore with the local police officer and was taken to a barbecue party on the sands. There was another stranger at the party, Dr. Reingold, an American zoology professor who had come up to Dungun for a week's research on the habits of the "great leather-backs".

The hostess introduced us and insisted on telling Dr. Reingold about my adventures, some of which even I found hard to believe. "You seem to have had a good time, so far," the professor remarked dryly. On hearing that I was spending only two days in Dungun, he said he was driving a few miles north of the town after the party to have a look at the great leather-backs, and would I like to go along.

Before I could ask what he meant by a leather-back, there was a unanimous chorus from the party that this was an opportunity I mustn't miss.

The ferry across the river Dungun stops running at dusk but there is usually a sampan owner knocking around to take people over. Dr. Reingold and I arrived at 1 a.m. and yelled for a boat.

Half an hour later our voices were hoarse. Nobody had stirred and our cries echoed up and down the river. The professor wasn't the kind of man to give up lightly. "Guess we'll have to borrow the police dinghy." There were no oars in it, so we decided to swim the boat across the river. Twenty yards off shore the current was too strong and we had to turn back. Of course the sampan owners had heard us and witnessed our failure to swim the police boat across but still they didn't pay any attention; for the longer we shouted the more desperate we must be to get across, and the more desperate we were the more we should be willing to pay. Deciding we had reached the ultimate stage of desperation, a sampan owner appeared miming the disturbance of his night's rest. He demanded eight dollars (£1), refusing to paddle us across for a cent less. We weren't in a position to bargain.

Dr. Reingold had taken his truck over on the ferry the day before. We hopped in and drove for a quarter of an hour, arriving at the beach about two o'clock. The professor left the truck by some palm trees, pocketed his torch and a tape measure and set out along the beach. I followed close on his heels like an inquisitive school-boy, wondering what kind of a monster I was looking out for. Dr. Reingold flashed his torch over the sand.

We had been walking along the tide line for several minutes when he stopped abruptly. He pointed to some marks about four feet wide. "Those are the tracks of her flippers. If there is only one set she must be somewhere up the beach; two sets mean she's returned to the water."

We followed the flipper marks up the sand beyond the high-water mark. Suddenly there was an enormous greeny-grey hump, like an upturned giant spoon, outlined against the sand. It was shining in the moonlight.

"The great leather-back turtle at a later stage in the excavations," I was informed.

Double flipper marks in the sand a few yards on indicated that one turtle had fulfilled her mission and was happily re-submerged in the Pacific. I asked the professor what made them choose this particular beach for a breeding ground. He explained that there was no coral reef off shore so that they had an unobstructed path-way from the bottom of the sea. "Then there's the gentle slope of the sand as well as its texture for excavating."

A wall of sand impeded one turtle's progress up the slope. She had chosen the wrong part for beach climbing. She hurled her full weight against the sand ridge, but the more she hurled the more the sand crumbled and the harder her tears flowed.

"For some reason she hasn't got the sense to give up and try another part of the beach," Dr. Reingold remarked. "She'll probably still be here when we return."

Further along the highwater mark, we came across a leather-back who had nearly finished preparing her nest. She was boring down and down, curving her flippers like a plough, and for every gigantic spoonful of sand there was a huge white tear. Digging was hard work. It was frustrating work too, for the walls of the hole caved in over and over again. Three feet down her flippers were unable to scoop out any more sand. The first part of her task was over. More tears rolled down her cheeks, and the first white egg went "plop" to the bottom of the hole. Another, then another, more and more streamed out, in batches of five or six at a time. After about fifty of them I thought the session must be over—but there were more to come.

"Catch one," called Dr. Reingold, and stretching my hand under a likely spot I clutched a warm white egg as it dropped from above. It was round, the size of a large duck egg, with a soft shell. "You can tear away the shell and break off the gelatine albumen," he said. "Now swallow the yoke." I made an ugly face and spluttered. It went down all right, but it was very sour and gritty. "Horrible! What happens if you boil it?"

"No good, the albumen never hardens."

Within three minutes she had laid a hundred eggs; after a hundred and twenty-five had been safely delivered, very much smaller eggs appeared—"without yokes," the professor told me. This meant that the performance was nearly over.

With the last egg out the turtle gave an immense sigh of relief. Then with motherly care she covered her nest with loose sand and rummaged about to disguise the spot where she had laid her babies-to-be. She must hide them very carefully because turtle eggs are a great delicacy for tigers which once prowled the beach. They also find a place on the Sultan's breakfast table. We turned back along the beach, and I asked how long they would take to hatch.

"About two weeks. The baby turtles work their way upward through the sand. When they break surface their instinct tells them to scamper for dear life towards the water before the gulls have time to swoop down on them. The mother may return to lay some more eggs, but only while the sea is calm. They keep away once the north eastern monsoon breaks and rollers roar up the beach."

Dawn was breaking when we found the other old girl still struggling at the foot of the sandbank, just as the professor had predicted. "She'll probably give up soon and try again tomorrow if the moon is up and she has enough energy."

So her children would have to wait till another day—still, what's twenty-four hours in a hundred years of life? We lay on the sand for an hour's nap. Perhaps there were a hundred baby turtles struggling for freedom two feet underneath us. Some way along the beach, the hump of a great leather-back was silhouetted against the rippled surface of the sand. She looked more like a legendary monster than anything I had ever seen. I wondered if she knew that her hours of labour were largely for the benefit of the breakfast table. Perhaps that accounted for the tears.

We were wakened two hours later. Standing around us was a group of sarong-clad children, clutching defenceless baby turtles a couple of inches long. The babies couldn't have been more than half-an-hour old. It didn't seem possible that in years to come they would be fifty thousand times their present size.

As the first 'tourist' to enter Malaya through Dungun, my appearance caused a stir amongst the sleepy immigration officials. No one seemed to know what stamp to put in my passport. The problem was left for the District Officer who had arranged to meet me in the Dungun club on the evening after the turtle adventure.

I was driven to the club by the local police officer, Mr. Fairey. We arrived just in time to see Audrey Hepburn falling into the arms of an unshaven Stewart Granger. The film show ended. The small European audience clapped dutifully and there was prolonged applause from a crowd of Malays outside who were enjoying a free show through the open windows.

The D.O. handed me a beer. "You're officially in Malaya," he beamed. "Hope you like the place." It was an easy entry. He apologised for not producing a stamp for my passport.

"Anyway, no one will ask to see your papers," he said.

The immigration ceremony over, Mr. Fairey drove me back to his house. "You're leaving Dungun tomorrow?" he asked.

I thought of hitch-hiking along the coast road to Kuantan, then across country to Kuala Lumpur and down to Singapore.

The officer was shocked at this idea. "Got to be damn careful. There're still a number of terrorists knocking around the place. If they saw a lone Englishman standing by the roadside they might take a potshot."

"How about going to Singapore by sea? Can I do it that way?"

He didn't think so. The coastal craft had left two days ago, and the next sailed in a fortnight. "Tell you what, though. I'll run you down to the first of the three ferries on the Kuantan road. That's about fifteen miles south of town. We should be able to pick up a truck for you there, going right through to Kuala Lumpur."

I agreed thankfully. Next morning Mr. Fairey placed his automatic in the front pocket of the car and we were soon bumping southwards along the road to Kuantan. While skilfully negotiating the potholes, he chatted about his years as a patrol leader in the jungle. So far he had never been let down by his Malay constables, of whom he spoke highly. "Once they've learnt to respect you and you in turn show confidence in them, there's a good chance of pulling through the thickest ambush. But without that mutual trust . . ." He shrugged his shoulders. "Last year my patrol was attacked and the terrorists shouted to the Malays—'Give us the white man and we'll let you go free.' They know that there's a chance the Malay will weaken under persuasion, and, believe me, it takes quite a lot of courage for him to refuse if he thinks his side is outnumbered."

When we pulled up at the ferry there were three trucks waiting to cross the river. Mr. Fairey only needed to say a few words to the driver of the first, the Pahang Mail, for me to be installed at once in the front seat.

"Cheerio," shouted Mr. Fairey as the truck moved onto the ferry. "You'll be all right on this one. She's running through to Kuala Lumpur. Probably be there tomorrow night."

Hitch-hiking must be rare in Malaya; the villagers were most curious when they saw me perched up at the front of the Pahang Mail.

We drew into Kuantan in the late afternoon. The driver indicated that we were stopping the night, that we should leave at five in the morning and that I was not to be late. I spent the night in the Rest House, one of the government-owned hotels which provide excellent food and accommodation at a price to suit even my pocket. I walked round the town and was surprised to see so many Chinese in the place.

A distant clock struck five. I struggled out of bed, dressed rapidly and ran to the garage. There was no sign of the truck. Had it gone? At 6 o'clock the Pahang Mail came spinning round the corner. It braked to pick me up. We all wished each other a *selamat pagi*.

The Kuantan–Kuala Lumpur road runs straight through the Malayan jungle and over the backbone of mountains that stretch from one end of Malaya to the other. In front of us was a truck carrying an enormous load of *rambutans*—a prickly tropical fruit tasting like a grape. Every time the lorry passed over a hump it sprinkled a few of these on the road in front of us. We didn't bother to stop for lunch, *rambutans* were quite as satisfying.

We roared into Kuala Lumpur in the late afternoon. The driver dropped me off at the railway station and even carried my luggage into the waiting-room. I untied the grip and pulled out two packets of cigarettes I kept for such occasions. "*Terima kasi banyak-banyak Tuan.*" He was delighted. I took an instant liking to the Malays.

In view of the warning given to me about hitch-hiking on Malayan roads, I enquired about the train service to Singapore, where I had a cousin to stay with. There was an express train leaving Kuala Lumpur at eight o'clock—three hours' time. I discovered at the booking office that there was no third class on the train, so I parted with two pounds for a second-class ticket. Kuala Lumpur station fascinated me with its Islamic-style architecture.

To kill time I wandered over to the bookstall. Suez was still very much in the headlines—I bought a newspaper. This concerned me, for if the trouble spread throughout the Middle East I should not be able to get to Europe that way. I must somehow by-pass the enormous traffic block of war. But then my original briefing for this world-tour gave me a wide choice of route, as was easy to be seen looking back. I could still vary within the limits imposed by the Suez situation, round the Cape on a ship or across Central Africa. An African safari appealed strongly to me but I quailed to think what it would involve in the way of fighting red tape to get the necessary visas. All the same I resolved to make enquiries the moment I reached Singapore.

Just then an English voice at my side asked for a *Straits Times*. In far-off places a visiting Englishman is over-joyed to meet a fellow-countryman. Not yet used to the Britisher's omnipresence in Malaya, I fell eagerly into conversation with this chap. Anyway, I was hungry and wanted to know where I could get a hearty meal.

"Of course, old boy. Delighted to show you a good restaurant if you can hang on a moment. I must have a hair-cut before the station barber closes; been putting it off for days. You wait in my Armstrong outside there—back in five minutes."

He disappeared through an archway. I found the Armstrong and presently fell asleep on the back seat.

"Come on, wake up." The owner had returned. I roused myself and apologised.

"Oh, don't worry. It's been hot and stuffy today. You say you've only just arrived here? Staying long in Kuala Lumpur?"

"No, I've just booked a seat on tonight's Singapore express."

"Pity. You won't see much of the place. Come far?"

"Oh, the Amazon," I said, vaguely thinking of the most outlandish place I had been to.

He laughed, disbelieving, and asked where I had arrived in Malaya.

"Dungun. On a Japanese freighter."

"Dungun! I've never met anyone who's done it that way before."

He seemed interested in my explanation. "By the way, my name's Tony Beamish. You're welcome to dine with us tonight."

We pulled up outside his flat and went in. "Stuart," he yelled from the hall. "Come and meet our visitor." An unintelligible reply came from the bathroom, but Stuart soon appeared in the doorway, foam dripping from his chin.

"Meet Alistair Boyd, a globetrotter I've just picked up at the station. Thought you might be interested in interviewing him."

"Yeah. What did you say he does?"

"Globetrots."

"O.K. I'll fix him up a broadcast tonight and he can tell the listeners how he does it. That all right, Mr. Boyd?"

I swallowed in astonishment. "Broadcast—tonight?"

Stuart laughed. "You seem rather surprised, old chap. Didn't Tony tell you who we are? The man who rescued you off the station is the Director of Radio Malaya. I'm his associate, worse luck."

At seven o'clock I was on the air fighting *piranha* fish, smuggling whisky on the Amazon and struggling with a raw egg at Japanese breakfast. I was £3 richer at the end of it.

Afterwards Stuart came forward with a good suggestion. "You can't possibly leave for Singapore tonight. We're driving down to Seremban tomorrow, to have lunch with the Chief Game Warden of Malaya. You'd enjoy meeting him. It's fifty miles along the Singapore road, not out of your way at all. Like to come with us?"

"Sounds wonderful. What about my rail ticket?"

"Oh, Tony'll fix that. He knows the station-master."

Midday Sunday we were having lunch with the game warden.

Tony explained that the object of the visit was to record the game warden's impressions of the Pahang river monster for a radioscope programme. The monster was supposed to have seven heads each one capable of swallowing a hippopotamus. The game warden's impressions of the monster were brief—seven heads of hot air.

Sitting on the verandah of the Seremban Rest House that evening the wife of the police training officer chatted to me about the years of emergency in the jungle. It had been a long tiring struggle, she admitted. One could never quite tell what the terrorists would be up to next. The movement seemed to be going underground. Now that their guerrilla tactics had failed it might well reappear in some form of political organisation. She didn't know what they would have done without the British army; it just showed how essential it was to keep a strong organised force in Malaya.

"I noticed some armoured trucks patrolling the road between here and K.L. Are they on duty every day?" I asked.

She shook her head.

"Oh no. The Number Two communist leader was killed yesterday. A patrol stumbled on him near here. The army are expecting a retaliation any moment."

I told her I thought of hitch-hiking to Singapore.

She looked horrified and said it was an idiotic idea. "Might be suicide. Give me till dinner-time and I'll see if my husband can do anything for you."

At nine o'clock the Rest House boy rushed up to my room. "Police station on the phone for you," he shouted through the door. I tore down and picked up the receiver.

"Hallo. Boyd speaking."

"Training officer here. My wife's just told me you want to travel to Singapore tomorrow. I've rung the air-base. They seem to have a routine flight going down there in the morning and say they'll be delighted to take you."

"Wonderful. Many thanks for asking them. What time should I be at the airport?"

"You needn't worry about that. They'll send out a staff car to collect you from the Rest House soon after nine. Hope you have a good flight. Best of luck for the rest of your trip."

I could hardly believe my ears.

An Auster plane was already warming up on the runway by the time the staff car reached the airport.

We were soon flying low over Malaya's green jungle carpet. The flight lasted over a couple of hours and we touched down in Singapore at midday. My cousin sent a car to meet me at the airport.

Staying with the people of foreign countries had been an exciting and rewarding experience. But by the time I reached Singapore I was quite ready to spend a week or two with people of my own kind. All the little worries of etiquette and the difficulties of conversation disappear on home ground. It was a welcome breather amidst the variety of oriental customs. I no longer had to remember to remove my shoes or pick my teeth or belch.

A globetrotter finds it difficult to earn his keep in the East. The heat and humidity are not conducive to heavy work, manual labour is poorly paid and the native workers of the country would probably resent the intrusion of a foreigner. The problem was solved for me by the *Singapore Standard* which agreed that I should write a few lines on my trip. The few lines became ten thousand words. My thirty-five pounds increased to sixty. My old camera was no longer taking recognisable pictures and at last I was rich enough to buy a new one for fifteen pounds. That left forty-five (in U.S. dollars, Straits dollars, hwans and yens). It was a great relief to be so affluent. The camera was an investment in that I could sell it if necessary without losing much on the deal.

Singapore teems with Chinese. They multiply in the oriental manner) 43 per cent of the population is under 15) and outnumber the Malays, Tamils and British put together. The Chinese run the city. They are the shopkeepers, the small business men and the wealthy merchants, always to be found clinching deals over a bowl of "sweet and sour". Through street doorways can be heard the clacking sound of the mahjong counters.

After two weeks in Singapore I grew restless. The urge to get moving again before I became too attached to the city spurred on my plans to depart. I would go to India first, then to Africa. The idea of returning home across the neck of central Africa appealed to me more and more. I planned a route through Kenya, Uganda and the Congo. There should be no trouble over entry permits for the two colonies, but getting into the Congo was likely to be as difficult as the South American republics. A day in the Belgian Consulate confirmed my suspicions. The Congo was a cocoon of red tape.

First, I had to have a good-conduct guarantee from England; next, find someone who was willing to put up a financial bond, and finally, produce evidence of a booked passage out of the country. Only then would the consul consider sending my visa application to Brussels for sanction. By the time the visa was ready I should have left Singapore long ago, so I would have to pick it up somewhere on the way.

We settled on Bombay, as that was on the direct route to Africa and I should have to pass through it on my way to Kenya. I arranged to call at the Bombay Belgian Consulate around October 15th.

There were hundreds of places I wanted to visit in the the East. Rather than rush round for brief glimpses of the lot, I decided to spend a few more days in Malaya.

An interesting invitation to see some Malayan aborigines arrived one morning from the Aborigine Department in Kuala Lumpur. I arranged to go along in a couple of days. In the meantime I was asked to a tennis party where I met three Thai (Siamese) students visiting Singapore on an economic delegation. They had all been educated in Britain and could speak English well.

"But you can't say you've been round the world if you haven't visited Thailand," remarked one at the end of a set.

Another, who introduced himself as Chandram, said,

"Won't you change your mind and include Bangkok on your tour? I'll be very happy to put you up in my home for as long as you are able to stay."

Nothing delighted me more than the prospect of a couple of weeks in Thailand. Eagerly I took up Chandram's offer and he said he would meet me at Bangkok's main line station in ten days' time.

"Mind you don't miss the Bangkok express. There are only two trains a week."

Next day I packed my bags and left for Kuala Lumpur. The Selangor State Protector of Aborigines met me off the night train at Kuala Lumpur and we drove out to a small village on the west coast.

"The aborigines here are quite a civilised lot," he said. "At least they wear clothes and recognise money as a means of exchange."

We were to buy some of their handiwork for the Malayan Agricultural and Horticultural Association's exhibition at K.L. Accompanying us was a rotund Chinese lady, middle-aged, with considerable surplus of avoirdupois. Her bottom was immense—so large and round that one couldn't help but stare at it. Her face was the same shape, though perhaps not quite so large, and it shone with joviality. Behind this bright beam lurked a good deal of intelligence. She could converse in Cantonese, English and Malay, and had picked up the obscure dialects of the "abos". When she bargained with them for their products, be it a violin or a model of a fish trap, she knew at once how much had been added to the price at which the seller would ultimately let it go. She had great powers of persuading the quantity we wanted from reluctant sellers. And she firmly refused any work that appeared roughly done.

We returned to Kuala Lumpur in the evening. I was dropped at the house of Dick Noone, Government Protector of Aborigines, a man who has spent most of his life dealing with the welfare of these people and with the problems of preserving them as a race. The years of emergency in Malaya aggravated his task. The Communists used the aborigines to secure food and other necessities as well as information. "Once we can safeguard their lives adequately they will remain loyal to us," said Mr. Noone. The department had already done a lot for their safety. Rehabilitation schemes offered them protection in hill-top encampments. This was also an experiment in community life, a fresh world to the aborigine after his isolated life in the jungle.

I visited an encampment where one little fellow gleefully showed me a wrist watch. When I asked him the time he grinned uncomprehendingly. It was just an ornament that sparkled in the sun, and as every *tuan* possessed one he was going to have one as well. Spectacles with plain glass lenses were all the rage.

Mr. Noone's assistant drove north to Ipoh. The main north-south road in Malaya is one of the best tropical highways in the world. Outside each town we came across barriers thrown over the road where vehicles and pedestrians were searched to prevent smuggling of food into the bandit camps. Cars of Europeans were sometimes signalled on, but it was unwise to take advantage of one's nationality and drive straight through without this signal.

The British Army had several contingents at Ipoh, the commercial centre of the tin mining industry in Malaya. After a beer session on my first evening, I was given introductions by several of the officers to their friends in Calcutta and Karachi.

The Ipoh State Aborigine Protector put me up for the night, and next morning we drove up-country. Of this excursion I can remember one outstanding personality. I met her in a bar of a hotel. She was an English woman, fortyish, rather tall and wearing a daringly low-cut dress. She had long "blonde" hair hanging straight down from a grooved centre parting. Around her stood a group of young admirers. She had been a reporter in Cyprus, an agent in the Chinese underground and a tourist to Alice Springs in Australia. During her non-stop commentary a young man next to me was letting me into the secrets of her love-life. She had a husband in England, one in Perak and yet another, he thought, within easy reach. She wore a chimpanzee carelessly draped round her shoulders, his hairy arm clutching her long white neck as though he would throttle her.

"Little darling," she drawled, while he polished off the contents of every glass within reach.

As this exquisite lady crossed the floor of the hotel, her grinning companion left a trail of ochre-coloured mounds on the carpet.

II

ORIENTAL PEARL

The Bangkok express had reached Padang Besar, the jungle village on the Malay-Thailand border. Customs officials of both countries swarmed aboard and toothcombed the baggage of everyone travelling up from the free port of Penang. Then we all descended and filed through the emigration office where travel permits and passports were scrutinized by the Malay officials. There was no fuss, no bother, for the drill was familiar to everyone. Everyone except me. When it came to my turn the officer made the inevitable comment on my passport. It had no record of the date nor even the place where I had entered Malaya. I explained what happened in Dungun.

"They had no official stamp," I said, "so the local District Officer kindly let me in without one." It was a perfectly genuine explanation, but I seemed to be the only one who thought so.

"What have you been doing in Malaya?" he asked suspiciously. "Business or tourist?" Just then I noticed lying on his desk the Sunday edition of the *Singapore Standard*, the paper I had written for. It looked pretty crumpled. The officer had obviously read it from cover to cover.

"What have I been doing in Malaya?" I repeated with sudden inspiration. I pointed to the article in the paper and next to it quite a recognisable photograph of myself. He looked up in astonishment.

"This you?" he exclaimed excitedly. I smiled back at him.

"I read your travel just before the train came. Very long journey. I hope you arrive home safely. Very happy to meet you. I am so glad you came to see me," and he handed back my passport in his excitement without any further interrogation.

The train filled up on the Thai side of the border. Siamese crammed the carriages and on seeing me seated in the second class they pointed to the first, thinking I had made a mistake. When I showed them my ticket they laughed heartily, patted me on the back

174

and introduced themselves. They seemed delighted that a foreigner should voluntarily travel with them rather than shut himself up in a first-class compartment.

Many visitors say that the Siamese are the most generous and hospitable people you could meet. I certainly thought so at this first encounter. Families travelling to Bangkok invited me to share their food and drink. I was surprised that so many of them understood a little English.

Thai customs officials interrupted the enjoyment by handing me a currency declaration form to sign. All visitors to Thailand could bring up to ten pounds cash into the country, any surplus being in the form of travellers' cheques. By that ruling I had now *too much* cash! In an attempt to avoid frustrating hours in a bank (it's unwise to explain to bank managers the origin or the destination of one's cash), I turned an innocent face to the official and said, "I no speak Siamese." The official grinned back and passed on.

Enormous baskets blocked the centre corridor, crammed with prickly *rambutans* like those I had seen in Malaya. The fruit was going to the market at Bangkok. Prying fingers found their way into the baskets and by the time the train had reached Bangkok, the carriage floor was littered with skins and the vendors had a fraction of the amount they had set out with.

In Thailand, as in the Peruvian sierras, train rides are considered holiday treats; ready-cooked meals can be bought on every station platform. The favourites are chicken, artistically pinned to triangular sticks, huge portions of rice served on dock-sized leaves, and the Thai version of a *bento* box.

By noon the next day the rice fields and jungle had given place to narrow waterways and clusters of wooden huts, and thirty-six hours after leaving Malaya, the Bangkok express slowed down for its entry into the "Venice of the Orient". We drew into Bangkok's main line station. Another eight hundred miles had been added to my journey.

I hopped off, and dumped my bags at the end of the platform. Chandram had promised to meet me at the station, but the train had run ahead of schedule. Ten little toffee-coloured kids squinted at me through minute almond-shaped eyes and hung around waiting for my next move. As they would all demand a huge tip for touching my bags I had to decline their offers of help. The youngest of them didn't take my refusals seriously. One hand rested on my suitcase while the other was outstretched palm uppermost.

"Hallo, Alistair," a voice hailed me from behind. I turned round to see a young wiry-haired Thai grinning all over. He was dressed in a pale-blue tropical suit with a bow tie to match. It was good to see an oriental face that I could recognise.

"Sorry I was a little late in getting here," Chandram apologised, "but traffic delayed me a bit. Rush hour here is as bad as London's, you know. I have my jeep outside so you can soon see for yourself. Good journey?"

"Uncomfortable, but enjoyable."

"Expect you could do with a bath after that train ride. Let's drive back to the house."

The house was in a residential quarter to the north-east of the city. Chandram's parents greeted me on the doorstep with the traditional joining of their hands and a graceful bow which I returned as best I could.

Chandram told me to remove my shoes and socks, and we both entered the living room barefoot. Upstairs he handed me a pair of bell-bottom silk pyjamas.

"What are these for?" I asked him, trying them on. I hoped my waistline would never measure the inches required to fill these.

"We wear them in the house. Much cooler."

Then when Chandram saw me in difficulty he showed me how to tie a fool-proof knot. Even then I lived in continual fear that they would suddenly drop to half-mast. There was a clean pair provided each day and night.

"The bathroom is outside." Chandram handed me an enormous silver bowl, and slipping my feet into bathroom sandals I followed him out of the house and across a stone courtyard. The bathroom was in the traditional Siamese style. There was no bath, only an enormous earthenware pot four feet high, brimming with ice-cold water. Antique silver bowls stood on a shelf for each member of the household. They were for scooping out the water.

An exotic meal followed—and none too soon for me. Curry was the main dish accompanied by salad and a dozen little side dishes each overflowing with spices and other indigestibles. During the meal I noticed a portrait of a distinguished-looking old gentleman on the wall.

"That's my grandfather," said Chandram, "Brother to one of our late kings." He laughed at my astonishment.

The hierarchy of titles and ranks in Thailand is very complicated and he tried to explain the system. The grandchildren of the King

15. Fishing boats at Dungun, Malaya. The sails are made from old flour bags.

16. A giant leather-back returns to the sea at dawn in Malaya. She is nearly five feet long, her head larger than that of a human.

17. A Malayan aborigine with his blowpipe.

18. Boatmen stand up to row on Bangkok's floating market.

were known as Mom Chao, the great grandchildren Mom Raja-wongse and their children, Mom Luang. The two lowest ranks Mom Rajawongse and Mom Luang came into use only fifty years ago during the reign of Rama VI. Few members of the royal family survived the last sack of the old capital Ayudhya and great grand-children were not considered royalty. Rama VI was worried that the royal family might die out and so great grandchildren and their children, were given the respective titles of Mom Rajawongse and Mom Luang. Today only those persons holding ranks above Mom Chao are given the title of prince and princess. "I'm only Mom Rajawongse," Chandram added modestly, "my grandchildren won't have any title at all."

I tried to figure out where Chandram came in line of succession to the throne but he assured me that he was a long way off.

I changed into more silk pyjamas and as I got into bed I couldn't help marvelling at my luck in meeting Chandram in Singapore. I might never have been able to take part in the Thai way of living or even see inside a Thai home.

In the morning Chandram drove off in the jeep to his Ministry of Finance office. Occasionally he taught English and Economics at the University and one morning he asked me to help him with a con-versation lesson. At the end of the class one of the students, named Ngam, offered to take me round the city, in return for help with his English. Ngam became my guide for the rest of my stay in Bangkok and Chandram kindly lent us his jeep during the day so that we shouldn't have any transport difficulties.

Bangkok is a young city, founded when the old capital Ayudhya was destroyed by the Burmese a hundred and seventy years ago. Much of the brick-work from the ruined temples of Ayudhya was shipped forty-two miles down-river to a little village called Kok. They became foundations of the new capital—Bangkok.

It is dominated by its Buddhist temples, their majestic pagodas rising well above the red tiled roof-tops. The temples are crammed with gilt and black stone statues of Buddha in various poses. There seems to be an element of competition between these eastern countries as to which can build the largest Buddha of all. "Bangkok has the longest," Ngam said proudly, and took me along to see the great reclining Buddha in the temple of Wat Po. It was carved in stone, covered with gilt and stretched a hundred and fifty feet down the length of the temple. Its toes alone were twice as large as my head. It filled me, a stranger to the Buddhist religion, with awe and reverence. It must be the grandeur, the mysterious air of majesty as well as the beauty, that fills the Buddhist with emotion.

Priests wandered round the temple grounds, each holding a fold of his saffron gown over one arm. There were many novices too, saffron clad and shaven headed, who like their elders moved about the courtyard with an air of indifference.

Ngam pointed out that there was no grass or tilled land in the temple area; he explained that a priest could not till land in case he killed a living creature. Every morning he trudges round the streets of the city with a begging bowl. He eats just before noon, then fasts until sunrise the next morning.

A curious feature of the pagodas of one particular temple is the flower ornamentation produced by breaking coloured plates into segments and sticking them onto the stonework, so that each piece makes a petal of a flower. The multi-coloured pattern is gaudy but effective. In some places plates and small bowls have been stuck on whole.

Motoring in Bangkok was a nightmare. Children ran loose by the thousand along thoroughfares and backstreets; reckless rickshawists jogged along with indefatigable tourists, and sweating trishawists cycled menacingly along the middle of the street. The worst offender of all was Bangkok's latest innovation—the motorcycle-shaw, which roared down the main street demanding sole claim to the crown of the road. Mudguards were the first things to drop off any of these two or three-wheeled vehicles in the city. Our jeep knocked two off a couple of rickshawists who came a little too close. In the heat of the argument between trishawists, rickshawist and inquisitive Thais, I was able to slip away unnoticed.

"The Venice of the Orient"—so say all the tourist brochures on Bangkok. Modern roads have replaced many of the old canals but there is still a lot of water traffic. Chandram's sister arranged a river trip for me one morning. The little motor craft left the Palace wharf at dawn. Half an hour later we were threading through Bangkok's floating market. The city's large floating population always paddles to this narrow waterway at daybreak. People buy and sell fruit, groceries, vegetables, clothes and household utensils. Canoes passed us with barely an inch of freeboard, piled high with small bananas, *rambutans* and pawpaws. There were umbrellas up to protect fish and other perishable goods from the watery sun. One craft was loaded with a multitude of spices meticulously set out in little trays. A floating coffee stall and a sweet shop had their oars entangled.

Then along came a leviathan of a wood barge, almost as broad as the river itself, pushing her nose through the crowd of small floating shops.

Thai boatmen stand up to row. A small barge has two oarsmen, one in the bows, the other in the stern. Their sixteen-foot oars are quite unwieldy in the market and cause a succession of water traffic jams.

One day Ngam suggested I should have a go at Television.

"What? Television in Thailand?"

"Of course," he smiled back. Life wasn't so primitive here as most foreigners thought. So off we drove to the T.V. studios.

Once inside the building Ngam soon enthused a programme producer with my story. "Just the sort of person we need for 'What's My Line?'" he said. Two nights later I was facing a panel chosen to guess my occupation—globetrotter. To my astonishment at the end of the show, a Swiss business man on the panel handed me a cheque—his own fee of two pounds. "I'm not allowed to earn anything outside my business. Usually give this sort of thing to charity; I think your cause is worthy enough."

I came away from the studios that night £5 the richer.

"The Amazon" was the topic of a second television broadcast a few days later. Unfortunately, between the interviewers and translators, things got slightly mixed up; "blowpipes" became "bagpipes" and "loincloths" were mysteriously turned into "kilts", and half the audience must have thought that I was roughing it in Scotland.

Chandram commiserated with me afterwards. "Cheer up, it's another three pounds towards your expenses and that's quite a lot of money in Thailand."

Between Thailand and Burma there is no railway, let alone a road. The infamous Burma-Siam railway attempted by the Japanese during the second world war was never completed. The two countries are divided by jungle-clad mountains whose few forest tracks are strangled by undergrowth. Their capitals are three hundred miles apart, but the sea voyage round the southern tip of the Malay peninsula is nearly two thousand miles and takes two weeks. I couldn't afford to waste that time at sea. It was either an air trip or nothing. I always anticipated the worst in asking airlines for a free lift.

Several of the international airlines said that they would be delighted to help me but . . . They would quote the usual deterrent—an agreement prohibiting them from granting gratis passages. I dropped in on the traffic manager of B.O.A.C., who only reiterated the theme. "Sorry, old chap, but we're in the same boat as the rest of them." However, he was just off to Thai Airways and said I could come along if I liked. "I'm not in a position to help you directly, but the least I can do is to introduce you to someone who might."

The smiling manager of Thai Airways required only the briefest explanation from me before deciding that now I had got this far, they would do all they could to assist me over the next stage. "You can go on next Friday's flight to Rangoon. That will be October 1st." The Thais who had given me a memorable two weeks inside their country were extending their generosity by giving me a lift out as well.

Though the flight lasted only 100 minutes I landed in Rangoon feeling that I was in quite another part of the world. In a sense my feeling was justified. The cultures of Burma and Thailand have a common origin, but their rivalry throughout the centuries has resulted in a striking contrast. Thailand, once completely oriental in its outlook and one of the few countries in South East Asia to remain uncolonised, has rapidly adopted western ideas and customs; but Burma, in stretching her legs as an independent nation, has shied away from new contacts with the old European colonial powers. In Bangkok there was an atmosphere of bustling prosperity. In Rangoon there was dirt and dishonesty, the fungi of lethargy and decadence. Filth and garbage were left to accummulate on the streets, symbolizing the incompetence of the administration. This was before the days of military rule.

I spent the night at the Green Hotel. This I was told was once clean and smart by oriental standards, but all principles of hygiene had disappeared with the Raj.

Brooding over my breakfast cup of coffee I wondered where to go for advice. Now that I was in Rangoon, the problem was to get out, and on to India. The sooner the better. In Singapore someone had given me an introduction to a Mr. Ohn Ghine, one of the managers of Mackinnon's, the shipping agents. He seemed to be the only person who might help me to pick up an India-bound freighter.

I made for his office after breakfast. The pot-holed streets were packed with people. A naked infant sitting on his mother's shoulders thrust out an arm at me and mumbled "dada, dada," the mother expecting me to press a few small coins in his grubby hand. Beggars, when they saw that I was a "new boy", trailed after me for the rest of the day, but received little for their labours.

I found Mr. Ohn Ghine busy at his desk, but not too immersed in work to listen to my plans. "So you want to cross the bay to India. We might be able to help you. You had better have a word with Mr. Hancock, our director." He lifted the receiver. "Hello, Ohn Ghine here; got a young Englishman who'd like to see you. Shall I send him along?" He rang off and called a boy. "Show this gentleman along to Mr. Hancock's room please."

The director seemed only too anxious to help. He felt sure they could find something sailing for Calcutta before long. "In the meantime you must come and stay with us. We've a spare room in our flat above and my wife and I would be delighted to have you."

From an absolute stranger this hospitality seemed unbelievable.

"Pity you weren't here last week," he went on. "Had one of our own ships sailing for India; still there are several others in port and there's no harm in asking their skippers."

The captains of two of these vessels were not interested. I tried my luck on a third, fully expecting to be rebuffed again. An impeccably-dressed Chinese steward stood like a waxwork, at the head of the gangway.

"The captain, please."

He bowed respectfully, beckoning me to follow him.

We found the skipper seated at the table in the chief engineer's cabin, surrounded by a battalion of empty bottles. "Who are you and what do you want?" he bellowed, sounding in a thoroughly bad temper. My hope dwindled still further.

In five minutes he knew my story. He also wondered how much of it was true.

"You want to go to Calcutta and say you are a student? Won't give me any trouble with the immigration officers if I decide to take you, will you?" He patted his midriff to ease down another pint.

"No, captain. All my travel documents will be in order. An Englishman doesn't need a visa for India anyway."

"Of course, of course, I know that. You don't need to tell me," he shouted. An awkward pause followed while he gazed vacantly at the diminishing pint in front of him. I hoped it might give him inspiration. If only the chief engineer would top it up.

"All right then, come back in the morning, early, mark you, and I'll let you know."

The night seemed to drag on interminably and I prayed that the Old Man would be in a better mood in the morning. It was getting on for dawn before I dropped off to sleep.

I arrived early as arranged. Not so the captain. He appeared at five o'clock in the afternoon. Even then he wouldn't say anything until he had gulped down a tankard of beer. Then he wiped his mouth on the cuff of his jacket and shouted, "Boy! . . . Boy!" a dozen times over, until a cringing Chinese steward appeared in the doorway. "Boy, bring another pint o' beer for our new passenger."

Relief!

"Here, sign this to say you're coming with us and that you've paid one *kyat* for your fare." That was 1s. 6d., not much to worry about. "You can forget about the *kyat*. Come on, drink up. Can't celebrate all day. We leave the day after tomorrow. If you're not on board we won't wait."

The British Council heard that I was in Rangoon. They realised that I should have to earn some *kyats* to keep alive in the city and promptly arranged a lecture for me in one of the Burmese schools, at a fee of three pounds. Afterwards I was taken to the University and introduced to some of the students. They were all standing about the courtyard involved in fierce arguments.

"No work today?" I asked one of them jokingly.

"That's right. We're taking the day off. We are on strike."

"On strike? Who called you out?"

"The Students' Union, of course. We want longer vacations and less work."

I laughed.

"The Union will stick up for our rights," the student assured me. Their rights appeared to be getting out of hand. I learnt that on one occasion the papers of an important examination had been published beforehand; if "rights" went this far there was no telling where they would finish up. Students in Burma seemed to hold the same fervent nationalist aspirations as those in Malaya.

I approached the influential *Nation* with a fifteen-hundred-word manuscript. The paper seemed interested, and generously parted with a hundred *kyats* for the article. They would have been more than welcome had I received them a little earlier, but as I was leaving the country the next day I should have to waste them on a night of riotous living. The trouble with that idea was that people just don't live riotously in Rangoon. Burmese *kyats* are no use outside Burma, and to change them into dollars or pounds inside the country was bad economy as one lost about half of them on the free exchange rate. Someone advised me to buy a ruby in the market, but it was likely that I'd walk off with a fine piece of coloured glass instead.

Mr. Ohn Ghine offered the best solution. "Why not buy some Burmese bronzes? They will keep their value wherever you go. I'll get one of my boys to show you the best place to buy a couple."

It was good advice and I sunk my profits (£10) in two heavy bronze dancing figures.

At sundown on my last evening in Rangoon I removed my shoes and trudged barefoot through garbage up the 166 steps to the foot of the Shwe Dagon pagoda that towers 326 feet above the city. It is built in tiers of gilded blocks surmounted by a giant pinnacle and at the very top glistens the Hti, the gold-plated umbrella inlaid with diamonds, rubies and emeralds. This immense edifice is the pride of the Burmese, "built over eight hairs from the head of Buddha." My guide said there was a rumour that the person carrying the hairs from Buddha's head, two thousand years ago, was robbed of them on his way to Rangoon, and was forced to substitute eight from his own head. Whatever the legend, the Shwe Dagon stands for the Burmese nation as the symbol of faith and it would be a national disaster if it were destroyed.

I saw an old lady in a corner struggling to lift a heavy stone.

The guide told me it was a wishing stone. "You wish first and then try to lift it. If you succeed your wish will come true."

"And if you don't?"

"You are demanding too much of Buddha."

Someone else knelt down to have a go, but I suspect she tried to lift the stone before having her wish, just to make sure it wasn't too heavy.

I was sorry not to spend a few days in Burma's up-country, for without a visit to the Shan States, to Mandalay, to the Lakes, or to Pagan—the ancient city of "four million pagodas", you get a lopsided idea of the Burmese people and their way of life. But I hadn't the time or the money.

Mr. Hancock kindly drove me to the docks. I lugged my bags to the top of the gangway and was about to disappear into this little new world, when someone called out my name from behind.

I turned round.

"I must ask you to come with me. The police wish to see you at once."

"The police? Oh, I'm sorry. The ship leaves in an hour or so. It'll have to wait another time."

"In Rangoon the police do not wait," he snapped back. "They insist that I bring you back with me." I had visions of handcuffs being whisked out at any moment, so refrained from arguing. His superior at the police station came straight to the point.

"Mr. Boyd, we have just read your article in this morning's *Nation*, but we have no documents recording your arrival. How did you enter this country? Who has your papers?"

"I arrived by Thai Airways five days ago. My papers are with the immigration authorities."

"They have no papers for you."

"Well, I'm sorry, they must have lost them."

"Let me see your passport."

After studying all the South American visas at length, he handed it back asking me to show him the Burmese one. When I pointed out the visa and the immigration stamp with "Rangoon Airport" scribbled all over it, he looked confused. Some wretched little official had slipped up somewhere. Taking the opportunity offered by the embarrassing silence, I asked if I could go now. "My ship is waiting for me if she hasn't already sailed," I added testily.

The officer apologised for the trouble that had occurred and drove me to the ship in one of the police cars.

12

" . . . AND INDIA MYSTIFIED ME"

October 5th, 6th and 7th. Three blank pages in my diary. Three carefree days afloat, about which I can remember little. Perhaps this was because of the drinking. There was lager from the Old Man, rum punches from Sparks, and beer, gallons of it, from the second mate who kept a steady flow going in his cabin. The boys of the China coast were the sort of chaps that give Britain a reputation in the orient. They were always very generous to me.

The "boys" taught me their signature tune, the printable verses of which went like this:

> When the home firms show a marked disinclination
> to fill your guts and pay your monthly hire,
> You are down and out, and so in desperation
> You write to Messrs . . . . and Esquire.
> You find them a most obliging sort of people,
> they pack you off to China in a trice.
> With a ten-pound note to spend on your voyage,
> ten more upon arrival—ain't it nice?
>
> So you join the band of booze-broken heroes,
> Well here's to the bran' new second mate.
> Sit down and have a whisky and soda while the
> Joys of the China Coasting I relate.
> Some evening perhaps you will lay a'dreaming
> On memories' wings perchance you'll homeward fly.
> When through your door a little voice comes stealing,
> "Secn'd Officer, what ting you wanchee my?"
>
> Ah, take no heed, be firm and shun temptation,
> For pain awaits you sometimes if you fail.
> Now I myself in one unguarded moment,
> But no! it pains me yet to tell the tale.

What's that you say? "Am I fed up with China?"
Well, guess one has oneself to blame,
But even then it has its compensations,
Press the bell, "Two-piece more boy, all the same."

In came the Chinese steward carrying two more glasses brimming with Scotch. Down it goes the same way as all the others and you retire to your cabin forgetting even the five-course lunch awaiting you in the saloon. In spite of our erratic hours the Chinese stewards continued to give us excellent service—far better than on any other ship I had known.

I discovered that one of the officers had been christened twenty-five years back by my father in Hendon Parish Church, and he had gone to the same school as my elder brother.

The second mate told me to watch out for bodies floating down the Hoogly river. We saw dead cattle, pigs and dogs borne seaward by a swift current, but nothing else, thank goodness. The second officer assured me that during festival time, human corpses were a common sight on this river.

A few hours in Calcutta reduced me to a state of irritable frustration. Indian immigration officials would point to a rule in a book with infuriating obstinacy. Taxi drivers would say, "Yes, I know where you want," and I would land up at some spot miles from my destination, that is if the taxi hadn't broken down on the way. An outstretched hand pursued me down every street and at night-time I stumbled over bodies lying on the pavement. I had over-estimated the attractions of Calcutta, it seemed.

Some three weeks before, in Ipoh, Malaya, I had been given an introduction to a family in Barrackpore, one of Calcutta's dormitory towns. I telephoned and introduced myself (I had grown quite un-abashed at doing this sort of thing now). Yes, they had heard from their Malayan friends, and would be delighted to see me. Within an hour of stepping ashore I was sitting before a delicious curry that gave me nightmares throughout the night.

Before breakfast next day I opened up my money pouch and spread out the contents on my bed—*yens*, *hwans*, Canadian and U.S.A. dollars, Straits dollars, *soles*, *cruzeiros*, *kyats*, *rupees* and ticuls, even a Russian rouble. At a rough guess I had about thirty-two pounds. A good sum, but not quite enough. There was still a fair part of the world to cover before I set eyes on the cliffs of Dover, and if I wanted to do any travelling in India, I should have to swell the money-bag, and that meant work. In India, like everywhere else in the East, it isn't profitable to take up a labouring job, even if there is one available. So I tried the usual resort.

At the *Statesman's* offices, I sat with an editor pouring out stories of my travels. "At the end of twenty hectic minutes," Desmond Doig wrote in the newspapers next day, "I was so saturated with news that my eyes would have been the better for windscreen wipers." He had accumulated plenty of material for an article.

He asked me. "How much do you want for all this information?"

"I don't want any cash. Just an air ticket to Darjeeling. After all it would be a great pity to be in India and miss the Himalayas, especially after arriving in such a roundabout manner."

The editor was flabbergasted.

"So you want an air passage to the hills. That's all!"

He stopped suddenly and smiled, "Well I suppose it would be a pity to miss the sight of Kangchenjunga, though there's no guarantee that you'll actually see it. There's a lot of cloud about at this time of year. The *Statesman* can help you get there. The rest is up to the weather."

I grasped enthusiastically at the offer before he had time to change his mind. "Can we telephone the airline company from here and book the passage straight away?"

Doig lifted the receiver and asked for Indian Airlines. Every seat in the Darjeeling plane had been booked for the coming week. I couldn't believe this. "I'm going round to see for myself," I told him. The editor wished me luck. He would be very surprised if I could pull anything off.

Why my case should demand priority I cannot imagine, but as I stormed into the offices of Indian Airlines, I was sure it did.

Few of the officials agreed with me. But surely I could convince the traffic manager that my case was sufficiently urgent for him to surrender a seat in the plane usually reserved for last minute V.I.P.'s.

"All right, ALL RIGHT!" he shouted in desperation after I had bombarded him for half an hour. "I've had enough. You're on tomorrow's flight."

My Darjeeling trip began at two-thirty p.m. the next day.

After flying at eight thousand feet over the flooded Delta lands of the river Ganges the 'plane dropped onto the runway at Bagdogra three hundred miles north of Calcutta. There wasn't a mountain in sight.

"Well, where's Darjeeling?" I sighed impatiently, dismayed at the flatness of the surrounding lands. A fellow passenger overheard my remark.

"We're only at the foot of the mountains," he explained and pointing northwards added, "Darjeeling lies over there."

I gazed at the rolling cumulus clouds, and concluded that was all I should be seeing of the Himalayas.

Outside the little airport there were a few shooting-brakes and trucks. "Did you book a car seat?" asked the passenger.

Nobody in Calcutta had told me about booking a seat.

"Try to squeeze into ours then," he suggested. A long argument ensued with the driver who insisted that he was contravening the law by taking more than six passengers in his communal taxi, but an experienced tea-planter handed him a few rupees and he soon forgot about the law.

Delip Bose, the *Statesman* correspondent in the hill station of Darjeeling gave me a great welcome at his home even though he hadn't known I was coming. I handed him a letter of introduction from Desmond Doig.

Delip Bose was a Nepalese of high birth and extremely polished manners. I think the air does something to people in the high Nepal. Perhaps typical of people living in a bracing mountain climate, he was extremely alert and intelligent. Black hair, curling a little at the edges, framed a deeply sunburnt face. His eyes reminded me of a shrewd old don who sums up pupils at one glance. He was smartly dressed in black ankle-length gaiters and a frock coat that ended just short of his knees. He talked very rapidly with complete mastery of English.

Folding up the letter with his long sinewy fingers, he said of course I could stay as long as I wished. "Desmond often springs surprise visitors on us but he has never sent us a young Englishman before. My son Arup will be home in a few minutes. I know he will be delighted to see you."

Like every visitor to Darjeeling, I sat on the summit of Observatory hill at five o'clock in the morning waiting for the celebrated view of the mountains to unfold. I had heard so many descriptions of the mystery of the Himalayas, and of the sunrise over their peaks. Now as Kangchenjunga glowed a deep red long before the sun broke the horizon, I had that electrifying sensation of excitement and awe. Slowly as the sun rose the snows changed imperceptibly through tones of purple, pink, orange, yellow and finally to a blue-white glow. Then the clouds, as though this sight was too much for human eyes, slowly rose from the valleys and hid the mountain, ending my brief glimpse of the forbidden lands of Tibet. This was the spectacle that had lured me into the hills.

When I returned for breakfast, Delip Bose said I must meet Sherpa Tensing before I left. "Why don't you call on him sometime before midday? He's sure to be in then. Arup will take you."

I was very interested to meet Tensing, who is a quiet, unassuming sherpa, living a comparatively simple and contented life with his family. He showed us round his home. He was running a mountaineering school, lending out mountaineering and camping equipment to amateurs. Arup asked him if he had any thought of giving up climbing. He smiled.

"No, not yet. There are still some peaks to be conquered. I keep in training on the smaller ones." They were the twenty-two- and twenty-three-thousand-foot size.

Another foreigner called on him while we were there. As with everyone who knocks on Tensing's door, he was welcomed like an old friend rather than a stranger. I hoped for Tensing's sake, however, that this man was not typical of his visitors, because he appeared determined to probe until he discovered whether Tensing or Hillary had reached the top of Everest first. "We did it together," came Tensing's patient reply, "but perhaps you have not read my book?"

The Siliguri-Darjeeling railway captivates all who see it for the first time. No one can resist the temptation to take a return ticket to Goom, the next station along the line, just for the fun of riding on it. A narrow-gauge railway, it starts at the foot of the Himalayas and climbs the 7,000 feet to Darjeeling. The engines must have been inspired by Emmett. Two men sat on a small platform at the front of the train as it came along Darjeeling's main street.

I asked Arup what they were doing there, and he seemed surprised at such a naïve question.

"Don't your trains have them?" he exclaimed in astonishment. "They sprinkle sand on the track to stop the engine slipping when the rails are wet. Most of them pinch a bagful or two of coal from the engine and sell it to their relatives along the track." The line follows the road most of the way. One of the hairpin bends is so sharp that the engine is on top of the bridge while the last carriage runs beneath it.

I found a couple of days of mountain air very refreshing after the debilitating climate of the lowland cities. Then Indian Airlines flew me back to Dum Dum, Calcutta. I hadn't been in Barrackpore five minutes before an officer of the Ghurkas invited me to watch the climax of the nine-day festival of the Dashera.

"The celebrations begin in about an hour's time, so don't be too long dressing," he said.

I hadn't much choice of dress, but rigged myself up in a green cummerbund with a borrowed pair of evening trousers.

The Dashera originated in the reign of King Dasrath in the Silver Age of the sun tribes. It commemorates two heroic fights, one between King Dasrath's son Ramchandra and the giant Rawan, the other between the goddess Durga and the giant Mahashishura. Ramchandra disposed of his giant easily enough but Durga's struggle with Mahashishura was long-lasting.

There was once a man called Rambha who had been granted a boon by the goddess Brahma. This boon was that no member of the opposite sex could resist him. Returning from a pilgrimage, Rambha attracted a most beautiful milk white cow, who followed after him. When the shepherds and the buffaloes saw what had happened they rose up and killed Rambha and placed him on a funeral pyre. During the sacrifice, the milk-white cow leapt into the midst of the flames and from their ashes was born a terrifying buffalo-headed demon, Mahashishura. Now Mahashishura himself asked a boon of Brahma, that he should not be killed by any member of the opposite sex. This granted, he set upon the goddess Brahma herself and overpowered her. The goddess at once appealed to the Hindu Trinity and in answer to her prayers a beautiful maiden appeared whose name was Durga, to slay this terrible monster. Durga had three eyes and eighteen arms, and each god gave her his own particular weapon until she had one in each hand. Mounted on a lion she set out to kill Mahashishura. On the eighth day of the battle, Durga fasted and made an offering of a black goat, and on the morning of the ninth day she rose up and slew Mahashishura with her *kukri*.

The celebrations commemorating this victory began with old tribal dances in Nepalese costume, men impersonating women. The climax of the Dashera came next day with the sacrifice of the buffalo. The Ghurkas tied the animal to the *maula*, a wooden post. The priest asked for blessings on the buffalo and on the *kukri* of the man who had been chosen to make the sacrifice. Then with one mighty blow of the *kukri*, the buffalo's head was severed from his body. There was a volley of firing from the squad behind the executioner, a burst of cheering from the onlookers. Mahashishura was dead.

After the festival one of the camp officers came up to me. "Heard you were hoping to reach Bombay," he said in a tone which suggested that he had constructive ideas on the subject. "I've an acquaintance in the local airlines who thinks he can get you an air trip. Told me to let him know by this morning if you wanted him to try for it."

I jumped at the opportunity.

"Thanks a lot for asking. Can you contact him now?"

"Certainly. Come back to the office with me and I'll put a call through."

I nearly missed the plane. Knowing what Calcutta's cab drivers are like, I ordered three different taxis to take me out to Dum Dum. One did turn up at the door, an hour late. The accelerator need hardly have been there at all. We jogged along the road at an infuriating twenty miles an hour whilst the time before the plane departure whittled away. We reached the airport with less than five minutes to go. I leapt out, handed the driver ten rupees and told him to keep the change.

"Thirty-five rupees," he shouted, leaping out of the cab after me. "Three pounds? Damn ridiculous," I snorted at him, handed over another ten rupees, and strode off. He spat a few oaths after me.

The aircraft taxied onto the runway just after I had clambered aboard and soon the lights of Calcutta glittered like bright little mosaics, several thousand feet below us.

We touched down at Jodhpur for one of those ridiculous early morning breakfasts that airlines delight in giving their passengers, at 2 a.m.

A comment on the smallness of Indian eggs started off a conversation with a fellow traveller. He introduced himself as Ted Godden and back in the plane we discovered that we had a mutual friend in England, which made talking easy.

"Let me know if I can be of any use to you," he said as we parted at Bombay airport. He was staying at the Taj and would be delighted to see me any time.

"Thanks. I'll make a point of looking you up when I've got everything fixed."

The airport bus dropped me off in the centre of the city. I walked to the Salvation Army Hostel and found a bed for the night. Then I turned to the ever-present question—the route back home.

Six weeks before at Kuala Lumpur station I had toyed with the idea of returning across central Africa. In Singapore the idea was nearer to becoming a reality. The consul there had posted my application for a Congo visa to Belgium. Letters of good conduct and financial guarantees had, I hoped, flown between London, Singapore and Brussels, and if nothing had gone wrong, I should be able to pick up the visa in Bombay. I arrived at the door of the Bombay Belgian Consulate, after journeying three thousand miles, within one day of the agreed date—October 16th. For once everything had gone as planned.

"Ah, Mr. Boyd," the secretary greeted me. "We have just received permission from Brussels to grant you a visa. The vice-consul here is very interested in your trip and he wishes you *bon voyage* through the Congo."

It was wonderful to find the consular authorities so co-operative for a change. I was ushered into the office of the vice-consul.

"What are your plans for reaching the Congo?" he asked me.

"I'm looking for a freighter sailing to the East African coast. Probably hop off at Mombasa or Dar-es-Salaam, then hitch-hike westwards through Uganda."

It sounded a bit happy-go-lucky to the consul, but it appealed to his imagination. I handed over four dollars, and page twenty-eight of my passport was immediately impressed with the Belgian Congo Stamp.

Bombay shimmered under a cloudless sky. It appeared to be siesta time, but I couldn't afford to rest until I had arranged something definite in the way of a passage to Africa. I thought signing-on a freighter here would be an easy task compared with my experiences of leaving England. I was over-optimistic.

To begin with only two companies ran a regular service to Africa. One of them had nothing leaving Bombay for a month. The other listed a vessel sailing for Mombasa in a couple of days' time, but nothing else for three weeks after that. I hurried along to the agents hoping they could squeeze me aboard. The assistant manager of the line saw me right away. He heard the whole story from small beginnings in Oxford down to the possibility of sailing on his ship. At the end of it he pointed out that I was a European, and couldn't possibly work on one of their vessels.

19. Two gentlemen guard an entrance to the temple of the reclining Buddha at Bangkok.

20. Prayer time at the Shwe Dagon, Rangoon.

21. Sherpa Tensing with his family at Darjeeling, India. Mrs. Tensing is second from the left.

22. On the Darjeeling railway.

"Could I travel as a supernumerary then?"

"Certainly not. We don't give free rides."

I held back a retort, and said instead that I might just be able to afford the deck passenger fare, depending on the charge.

"Depending on nothing of the sort," he snapped. "Deck space is reserved exclusively for non-Europeans."

I was thwarted at every turn and began to lose patience. But one had to be humble about asking favours, so I tried to keep calm.

"Can you give me just one helpful suggestion?" I asked meekly.

He couldn't, and in desperation I asked to see the manager.

He didn't think that would help me. We sat looking at each other. At last he broke the silence.

"Actually, you know, it's not that we don't want to help you. And it's not the company's fault. When you reach Kenya the authorities will ask to see a letter guaranteeing you a bond of a hundred and fifty pounds. Without that they won't let you in, and so no shipping company will consider your application for a ticket."

This surprising piece of news gave the situation an unexpected twist. That a British subject couldn't enter Kenya for one week without putting up this colossal bond was the very last restriction I expected. Hurriedly I scribbled off a letter to a school friend in Kenya asking him whether his father could put up a bond for me, but for all I knew the family had probably left the colony years before. They were the only people I knew there.

It would take a week at least to get a bond from Kenya; a speedy departure from Bombay was out. I could be sure of one thing, it would not be easy to leave for Africa by sea.

That day my financial troubles came to a head.

They had begun about a week back when I had unofficially changed my Straits dollars, some twenty pounds, into Indian rupees. Now, when I tried to convert the rupees into sterling or U.S. dollars, at a rate that I considered economic, the money changers were unwilling to part with their meagre hoards of dollars and pounds without making hugh profits for themselves. In desperation I rather unwisely called at the Federal Reserve Bank for advice. Before I knew what was happening, I found myself in the presence of the chief cashier. There was no escape and I had to tell him of my plight. Then came the awkward questions.

"Where did the money come from in the first place? ...

"Why haven't you the currency declaration form that all visitors complete at the port of entry?" I had no answer.

"Of course," continued the cashier, "you realise that foreigners can only bring ten pounds cash into India?"

Of course I realised, and it would be foolish to deny that I had broken regulations because I had twenty pounds in my pocket which I wanted to convert. I couldn't say I had earned it in the country because that would be another regulation broken, as non-immigrants are not allowed to work for payment. I admitted my mistake, and awaited the results.

The cashier evidently appreciated my frankness. He ended the interview by handing me twenty pounds in travellers' cheques in return for my bundle of rupees. My faith in human kindness was revived.

Now for the main objective—Africa.

Back in the hostel, two Nepalese students came over to my table and asked me what I was doing that evening. They were going to the Bombay Youth Congress, and asked me to join them. The Youth Congress was a form of students' Union.

Off I went for a lively evening's discussion with Bombay students and forgot the setbacks of the day. Most of the students I met were full of praise for Britain and her services to India. Some even appeared to regret her departure.

Early next morning I walked into the Taj Mahal Hotel, and asked if I could see Mr. Godden. The receptionist telephoned his room and back came an invitation for me to join him over breakfast.

"Hullo. Good to see you again."

"You, too." I sank into a luxurious armchair.

"Well, what's up?" he asked. My face must have looked very gloomy. "Something wrong?"

"Everything's as wrong as it could be. I'm no nearer to Africa than when we parted at the airport."

He was sympathetic over my difficulties.

"Tried the airlines at all?"

I brightened at this suggestion. "Hadn't really thought of it. They're usually the last resort."

"Well, it looks as though the time has come to try the last resort. I know the manager of Air India International."

I stared at him in astonishment.

"When we're through with breakfast I'll take you along to meet him."

But at the A.I.I. offices that old, familiar regulation reared its ugly head. They were not allowed to grant me a concession passage. But at least they had some suggestions.

"How about tackling a travel agency or trading merchants? Jeena and Company for instance, importers, travel agents."

"Jeena's!" interrupted Mr. Godden. "Of course, why didn't I think of them before? Know them very well. Just the sort of firm which might be glad to help."

Mr. Godden certainly had some useful contacts, and as we walked out of A.I.I. and into the offices of Jeena and Company, I prayed that this one would carry the day.

The director, Mr. Katgaran, listened politely while his friend outlined my problem.

He was astonished that I had managed to reach Bombay at all on five pounds and looked encouragingly impressed, but that may have been due to Mr. Godden's enthusiastic narration.

Mr. Katgaran turned to me, beaming. "Well, suppose we decide to help you reach Africa. How would you set about repaying us the seventy-five pounds' worth of kindness?"

How on earth? I realized that the whole success of my venture depended on my answer, but I felt that nothing I could say would win me a ride three thousand miles out of Bombay. But I had to say something and it was worth a try.

"Of course, the article I'm writing for a Bombay newspaper," I replied, warming to the theme, "could end up with 'the kindness and generosity of Jeena and Company has saved me from the dismal prospect of walking the streets of Bombay'."

Mr. Katgaran looked at Mr. Godden and they both laughed.

"All right, Mr. Boyd. It's as you say. Through the kindness and generosity of our company you will be having tea in Nairobi tomorrow. Good afternoon, gentlemen."

13

SNOW WHITE

The Air India plane touched down on the city runway. We arrived, as Mr. Katgaran had promised, in time for tea. The immigration officers held me up at the airport, tackling me about the financial bond the moment I stepped off the plane.

"I haven't procured it in writing yet," I hedged, "but I know Colonel Rubea and I'm sure he'll let me have it the moment he hears that I've landed."

"That's no good to me," retorted the officer. "You should have obtained the bond before you left Bombay. I can't let you into the country until I have the guarantee from this Colonel whatever-he-is."

"Oh, yes you can, officer," a voice suddenly boomed out from behind me. I turned round to see who had come to my aid and collided with a six-inch handlebar moustache.

"Cool down a bit, officer," its owner continued. "Never heard such a fuss. Of course you can stamp the lad's passport. I'll guarantee his bond here and now."

"Oh, thanks very much, sir. . . ."

"Nothing, nothing at all," he swept aside my thanks. "So happens I know the colonel," he added, flicking imaginary dust from his lapel. "Delighted to help a friend of his. The name's Carr Saunders," and he handed me a handsome card bearing the inscription "Carr Saunders. Big Game Hunter". I was speechless. He flashed me a crocodile-size grin, ignored the officer and strode off. I got into the A.I.I. car and we made for the town.

Children, black and white, thronged the pavements of the city waving Union Jacks. I smiled and waved back. Nairobi's streets were decked with multi-coloured bunting and striped awnings. Enormous signs stretched across the road proclaiming "Welcome, Welcome to Nairobi". As our car entered Delamere Avenue still larger crowds of children and even groups of adults craned their

196

necks as if to get a good look at me. All the time I was aware of a complete absence of any other traffic. Suddenly, halfway down Delamere Avenue, the chauffeur braked. We stopped within a few inches of a huge white glove. The policeman strode towards us. "Excuse me, sir," he said pompously. "Unless you are on priority business I must ask you to leave the boulevard at once."

"Well, judging by the number of people who've turned out to welcome me to Nairobi," I answered jokingly, "I'm beginning to think that my business must be of extreme importance."

The policeman did not appreciate the joke. His eyes nearly burst out of his head. "I don't know what you are talking about. But I should be obliged if you would leave this route at once." He rattled off something in Swahili to the driver.

Then he stuck his nose in the air, and proclaimed in a voice louder than was necessary, "We are expecting Her Royal Highness, the Princess Margaret through here at any moment."

Just as he made this dramatic announcement faint cheering started in the distance.

We retired in confusion.

The Air India driver dropped me at the Woodlands Hotel. "This place very good, not too much money."

I lugged my bags up the stairs and rang the bell. The door was thrown open.

"Did you see her? Wasn't she lovely? Just like her Mum."

I recoiled from this gushing outburst.

"A room for three days?" the receptionist babbled. "Certainly. She looked radiant with beauty at the railway works. You did say you wanted it for three weeks? Been there all morning, she has. Didn't you know?"

"Poor soul," I sympathised with the Princess. "She must have been bored stiff. Walking between rows and rows of bogey wheels."

The receptionist looked shocked at my comment. "Never thought of it that way before. 'Course, it must be a tremendous strain on royalty and the like. Still, wouldn't mind doing it myself for a bit, would you?"

"Well, don't know that I could smile for that long."

"Oh, but she does it marvellously. Just like her mother."

She was off again and during the four days I spent in Nairobi no one could talk of anything but Her Royal Highness—how she looked, what she wore, whether she could remain "such an idol of loveliness" under the strain of her ridiculously overcrowded tour.

Nairobi was getting on my nerves already, though it wasn't fair to judge the place under the present circumstances.

Saturday was the great day of the tour for the Europeans in Kenya, who had practically all been invited to the Garden Party.

"You'll be sure to find him at the Party," my landlady told me when she heard that I was looking for Colonel Rubea. I hadn't been invited but I unpacked my tropical suit and ironed out the creases. Government House was just round the corner. Ignoring the coloured arrows directing people and cars to various enclosures, I walked up to a police officer and asked him how to find the Colonel. He took me along to Government House.

After walking through a number of check points, he whispered confidentially in my ear, "We are now outside the V.I.P. enclosure." I hoped that my suit looked up to it.

"Colonel Rubea?" repeated one of the Governor's A.D.C.s. "Yes, he's just arrived. I expect he's in the Royal Enclosure. Is it urgent?"

I paused to rally up enough courage to reply in a grave tone, "Yes, very."

"Follow me through."

We stopped at the enclosure entrance.

"Your name please?"

I pretended not to hear. "Colonel Rubea," I called out across the enclosure.

"Your name, please?" persisted the A.D.C.

"Mr. Boyd, Alistair Boyd," but before he had time to make anything of it, a portly gentleman strode towards us. A detective standing close by was about to turn me away, but the Colonel averted that ignominy.

"Don't worry, officer. Friend of mine, what? I say! Glad to see you again, my boy."

I started on an explanation.

"I'm the chap going round the world and I . . ."

"Oh, so you're the lad who wanted me to put up a bond, eh? My son told me all about you. Your letter from Bombay only arrived this morning. How on earth did you get here so damn soon? And what about the guarantee? Who's done that for you?" I told him what had happened.

"Well, I suppose you're looking for a place to stay. You'd better spend a day or two with us. We've got a place in town for a week."

So Monty Rubea became my host in Nairobi. Like most planters he is usually too preoccupied with what goes on at his estate to spend much time in the city. He prefers to visit his planting friends for tea and thinks nothing of driving a hundred miles for an evening game of tennis.

Nairobi is no longer the home of the planter. Many of today's inhabitants are recent immigrants, engaged in distribution, servicing trades and manufacturing. They have little direct interest in the soil, with the result that the colonial life characteristic of the place in pre-war years had largely disappeared. There is also an un-popular resident in Nairobi—the "poor white", who has settled there for no particular reason but want of somewhere better to go. There will always be a place for him, at the expense of the more intelligent African, in a country where white still dominates black. The "poor whites" are spreading like an infection over Africa and their presence constitutes one of the serious dangers to race relations.

Living in Nairobi was becoming a luxury that I couldn't long afford even with the Colonel's hospitality. Within four days I had run through eight pounds and I'd have to meet increasing expenses somehow. Manual labour is plentiful in Africa so I couldn't resort to that. Instead, I took the usual course and tried a newspaper as well as the radio network run by Cable and Wireless.

Both organisations pleaded poverty. The newspaper's circulation wasn't large enough to warrant a payment of more than three pounds for an article of fifteen hundred words. Fifty shillings was all the radio network ever paid for a talk. This wouldn't get me far in a town where ten shillings barely covered a meal. But I couldn't grumble. I wasn't a journalist—far less a radio star. The Colonel agreed prices were high in Nairobi. The reason was simple, he explained. "We haven't yet attracted the manufacturing trades to the colony. Most things except food have to be imported. If it comes from the west it's good but damned expensive, and most of the cheap stuff that comes from the east suffers from shoddy workmanship. The only way you can mend the hole in your pocket is to leave the place. What's stopping you from striking westward tomorrow?"

Only one thing was stopping me—the usual thing; my visa for French Equatorial Africa wasn't ready.

Monty advised me on the route I should take to the west coast of the Congo. My best way for hitch-hiking lay through Ruanda and Stanleyville. "Stanleyville is about a thousand miles from here.

Should take you two weeks, maybe more; depends on the state of the roads. If there's been much rain, traffic comes to a standstill. A friend of mine transports petroleum for Stanvacs, the Mobiloil people; I'll find out whether they're sending anything through in your direction."

My visa came through the following day. At the same time Colonel Rubea managed to fix up a lift for me in a Fiat leaving Nairobi next morning.

Instead of the little Fiat miniature car I had imagined, it was a petrol carrier loaded with five thousand gallons of high octane. Sharing my wooden perch was a negro twice my size.

The driver was an Italian who understood nothing but his own language and a smattering of Spanish, so our conversation was strained. He had christened the vehicle Brunetti. He was no speed merchant, and the needle flickered round 12 m.p.h. most of the way except when there was a straight downhill stretch of road. A number of vehicles whipped past us and it would have been well worthwhile getting out and thumbing one of them, but I didn't want to offend the driver after he had specially made room for me.

To my relief, however, the truck gathered speed as it crossed the flat floor of the Kenya rift valley. Giraffes poked their crazy necks above the bushes to see who was coming and dust trails rose into the air as the frightened herd took flight.

The Italian said nothing but sang operatic arias as he drove along the Eldoret road well into the night. Twenty miles beyond Nakuru he jammed on the brake at the signal of a lone policeman.

"I'm sorry you can't go further tonight. There has been heavy rain over the mountains and the road is thick mud. You should be able to continue early tomorrow morning."

"But if the rain starts again, what then?" I asked. The policeman just smiled and shrugged his shoulders.

This kind of delay was bound to happen in East Africa. Resigned to the fact that I had made a great mistake in hitch-hiking on Brunetti in the first place, I pulled out my hammock and slung it between the truck and its tender. We were about six thousand feet up. It was bitterly cold. Every time I began to swing, my bottom grazed the rain-soaked grasses, and after a while the damp began to seep through my layers of clothing.

At six o'clock I could no longer kid myself that staying in bed was a pleasure, but we had to wait for three hours before the police would let Brunetti through the barrier, together with six other trucks which had rolled up behind us during the night. Brunetti of course, was the slowest of the bunch and soon found her customary position of last in the convoy.

Only sixty miles had been gained by tea time. There were nine hundred still ahead of me. At this rate of progress I would land up in the Congo around mid-November. I sank into a depression. Then came the rain. We had exchanged the tarmac surface for mud a long way back and now Brunetti started to skid dangerously. We stopped at once.

The driver apologised in his broken Spanish when he saw my dejection, but said we could not drive under these conditions with such a load.

He got out his kettle, collected some damp wood together and ensured a successful fire by flooding it with petrol.

"Tea," he grinned at me. "You like some?"

But I couldn't whip up much enthusiasm for tea at that moment. I asked him whether we'd be on our way again tonight.

I could see his point that we couldn't rush it with 5,000 gallons of petrol, and without more ado I decided to leave Brunetti and hitch-hike a passing car into Kampala. The Italian understood and wished me good luck.

Two National Service boys picked me up in a Citroen and dropped me at Kisumu on the shores of Lake Victoria. I spent the night at a hotel in the Indian quarter.

"Sleep there at your own risk," a police officer had said. "And don't blame me if you get into trouble with the Indians."

Nothing happened, but then that policeman stood on guard outside all night.

The following night I was given a lift into Kampala, largest town in Uganda. The manager of the Imperial Hotel came up to me at the hotel desk. I had been hitch-hiking with a friend of his so he knew all about me. He would be delighted for me to stay the night as his guest.

This generosity saved me from an uncomfortable night on the floor of the local police station. An enormous dinner was included, my first meal in twenty-four hours. The manager suggested that I should leave a note on the hotel notice board asking for any lift in the direction of the Congo. I retired to bed, hoping to make up some sleep.

Next day I was speeding south in a Ford. I hitch-hiked another lift through Ruanda-Urundi, and for the first time on an international frontier line, I wasn't bombarded with questions about my nationality or integrity.

The Belgian mandatory territory of Ruanda-Urundi lies in the very heart of Africa, eight hundred miles from the sea. Its frontiers march on Tanganyika, Uganda and the Congo. A land of volcanoes, simmering and sleeping, it has five and a half million people. The traditional occupation is cattle ranching, but today many of them scratch a living from the terraced mountain slopes. In this 'Switzerland of Africa' old and new live side by side. Against a background of primitive settlements stand the latest in up-to-date hotels; the bamboo round huts of the Watatsi and Batwa look onto striped beach-huts, the ancient fishing craft and thirty-knot speed boats mingle in the same waters. Lake Kiva, once the scene of an old Ruanda-Urundi civilisation, is the playground of the present-day European settler in Central Africa.

The journey through Ruanda-Urundi lasted six hours. We crossed over to the Congo in the late afternoon and I was set down at Rutushuru, a small village.

Truck travelling in the Congo was not cheap. Most lorry drivers demanded payment equal to a pound per hundred and fifty miles. Lorries were few and far between, private vehicles even more so. I stood three hours by the roadside at Rutushuru before having any luck. European hitch-hikers were seldom seen in the Congo. I was accorded the usual open-mouthed interest given to rare specimens, and was becoming rather embarrassed when at last a Belgian stopped and picked me up.

The lift took me as far as Ruindi camp, in the centre of the famous Albert National Park. Our car drew up inside the palisaded encampment and we were greeted by the manager of the camp. He cordially invited us to lunch, for which afterwards I had to pay fifteen shillings.

When I learnt that this was a moderate price for a meal, the hundred and fifty U.S. dollars in my pocket looked very paltry. One month in the Congo might find me on the bum sooner than I expected.

Now I was in the park, I wanted to see some game. I hadn't met a tiger, leopard or a lion yet.

The manager explained apologetically that there wasn't a seat available in either of the cars which took visitors round the park.

"If you had been here last week we could have squeezed you in, but they're both full now. We've two lots of German tourists staying here."

I was very disappointed. A man sitting alone in the corner overheard our conversation. He called me over to his table. A nervous middle-aged Belgian, he introduced himself as Ludvig. He apologised for listening and said he'd have liked to show me the park himself, but must press on north tonight. "I'm going to a small town called Butembo, on the way to Stanleyville, so if you don't mind leaving the camp now you're welcome to come with me. We should see some game on the road."

I agreed to this kindly suggestion at once.

Within a couple of minutes of leaving camp I spotted a herd of elephants. They seemed oblivious of our approach. "Look! elephants!" I said. Ludvig looked round nervously and trod hard on the accelerator.

"Hey, please slow down a bit," I pleaded. "Can't possibly take a picture while you're doing seventy."

"No, no, impossible." He looked terrified. "They are dangerous animals." He told me that last year his brother had stopped for a photograph, only to get an elephant's huge foot stamped through the roof of his car.

My photograph turned out to be a panorama of blurred grasses with no elephant in sight.

The road rose tortuously above the savanna lands of the Albert Game Park. On mountain tracks in the Congo the road divides at the S-bend corners. This was just as well with such a nervous person behind the wheel. I was relieved to arrive intact at a small hotel in Butembo.

A friendly fire blazed in the hotel and we were glad of the warmth although we were on the Equator. The eastern highlands of the Congo are chilly at night. There were a number of other travellers dozing in the chairs round the stove. The atmosphere was one of sleepy serenity, of deep relaxation after the exhaustion of a hard day's driving. Someone switched on the wireless but few bothered to listen. Between the atmospherics I could just make out a hit parade tune over the French programme from Brazzaville, a thousand miles away to the west.

The snow-capped Ruwenzori Range was now to the east and the track dropped down into the tropical forest of the Irumu. At one point Ludvig braked hard as a family party of baboons strolled across the road just in front of us.

"Quick, get the gun from the boot! We go after them." But by the time we had clambered out the baboons had carefully hidden themselves in the greenery. Ludvig fired a few random shots into the jungle but the animals stayed put.

Further on there was a long black line across the road.

"What's that," I asked, "a snake?"

"Ants."

"Ants? Mind if I go and have a closer look at them? Won't be a moment." Ludvig grabbed me back from the door.

"Do not go near. They are deadly creatures. They eat through you very fast."

He drove slowly over the ant trail. There were millions of them, black, the largest half an inch or more in length. With the outsizes flanking the smaller ones in the centre, the deadly column pushed relentlessly across the road.

"How long will that go on for?"

"Days, maybe weeks. I have known trails fifteen kilometres long. Eat anything, everything. And if their trail goes across a village, *c'est la fin*."

We bumped along the mud and gravel road towards Mambasa, swerving to avoid fallen branches and the occasional elephant pat (three feet in diameter). About a kilometre short of Mambasa the car broke down.

The half shaft had broken. "Something like this always happens when you are in a hurry," Ludvig moaned. We were lucky to be near a village, so abandoning the car we walked to Mambasa.

A young planter met us on the road and Ludvig told him what had happened.

"Tough luck," he commiserated, "come and spend the night on my plantation."

Ludvig declined the invitation, preferring to stay in the village hotel, but I accepted eagerly. There was nothing I could do to help Ludvig and he advised me to push on to Stan by myself as it might be a few days before the car was on the road again. So we parted company.

The young proprietor of the plantation, Jean, lived in a wooden chalet. He didn't mention any other inmates; half-way through the night I heard a baby cry, but I thought it tactful not to enquire.

We sat down to a very early breakfast the next morning. "Just started this kind of work, Jean?"

"Yes. At the moment I'm clearing the ground for the coffee trees. I employ about a couple of hundred hands. Pay them fourteen francs—two shillings—a day."

"Is that all?"

"Yes, and that's quite enough. Sounds cheap labour to you, but it's not really. They're lazy and most of them give me so much trouble that they're not worth any more."

Mambasa is a small route-way village straggling along the "main road" at the junction of two routes to Stanleyville, one from Irumu and the other from Beni, on which I had just travelled. Realising that any traffic leaving Mambasa would start early in the day, I dumped my bags on the highway at dawn. Nothing left the town all morning. I waited for midday traffic from Beni and Irumu to roll by. Four trucks came along but not one of them stopped for me. No other vehicle attempted the difficult route to Stanleyville. The blackening cumulus clouds, massing over the brilliant green of the jungle roof, told me the reason. There came the familiar smell of rain—sour, rotten, stifling. A sudden crack of lightning shattered the stillness, and a million birds soared upwards, their cries lost in the roar of the cloudburst. This was the climax of the rains that had turned the Irumi forest into swampland. Any traffic on the road would be stranded, sunk in deep mud. I was soaked to the skin.

No point in waiting by the roadside hoping for more traffic while this lasted. I ran back to the Hotel Les Pygmies where Ludvig had spent the night, and asked if he was still there.

"Sorry, no. Someone called for Monsieur three hours back. To do with his car I think."

I ordered a beer and omelet, and sat down at a table. Pity I had missed Ludvig, but I was glad someone was attending to his car. That made me feel a little less guilty at leaving him here. Now I must seize any opportunity of a lift to Stanleyville. A Belgian army convoy drew up outside. A captain leapt out of the leading jeep and strode up to the bar for a pint. The *maîtresse d'hotel* told him I wanted a lift and he came over to my table.

"Very sorry, we're driving to Butembo, otherwise we should have liked to help you. The road from Stanleyville is very bad. A dozen trucks are down to their axles in mud. They have been there two or three days." He finished his pint, "*Avant santé* to the success of your trip, though I do not think you will make Stanleyville this week."

The kind-hearted *maîtresse* offered me a room without charge, realising that I was forced to stay in Mambasa.

One trucker ignored the advice of his mates and decided to attempt the journey to Stan the next morning. By the time I found him the cabin of the truck was already overflowing with negresses.

"You ride up there," the driver pointed to the cramped space above the cargo. I climbed up and joined another bunch of crouching Congolese. The top deck passengers sat on bags of dried fish and squabbling chickens; from under them came the grunting and squealing of pigs. The smell intensified as we rumbled along. All top passengers were expected to descend and pick jungle greenery for the animals when we stopped. We spent most of the time ducking to avoid the overhanging branches of the jungle.

As we rounded a corner a torrent of water swept across our track. The driver braked, mud oozed up to the wheelhubs and we stuck. Further progress that day was out of the question. I was becoming quite expert at choosing the wrong time of year for my little trips.

I had just hopped off the truck when round the corner glided a low sleek American limousine, scattering watery mud in all directions. It braked suddenly on seeing the river and skidded to a standstill only a few feet from the truck.

I rushed up to the driver's window. "Stanleyville?" A familiar face smiled back at me from behind the wheel.

"Why hallo, Ludvig. Fancy seeing you again."

He grinned. "I did not expect to see you again either," he smiled.

I admired his new car. "Not mine," he explained. "I've borrowed it from a plantation owner near Mambasa. What has happened here?"

"An unmapped river."

"There is one born every day here at this time of year. Come in and we will return to Mambasa. Tomorrow we can try the diversion. It is only two hundred miles out of our way." Ludvig went back to his friends and I spent another night in the Hotel Les Pygmies.

Belgians got moving when it came to road clearance. By the time Ludvig called for me at daybreak the police had announced that yesterday's river had been diverted and the road was fit for light vehicles. We left straight away.

The route to Stanleyville took us through pygmy-land. The pygmies are no longer hidden away in their jungle hide-outs.

They come out on the roads, and many have succumbed to commercialism. The big-hearted tourist says, "Poor little souls, let's give them something," and a handful of francs are thrown from a car window. Easy money. The pygmy decides to look pathetically at the next passer-by. The next passer-by feels sorry, and so does the next, until a hundred-franc note and a packet of cigarettes is considered a mean offer for even one photograph. Cursing all the tourists before me, I followed suit and gave them the customary "little something" for a photograph.

The pygmies make a living out of the forest with the skill of bow and arrow forgotten by most other natives of the Congo. But soon even the pygmies will have no need to remember. They will be able to exist on their tourist trade.

Within a few miles of pygmy-land are the hunting grounds for the okapi—half zebra, half horse—an animal found only in the Congo. Further along the route we drove through Bafwasewende, home of the Mambela and Angote leopard men of the Congo. Ludvig told me that up to this century tribal dissensions and even personal quarrels were solved in a strange manner. The attackers disguised themselves as leopards, wearing real skins and carrying pronged sticks to reproduce the pad marks of a leopard on the ground. Their hands were tipped with metal claws, to tear the flesh off their human prey. By all visible evidence the deaths could be attributed to attack by a leopard.

Midnight chimed across the rapids of the River Congo as we drove into Stanleyville. I was dropped at the door of a Greek hotel-keeper to whom I had been given an introduction by someone in Nairobi. After my repeated thanks, Ludvig accelerated away down the street. That was the last I saw of him.

14

THE CONGO

Stanleyville lies a thousand miles up the Congo. Above the town are the Wagenia Rapids which Stanley discovered on his journey across Africa in 1855. These prevent further navigation up the river.

The town has grown from a nineteenth century colonial outpost into the modern centre of north eastern Congo. Even so, her communications with the rest of the country are very poor. There is no through road to Leopoldville. Traffic goes by air or water.

One day I met an Englishman working for an Indian company that went by the name of Nasser. He learnt that I hoped to pick up a boat going down river to Leopoldville.

"May take the Nasser brothers quite a time to fall in with the idea," he said, "but there's no harm in asking them to help."

The Nasser family lived in a monstrous castle known by most people in Stanleyville as "Nasser's Palace". It breathed opulence. The gardens contained a galaxy of fountains, statuettes and wrought-iron creations. The furnishings inside were equally sensational: geraluminium beds (gold and silver coloured), camphor-wood chests and wall pictures in relief with lights behind them. The clumsy furnishings in most rooms contrasted strangely with one delicate Japanese-style room. A member of the family remarked that they had aimed at contrast in colour and design.

This lavish display of wealth was not reflected in the appearance of the down-town storehouse, which looked like a chaotic antique shop. In the midst of great confusion stood the Nasser brothers' private office—a little tabernacle of a room without windows, draped on all sides with black velvet curtains. Mr. Wilcox took me through the curtains and glass doors. The Brothers Nasser were "at home". Within a few seconds of stepping inside I was freezing. A modern air-conditioning unit had reduced the temperature to arctic conditions. Tennis shoes, elephant tusks, old ladies' garments, shaving cream, fountain pens, watches, trunks and yards

23. Snow White and the Pygmies in the Congo.

24. "In a while . . ." Crocodile stew was sometimes served on the *Colonel Vangele* in the Congo.

25. The paddle steamer *Colonel Vangele* often stopped for firewood.

26. The last voyage —aboard the *Holmgar*.

and yards of cheap printed cloth were all piled high on their modern roll-top desk. But a wide range of private spirits and wines on a shelf implied that business was brisk. The brothers sat with feet up on the desk.

"So you want to reach Leo?" said one of them, removing a long pipe from the corner of his mouth. "I suggest we call on Otraco's, the shipping company. Shall we go now?"

A suffocating blanket of moist heat hit me in the face as we emerged into the 90° F. outside, but the Nasser seemed unaffected.

Our mission to Otraco's was unsuccessful. "My hands are tied by the authorities in Leo," said the Port Administrator. It was obviously the stock answer to an age-old enquiry. Of course if I wanted a cheap trip, he said, I could travel on the negro barge. My enthusiasm was cut short by Nasser's angry dismissal of such a suggestion. But the Administrator wasn't going to help any further. Nasser was very angry and refused to admit defeat. He sent a telegram immediately to the shipping company's head office in Leo, demanding a student concession passage. I wasn't surprised to hear that, "They were sorry but . . ."

"It is always but, but, BUT," Nasser crumpled the telegram between his gross fingers, outraged and humiliated that his name hadn't carried any weight in the company's decision.

After calming down a little he advised me to go straight to the docks and talk with one of the captains, who were better people than shipping managers.

Mr. Wilcox offered to drive me down to the quay and ten minutes later I was sitting in the captain's cabin aboard the s.s. *Colonel Vangele*.

The captain was surprisingly sympathetic and nodded his consent, though officially his hands were tied by the same regulations.

"We shall be glad of your company. We leave tomorrow; the exact time depends on the stevedores."

I told him it was a great relief, and asked how long the journey would take.

He thought about two and a half weeks. The passenger craft did it in five days, but this old tub was only a cargo vessel which stopped at most of the settlements along the river. "She's like an old Mississippi stern-wheeler, the last of her kind on the Congo. Her fuel is wood. We have to collect logs from the forest every other night which always takes a few hours."

The *Vangele* was 120 feet long, square in the bows with a huge paddle in the stern. Her boilers were on deck beneath the wooden-shuttered cabins and the open bridge. The deck round them was cluttered up with tree-trunks. A tall, slender chimney-stack towered above the vessel with wire netting over its flue to prevent pieces of charred wood from flying into the air.

"Please remember you're not on a luxury liner," said the captain. I quickly assured him that as long as I reached Leo safely he wouldn't be hearing any grumbles.

When I returned to the ship with my bags next morning, the two captains (there was an extra captain and co-pilot) and their wives and families were waiting to greet me on the upper bridge, with glasses of beer. In the rush I had forgotten to bring food for the trip. "I'd better dash ashore and get some," I offered, but the captain's wife protested.

"No please. You must come and eat with us on the bridge. There's plenty of food aboard."

Great thumping sounds came from below us all morning as the furnaces were stacked up for our departure. Secured to our starboard was a double-decked negro barge, *Budja*, which we were towing to Leopoldville. She was a removal van as well as a passenger boat. Many of those aboard were moving permanently to Leo in the hope of making a fortune there quicker than in Stanleyville where wages were low and unemployment widespread. At midday the *Vangele* had full steam up and half an hour later she slipped moorings and headed downstream towards Leopoldville.

On most ships, the bridge is the sacred part of the vessel. Officers are addressed as 'sir', conversation is about nautical matters (including women), and but for the officer on watch and the helmsman, who often seem oblivious of each other's presence, everyone stays well clear until his turn for the watch. But on the *Vangele* the bridge was the living quarters for the senior captain, his wife and baby. Meals were served at a table conveniently placed in the centre of the wheelhouse, so that the captain could see during meal times where the helmsman was taking us. "Our helmsmen do not understand 'port' and 'starboard' and are always steering in the wrong direction," he explained.

But it wasn't altogether the fault of the helmsman that the *Vangele* led an erratic course. On one side of him stood an extremely noisy refrigerator that was always going wrong and on the other side a monkey and a cat chased each other around a chair. The baby's toys were scattered in every direction. Some of them littered the base of the telegraph so that every time the captain had to alter speed another treasure was crushed under his foot. The baby's yells were merely intensified when the burly negro steward patted his head. Sometimes when papa wasn't looking, baby decided to take complete control of the *Vangele* by climbing onto the chair and pulling the telegraph backwards and forwards from "full astern" to "full ahead". The exasperated engineers below could only be pacified by an apology from the captain in person.

The captain's wife prided herself on being the cleanest person on board. There wasn't much competition. On alternate days she strung the washing across the entire width of the bridge. This always annoyed the tally clerk who, for some curious reason, had a passion for gazing soulfully into the forest as the boat slid by the river bank. Baby was quite uninhibited, and when wee "accidents" happened on deck they were usually blamed onto the monkey whom no one dared scold on pain of having blood drawn from his arm.

Navigating the Congo was a comparatively easy task compared to the Amazon. The river was sign-posted most of the way, so that you couldn't miss the channel unless you fell asleep. When night fell at six-thirty, as it nearly always does in the tropics, our powerful searchlight easily picked out the illuminated boards against the dark green of the river bank. With these aids, there was no need for a pilot.

The *Vangele* often stopped at small river posts to pick up nuts and sheets of rubber. In these out of the way places labour was so cheap that most of the bulky cargo was shifted by hand.

The captain told me it was more profitable that way. The natives worked on a piece basis. I pointed to a small boy struggling under a hundredweight bag of scrap rubber. "How much do they get for doing that?"

"About a quarter of a cent." That was just under a halfpenny. When there were bags of nuts to shift, stevedores surreptitiously enlarged any small holes in the bags.

At dusk we pulled up by one of the wood piles on the bank. These were stacked by casual employees of the company at intervals of about fifty miles along the river. The procedure was the same at each logging station. For three, five, sometimes seven hours the great sinewy Congolese gathered armfuls of trunks and threw them on to the hollow iron deck, making a loud metallic thud. You soon gave up any thoughts of sleep with that going on. Sometimes I went out and tried to help, struggling hard to lift a single log.

The swift current of the Congo answered the negroes' impatient desire for their womenfolk at Bumba with a speed of twelve knots, bringing us to this wood-and-plaster town in the middle of the afternoon. Twenty yards from the bank three deckhands dived over the side with the mooring ropes and swam towards the shore. There was always a competition to reach the bank first. On this occasion, a dead heat resulted in a scrap.

"*Ah, les femmes!*" exclaimed the tally clerk the moment the boat was secured alongside. "You come too, Mr. Boyd?"

"Where to?"

"The dance hall. Come with us."

As the only European aboard not concerned with the running of the ship, I had been treated in a friendly way by the Congolese who came to me with their grumbles against the captain. Wanting to remain on this friendly basis, as well as curious to see negroes dancing, I agreed to go along with the tally clerk.

The dance hall lay in a quarter of the town reserved for natives. It was open to the elements and lit by a few oil lamps suspended from trees. A few pieces of wood nailed together served for a floor. The men in semi-European clothes and the women in their gaudily printed drapes, danced feverishly as the tom-tom and flute band whipped up the tempo. I was the only European in the hall. Several members of the ship's negro crew were hanging round the entrance when I arrived, debating whether to part with five francs and join the fun. They were wreathed in smiles when they saw I had been persuaded to come, and greeted me with exaggerated warmth in the hope perhaps that I might take them all in.

To the Congolese all white men are wealthy and I had learnt not to display too much money in front of them. I pulled out a five-franc note. Immediately came cries of "Hey, mister, take me in," and "Captain, he pay me money in Leo; I give back."

A wave of generosity took hold of me and I treated them all. No sooner had we sat down than we were joined by the other members of the crew who had been rich enough to pay themselves in but were now broke. No one made a move to order more drink. It was up to me to do my little bit.

"Ten bottles," I shouted to the bar-boy, and suddenly my relationship with those around me became a grand *bonhomie*. Several strangers came up to the table, patted me on the back and gazed dreamily at the bottles, but the *Vangele* crowd made sure that they didn't get away with any swigs.

It doesn't seem to make much difference in the Congo whether you dance solo or with partners. Just keep jigging your arms, legs and bottom in rhythm with the music and you're doing fine. My companions persuaded me to get up and dance as well, but the moment I stood up a dozen negresses flashed enticing smiles towards me and started to wiggle, each hoping I might be induced to favour her. Most couples danced yards apart. This was to allow the lady to swing her hips and revolve her behind, but I soon taught them the European way.

With ten dances to my credit they considered me less of a freak than at first, but they couldn't quite forget that I was white and they were black. At the beginning of the eleventh number, jealousy got the better of two women who had previously danced with me. They began clawing at each other. In the Congo, minor squabbles very quickly turned into heated battles. A negro stepped in between the women in a noble effort to break them apart, but at this intrusion a second leapt up, followed by a third, then a fourth, more and more until they were all on their feet, cat-calling and shaking fists. One smashed a bottle on the table and menaced me as the cause of the trouble in the first place, brandishing the jagged edge of the bottle high above his head.

The dance floor quietened. The patter of tom-toms faded away. Everyone stood waiting while this herculean negro poured forth a volley of oaths. Their meaning was utterly lost on me, which enraged him more than ever. He was about to hurl the bottle when one of the *Vangele*'s crew grabbed his hand from behind. The general uproar recommenced and two or three of the crew hurriedly escorted me out before it was too late.

I sank into my bunk. Just before I dropped off to sleep the captain knocked on my cabin door.

"Ah, I am glad to see you back without any injury."

"What do you mean, captain?"

"I noticed you went ashore with a crowd of Budjas. They are all Budjas in this town, it's their territory. Some of them are savages, believe me. If they have a grudge against a white man they will take vengeance on any white man at the first opportunity. However," he grunted, "I am glad to see that you didn't have trouble. Good night."

"Good night. Thanks, captain."

The story of the Congo's development before its independence in 1960 is largely a story of the missionaries. Above all others they dedicated their lives to civilising and educating the Congolese of the bush. The Baptists were the first to set up stations along the banks of the river. They persuaded the negro to forsake the forest and live in a community where he could enjoy the benefits of a civilized life, leading him from slavery under the witch-doctor to the freedom of the Christian faith.

One of these missionary stations was Lukolela, founded by Stanley in 1883. For the *Vangele* it was just one of those many stops on the river to collect wood, hand over a packet of mail and take on a few goods for delivery at Leo. For Mr. and Mrs. West, the English Baptist missionary and his wife, it was a rare occasion.

"My wife and I have few visitors and an Englishman is almost unheard of in these parts unless he is connected with the mission," said Mr. West as he greeted me at his door.

I asked Mr. West how long he had been here.

"About thirty years. My appointment is up in January. Be quite sorry to leave after all this time. I'll take you round the mission grounds so you can see the sort of work we do."

He invited me to lunch. I hesitated, imagining that visitors would have to be catered for in advance.

"We're all right this week," Mrs. West hastened to assure me. "The joint from Leo came the day before yesterday." As we were settling down at the table, a tall negro entered the dining-room holding an enormous bare white bone.

"How are we going to eat that?" Mrs. West asked. The boy shrugged his shoulders in typical negro fashion, frowning a little, then grinned showing two rows of gleaming white teeth. Mrs. West went into the kitchen, to find the meat lying on the draining board ready for the dustbin. "Perhaps that's because he served our last joint covered with ants and I had to throw it away," she smiled. "Still you mustn't judge Congolese intelligence by this boy. He's particularly backward. Many of them are quite bright fellows."

Outside the mission house was a score of jabbering children who had got to know of my arrival. They followed close behind as we set off at a brisk pace down the sun-baked village street.

Aged inhabitants came out of their adobe huts to see what all the excitement was about and we stopped to chat with them. We found one woman kneading dough from the cassava root and another chopping it into four pieces and placing a banana leaf round each to stop coagulation when baked in a pile of charcoal. Next to her was a girl cracking open the oil palm nuts and separating the kernels from the sticky shells. "When she's packed up a bag or two of those," Mr. West said, "we'll send them off with some others to the factory in Leo." Beyond was a cripple, walking on her knees planting a bed of onions. "She's been like that all her life; now she's doing something useful she feels she's wanted, and of course is much happier." Others came out of their huts and gave me eggs, pineapples and bread. Every time Mr. West stopped to explain to them what I was doing, his words were greeted with buzzing tongues and shrieks of surprise. I asked Mr. West why they were all so excited.

He laughed and explained that a white man without any money was beyond their imagination. "They can't believe you have to work your way from place to place. Also, Congo families stick together and young men don't leave home until they're at least thirty. Some of them think you're very young indeed."

"Why's that?"

"Because you haven't acquired a middle-aged spread. Out here it's a sign of respectability and maturity. Hence you see," patting his own midriff, "why I've grown a bit lax."

Copying the example of the mission house, the negroes in the encampment and neighbouring villages had tried their skill at interior decorating. Many of them were justly proud of their clean bright houses. Congolese, like most Africans, love pictures, particularly photographs of themselves.

Back in the mission house, we discussed the problem of what the Congolese would eventually do with their education. Mr. West's observations are now loaded with irony, in view of the tragic events which have since taken place.

He told me that the Belgians were aiming at real democracy in the Congo, at partnership with the Africans, and thus stressed the need for local education. In his opinion they had always allowed the African to occupy a position equal to his ability, a policy which had culminated in the establishment of an African university.

Before leaving Lukolela I met the mission's oldest inhabitant. He professed to remember the day when Stanley arrived at the village eighty years back, and he certainly looked convincing.

In the afternoon on our nineteenth day out from Stanleyville the *Vangele* entered Stanley Pool, a wide navigable stretch of water above the rapids of the lower Congo. On the north shore of the Pool lay Brazzaville, the decadent capital of French Equatorial Africa.

On the south was Leopoldville, mushrooming capital of the Congo. Reaching up with its skyscrapers Leopoldville is something of a fantasy for the Congolese to describe to their friends back in the mud huts up-river. For me it was civilisation again.

Prices were high in the Congo and in Leopoldville they were that little bit higher still. The Belgians had brought their own living standards with them, so most European goods could be bought in the capital.

"Yes, things are expensive," the captain agreed when he heard me complaining, "but salaries are compensatingly large." The minimum for a European was about £1,700 a year and most Belgians earned upwards of £3,000. This was no consolation to me.

Leopoldville may have lacked some of the luxurious amenities of other cities, but it was still no place for an impecunious globetrotter to stay. Any hopes of earning some ready cash vanished when, after I had gone to the trouble of getting an attractive blonde to type out my story in French journalese, the editor of the newspaper refused to publish it since I was not a famous journalist.

But my luck held. The Baptist Missionary Society kindly offered to put me up for a while. Then I received an invitation from an American director of the Mobiloil Congo Belge, to move into accommodation belonging to the firm.

He had received a letter from the company's office in Nairobi and welcomed me with typical American generosity.

My Leopoldville digs were fabulous. They ran to an air-conditioning unit in the bedroom, and included all meals, of American size. Without any hand-to-mouth worries to bother about I could concentrate on the last great problem of my journey—the return to Europe.

15

WASHING UP HOME

I had been in Leopoldville a couple of days when a letter from home via the British Consulate brought important news. My twin brother was to be married in early January and he wanted me to be best man at the wedding. Six thousand miles came between me and home and I had just six weeks to cover them. The race was on.

The English community in Leo were very helpful, introducing me to influential people. But one day it would be, "the airlines have offered to fly you to Europe", and the next day, "the decision has been over-ruled by headquarters in Brussels" (or Lisbon, or Paris). Meanwhile the shipping companies were busy telling me that they dare not put me on this or that ship "for fear of getting into trouble". The power of the Unions had a strong hold even in the Congo.

One school of thought said I should pack my bags for Matadi, the premier port of the Congo, about three hundred miles west of Leo; the other was quite certain I should stand a better chance of picking up a ship from Pointe Noire in the French part of Africa. Then a Belgian who had already been most helpful rang me up to say that he had arranged a flight for me to Pointe Noire.

Early next morning he telephoned to say he was sorry, the trip had been cancelled. Everyone was trying to be helpful but nothing seemed to come of it. Now the wedding was five weeks away.

One evening I got back to the flat to find a message from a Monsieur Demets who was taking his private plane down to Matadi. There was a spare seat and if I wanted to make use of it, I should be at the airport midday tomorrow.

My last memory of civilised living in Leopoldville is a bunch of daffodils. They were a gift to me from one of the Belgian Mobiloil employees. I thought I was seeing things. "Didn't know you could grow daffodils here in this heat and humidity."

"We don't." He grinned. "They came out on the overnight flight from Brussels."

Each stem had cost 15 francs (2s. 6d). I did not see how anyone could afford them, even in Leopoldville.

"Oh, well, I'm married," he explained.

"But that should make you worse off."

"Not out here. I have eight children. For every child there is a State allowance which increases the more children one has. We are mostly Catholics here and we have very large families."

The reason for this lay in the hope that many of the children born in the Congo would stay there, thus helping to develop the country.

I went to say goodbye to my host and tried to thank him adequately for everything he had done, then was driven to the airport in one of the company shooting brakes. Within an hour I was flying.

Stretched out beneath us was the rolling savanna country, broken by heavily-forested valleys eating their way back into the highlands. The pale streak of the Congo cut across mountain and valley, imprisoned between high banks. Stanley Rapids on the lower Congo glinted in the sunlight. This series of waterfalls is the result of a geological phenomenon more than thirty million years ago, which uplifted the rim of the continent like a gigantic spoon. But for its hundred miles of unnavigable water, the history of the great river and its gigantic basin behind would have read very differently. Four hundred and fifty years ago, the early Portuguese explorers Diaz and Cao discovered the mouth of the Congo. Had they been able to push on beyond the rapids the interior would have been opened up in the early days of African discovery. Instead, it was left to Stanley, three and a half centuries later, to make the heroic first journey into the heart of the continent.

"Hold on," Monsieur Demets yelled in my ear. "We are going to land."

Acres of jungle rolled below us. There wasn't any sign of a runway.

"Where?" I shouted.

"On the road, about a couple of miles ahead."

He saw my expression. "I am putting through a new stretch of gravel from Matadi to Leo, there is no tarmac yet. If the Congolese have done what I told them it should be just wide enough to land on."

He pushed the joystick forward. We swished over the tree-tops and landed on the bumpy road, pulling up just before it took a sharp left turn.

"They have made the road wide enough," he remarked, "but the runway should be a little longer."

A crowd of negroes sprang out of the bush and gaped at the glittering machine. We clambered down, secured the aircraft to the ground with ropes and stakes, and got into a waiting car.

Half an hour later, we were in Matadi, port of the Congo. Monsieur Demets dropped me at the house of Mr. Strugnal, the manager of the local retail food stores. Mr. Strugnal was the sole Englishman in the town and pleased to see a fellow countryman.

"Come and stay a while," he suggested. "It may be some time before you find a boat." Yet another instance of spontaneous generosity from someone who had never seen me before. I accepted the offer gladly.

Three of the five vessels in port had sailing orders for Europe, and I visited them all first thing next morning. The captains of the German and Italian freighters couldn't help me, but the skipper of a Danish fruit boat said he would take me to Hamburg. "We won't be in Europe until the beginning of the New Year, maybe later, if the weather is bad," he warned me. "I must hope for favourable winds and trust to luck." As the ship wasn't leaving for a week I waited in Matadi in case any other Europe-bound vessel arrived in port.

December came and I prepared to join the fruit boat, resigned to the fact that I shouldn't be home for Christmas, maybe not even in time for my twin's wedding. The thirty-eight pounds in my pocket seemed useless. It wouldn't buy me a ticket even half-way back to Europe. My experiences in Lima and Stanleyville should have taught me that it doesn't pay to step off the busy shipping routes of the world.

The telephone rang in the midst of my despondency.

"Will you answer it?" called out Mr. Strugnal from the kitchen. I lifted the receiver.

"I wish to speak to a Mr. Boyd." The voice sounded sinister, and I mumbled a reply.

"I am the chief engineer of the *Scharnhorst*. My captain said that he could not take you back to Germany, no? You come in the engine-room. Few people will know. I come ashore tonight. If you wish to come, meet me in the Bar Academie at nine."

He rang off and I was left foolishly holding the receiver wondering if I should grab the offer or whether it was just a hoax. I had nine hours to decide.

The 'phone rang again and Mr. Strugnal picked up the receiver. I prayed it wasn't the same man.

"Yes, yes, that's right. He's staying here. Hang on a moment."

"It's for you Alistair. Monsieur Guy de Clippelle, of the Agence Maritime Internationale."

Ten minutes later I was sitting in the offices of A.M.I.

"Ah, Mr. Boyd," said M. de Clippelle, "I am glad you have not returned to Leo. Do you remember last week I told you about a tanker called the *Holmgar* lying down river at the petrol port? She was leaving for Venezuela."

I remembered vaguely.

"We have received a priority cable half an hour ago from Brussels. One of the company's tankers has been held up because of Suez and they want the *Holmgar* back in the Mediterranean. She sails in a few hours."

I must get aboard her, somehow.

At that moment the captain of the *Holmgar* strode into the office to receive his final orders.

"Ah, capitaine, you have come at the right moment," exclaimed M. de Clippelle. "Mr. Boyd here is in desperate need of a lift back to Europe. Have you a spare place for him?"

"I do not think so. What can he do?"

"Anything," put in de Clippelle before I had time to answer. "Anything at all, on deck or below. I can answer for him. He——"

"Very good," interrupted the captain, "if you say he is all right, you need say no more, and I shall take him. We are short-handed and he can make himself useful in the galley." He turned towards me. "You can come with me now and clear away the breakfast."

So I was galley boy, mess boy, call it what you like and working in the crew's mess aft. My job was to wash up filthy plates, one pile after another. I got up at five-thirty and finished at eight in the evening. I was working for my passage only, no pay. But I couldn't complain; every revolution of the propeller was sending me in the right direction.

The crew weren't a bad lot either. Swedes, Norwegians and Germans, quite a change after the negroes on the *Vangele*. There was one old man who had walked from the Cape to Cairo in his youth.

One morning the captain found me scrubbing out the mess. "We are going to Sicily," he said. Sicily, Italy, Holland, they were all the same to me. They were Europe, that was the great thing.

"When do you think we'll get there, sir?"

He said it depended on the weather after Dakar, but even allowing for the worst at this time of year, it shouldn't be later than December 22nd.

The nearer to home the *Holmgar* bore me the slower dragged the time. The mountain of dirty cups, saucers and plates seemed to rise higher and higher. Given three clear days I could reach England before Christmas—a blissful thought. But what if we broke down in a full gale? And there was always the faintest chance, as the captain had warned me, that being a tanker the *Holmgar* could be re-directed anywhere at the last minute. Surely fate wouldn't intervene at this stage. I had said that before.

On December 15th we steamed past the Straits of Gibraltar and then I knew I should be home for Christmas. Three days later the *Holmgar* dropped anchor in the harbour of Augusta, Sicily, and after dinner on December 19th I hung up the tea towel for the last time.

I went up to the Captain's cabin to thank him for taking me.

He pulled a bundle of notes from his safe and handed me nine thousand *lire* (£5), "pocket money".

I boarded the morning train to Rome and Genoa. It was chilly after so long in the tropics. The only decent bit of clothing I had left was my tropical suit, not much protection in this weather. I stuffed myself into layers of underclothes. The sight of someone travelling across Europe in winter in a crumpled linen suit drew forth a few stares and comments. I had good reason for wanting to avoid attention; there were two ivory crocodiles tucked into my knee-length socks. Whenever I bent my legs the bulge would show through my trousers. In the Congo I had developed a convincing limp and walked bow-legged, but that wouldn't fool the continental customs officials. To cover both tropical suit and crocodiles, I bought an extra-long plastic mackintosh in Genoa.

The train crossed into France at midnight. "*Les passeports! Les passeports!*" The French immigration officer took my passport and thumbed through its pages in a fruitless attempt to find a place for his stamp.

"Monsieur, there is no room," he complained. "I will have to overstamp somewhere." I showed him a small space just below the tiny red stamp of the U.S.S.R.

Paris, Amiens, Calais, the cross-channel steamer, and I fancied I could see the White Cliffs of Dover poking through the mist ahead. Yes, there they were.

"Home," I said in a loud voice.

"Yes, luvly to be 'ome, ain't it, Guv?" the man standing next to me agreed enthusiastically.

"Yes, lovely."

"The wife and me've been on a day trip to Calais. Cor, what a lark if you like. We enjoyed our little ole selves, mind you, seeing all these Frenchies on their home-pitch. The way they talks and goes on, excited, proper rattle all the time. Same in the shops and caffs. Well, it's worth seeing and now we know, but one day's enough, plenty. Start missing the old beer after that. Where've you bin, Paris?"

In the train to London I didn't want to talk to anyone, least of all to my neighbour about her husband's arthritis. Why, I didn't need to talk to anybody now. I was just beginning to realise that there were no more battles ahead of me with obstinate officials, no useful contacts to be chased after; all my multi-coloured destinations had merged into the simple one of HOME. At long last the brakes were being gently applied to my journeying—that's how it felt. The drive of my will that had pushed me round the full circle of the globe was falling off. I was strangely content just to relax and to listen to the conversations going on around me. Yes, and it was an odd sensation, come to think of it, to hear those strangers talking English. I wanted to break in and say, "What a funny thing, I speak English too." But no, sit back, this is home.

Fifty years ago international boundaries were lines across which people and ideas could flow and intermingle. Today these lines have grown into formidable barriers that seem specially designed as as a deterrent to globetrotters.

"And how did you find the world?" everyone would ask. As if one could answer just like that. Where to begin, where to end? Better just to say, "Wound round with red tape but filled with good people."

Seated opposite me were a couple of tourists complaining loudly about their discomforts during a week's holiday at a hotel in Rome. Goodwill begins not with the exchange of political formulae, but with understanding and an attempt to see the other chap's point of view and to make allowances for race, creed and custom. Too many tourists and visitors abroad expect to find everything just as it is at home or perhaps a little more luxurious. They are horrified at anything a little different from what they are accustomed to. If they don't like unusual food, or happy-go-lucky trains, why don't they stay at home?

The boat train was filled with noisy families and excited couples, returning home for Christmas. I was alone just as I had been all along. At times I had missed the excitement of sharing a breath-taking experience, yet I had never felt really lonely. I could always find someone to talk to, someone bursting to unravel his life's history to a complete stranger. I was glad that I had globetrotted alone. Much of the hospitality and personal contact might otherwise never have come my way. Alone, I had no option but to talk with foreigners. They appreciated my effort to talk in their own language though they often replied in good colloquial English. Above everything else I had to be free to travel where opportunity took me.

"Coffee, sir?" A waiter interrupted my thoughts. I dug into my pocket and pulled out a bundle of foreign currency—much more than five pounds worth now. No need to hoard it any longer. It was a good idea of the Duke's to start with a fiver; made me so much more dependent upon others, though of course, there was always the danger of imposing myself. I hope I was forgiven wherever circumstances forced me to do that. The object of the challenge, after all, was to meet people on their own soil and by working amongst them to appreciate their ways of life.

My journey made me realise that Britain is more than a group of islands stuck on the edge of Europe, that our country is as large as any other, not in size, but in its function as one of the most highly developed and influential states of the world. I discovered that physically Britain looks tiny from abroad but that "made in Britain" can be found on an article be it a thousand miles up the Amazon or in the heart of the Congo; that Britain's voice can be heard by press and radio from Siberia to Bolivia, even if the facts are some-times distorted, and that her actions are the subject of world-wide controversy. The most widespread criticism I heard was that we seem ignorant of what is going on inside other countries. We are amazed to learnt that Thailand has television and Venezuela ten-lane highways; that modern architecture in South America can be more imaginative than anything we seem capable of producing.

This is a world of juxtapositions, wealthy and poor, the highly civilised and the primitive; those living on luxuries drawn from all over the world, those existing at subsistence level who are entirely self-sufficient. Travel can give you an understanding of a million types of people. Perhaps the penniless globetrotter helps to create a little understanding between them, for he is neither a tourist nor an ambassador, but a bit of both.

We must be half-way to London by now. I hadn't realised quite how much I appreciated England. I wondered if the wanderlust spirit would ever return. There are many places in the world I should like to have a longer look at. Kenya with its healthy climate, Thailand with its hospitality, the United States with its unrivalled generosity and Peru with its archaeological gems and its señoritas. But considering everything together—old friends, home comforts, security, just familiarity again—all these would pull me back to England.

For me, the world remains as large as ever, and I was glad to find it that way. The world is a mine of friendship if you are hard-working, even if you are hard up. It took me five pounds to find that out, and I have come back rich in new friends.

But here's Victoria, the same old Victoria Station, looking just as ugly as it did fourteen months ago. Yes, and there's the Underground, admired the world over for its efficiency, and the man with the bowler hat coming down the platform giving his tightly-rolled umbrella a little twiddle, just for the hell of it. Perhaps sometime in the future I might be coming along Victoria Station myself in a bowler hat with a tightly-rolled umbrella.

I fancy I can smell the smog now, but perhaps I'm imagining that. I walked into the nearby hotel to telephone home—to say that after travelling fifty-two thousand miles, I was safely back.